Will the
Non-Russians Rebel?

Studies in Soviet History and Society

edited by Joseph S. Berliner, Seweryn Bialer, *and* Sheila Fitzpatrick

Will the Non-Russians Rebel?

State, Ethnicity, and Stability in the USSR

ALEXANDER J. MOTYL

CORNELL UNIVERSITY PRESS

Ithaca and London

First published 1987 by Cornell University Press.

International Standard Book Number 0–8014–1947–6
Library of Congress Catalog Card Number 86–24386
Printed in the United States of America
Librarians: Library of Congress cataloging information
appears on the last page of the book.

The paper in this book is acid-free and meets the guidelines for
permanence and durability of the Committee on Production
Guidelines for Book Longevity of the Council on Library
Resources.

To Irene

Contents

Tables

FIGURES

Preface

How stable is the Soviet multinational state? How explosive is the USSR's nationality question? Is the empire in decline, or is developed socialist society relentlessly moving toward communism?[1] How likely is it that the non-Russians will actively and massively oppose Soviet power? To ask the question that goes unstated in most studies of Soviet nationality affairs: Will the non-Russians rebel?

Scholarly opinion is divided. Soviet authors insist that the nationality question has been solved, "irrevocably and finally," and that remaining tensions are due either to "subjective" mistakes or to "non-antagonistic contradictions." Western students of Soviet ethnic relations are divided into what one scholar aptly calls the "disintegrationist" and "nondisintegrationist" schools.[2] The disintegrationists see nationality problems as an increasingly unmanageable issue that is likely to lead to the decay and eventual collapse of the USSR. The nondisintegrationists believe that ethnic issues, although prob-

---

1. Hélène Carrère d'Encausse, *Decline of an Empire: The Soviet Socialist Republics in Revolt* (New York: Newsweek Books, 1979).

2. I am grateful to Irwin S. Selnick for this picturesque distinction. For prime examples of the disintegrationist perspective, see R. V. Burks, "The Coming Crisis in the Soviet Union," and Alexander Shtromas, "How the Soviet System May End," *The World & I*, January 1986, pp. 305–50. For a nondisintegrationist view, see Gail Warshofsky Lapidus, "Ethnonationalism and Political Stability: The Soviet Case," *World Politics*, no. 4 (July 1984), pp. 355–80.

lematic, are not about to develop into a system-threatening factor. Quite the contrary, these scholars argue, just as the Kremlin has succeeded in managing its ethnic groups in the past, so, too, it will be successful in the future. Who is right? Which argument is more plausible? This book provides what I hope are useful answers to these questions.

The Soviet Union's stability is inextricably related to ethnic concerns, as the question of disintegration or nondisintegration is a question of stability. Before we can ascertain the likelihood of rebellion, we must first determine how the USSR has managed to weather past crises and why, in the post-Stalin era, it has come to enjoy what all scholars regard as a remarkably durable stability. True enough, it seems, but what is stability? Most definitions refer to the "maintenance" or "survival" in some form of the "political system." No wonder, therefore, that studies of stability tend to be afflicted by the lack of focus decried by Roy Macridis—the tendency of systems analysis to downplay the sphere of politics consisting of individual and collective actions.[3] Without suggesting that the entire blame for the conceptual fuzziness surrounding stability lies with the systems approach, one can legitimately argue that changing the unit of analysis may resolve some problems (and perhaps create new ones). At the very least, this procedure should be an interesting intellectual experiment.

If the political system is not to be our focus, then what? The concept of the state, as used by Karl Marx and Max Weber and as recently resurrected by a variety of scholars, immediately comes to mind.[4] States, unlike political systems, are willful human agglomerations that actively implement policies; one of their policy goals is stability, or the effective pursuit of survival vis-à-vis adversaries. Specifically, states prevent and contain antistate collective actions against the pat-

3. Roy C. Macridis, "Comparative Politics and the Study of Government: The Search for Focus," *Comparative Politics*, no. 1 (October 1968), pp. 79–90.

4. Philippe C. Schmitter, "Still the Century of Corporatism?" in *The New Corporatism: Social-Political Structures in the Iberian World*, ed. Fredrick B. Pike and Thomas Stritch (Notre Dame: University of Notre Dame Press, 1974), pp. 85–131; Alfred Stepan, *The State and Society: Peru in Comparative Perspective* (Princeton: Princeton University Press, 1978); Eric A. Nordlinger, *On the Autonomy of the Democratic State* (Cambridge: Harvard University Press, 1981); Theda Skocpol, *States and Social Revolutions* (Cambridge: Cambridge University Press, 1979); Nicos Poulantzas, *State, Power, Socialism* (London: Verso, 1980); Stephen R. Graubard, ed., *The State* (New York: Norton, 1979); Stephen D. Krasner, "Approaches to the State," *Comparative Politics*, no. 2 (January 1984), pp. 223–46; Howard H. Lentner, "The Concept of the State," *Comparative Politics*, no. 3 (April 1984), pp. 367–77; Bertrand Badie and Pierre Birnbaum, *The Sociology of the State* (Chicago: University of Chicago Press, 1983); John Breuilly, *Nationalism and the State* (Manchester: Manchester University Press, 1985).

terns of authority inscribed within them and generated either internally, by states themselves, or externally, by such societal forces as classes and ethnic groups. Another policy goal is the maximization of autonomy—a state's determination to minimize the environmental constraints on its behavior which are exerted by substate elites, society, and other states. From this state-centered perspective, the important questions are: How does the state deal with its opponents? How does it interact with ethnicity? And how does it reconcile the imperatives of survival, or self-maintenance, with those of autonomy? The state-ethnicity-stability triad forms the basis of a largely conceptual discussion in Chapters 1 and 2.

Chapter 3 examines the Soviet state's interaction with Russians and Ukrainians. The Soviet state, I argue, is highly autonomous and Russian, in that its Russian pattern of authority is generated both by the autonomously acting state and by the societally hegemonic ethnic power of the Great Russians. The major challenge to the Soviet state's ethnic stability, therefore, comes from the regional hegemonies of the non-Russians in general and the Ukrainians in particular. Why the Ukrainians? Their indisputable economic, political, social, and demographic importance, as well as their frequent involvement in nationalist movements, have combined to make of the USSR's second republic the key to the nationality question.[5] Despite the recent interest in "Homo Islamicus" and the "Islamic threat to the Soviet state,"[6] if the Ukrainians will not or cannot undermine the USSR's ethnic stability, then neither can any other non-Russian nation.

Chapters 4 through 7 examine how the Soviet state has managed and continues to manage the disruptive capacity of the Ukrainians and, by extension, of other non-Russians. Chapter 4 focuses on the prevention of undesirable attitudes by instrumental means. Chapter 5 discusses how Russian authority patterns are concealed in an elaborate ideology. Chapter 6 deals with the privatization of antistate attitudes and the concomitant prevention of antistate behavior by Russification policy. Chapter 7 examines how the state prevents the formation of autonomous collectivities and elites by employing coercion and pursuing control of the public sphere.

The next two chapters approach the problem of the USSR's ethnic stability from the viewpoint of its opponents. Chapter 8 centers on

---

5. Yaroslav Bilinsky, *The Second Soviet Republic: The Ukraine after World War II* (New Brunswick: Rutgers University Press, 1964).

6. Carrère d'Encausse, *Decline of an Empire*, pp. 249–64; Alexandre Bennigsen and Marie Broxup, *The Islamic Threat to the Soviet State* (London: Croom Helm, 1983).

past forms of non-Russian antistate activity and the reasons for its failure. My conclusion—that resistance to the establishment of Soviet power has been relatively common in the USSR's history, while rebellion against established Soviet power has not—may demoralize non-Russian rebels in search of precedents. Chapter 9 discusses the potential for external instigation of or aid to internal rebellions in the USSR. Finally, Chapter 10 considers the question of Soviet ethnic stability in the context of the USSR's current economic ailments. How will the crisis or crisis-like situation that besets the USSR affect the non-Russians' capacity for rebellion? How will these problems affect the Soviet state's ability to prevent rebellion? The answers are of critical importance both to scholars and to policy makers, in the Soviet Union and in the West.

A final word on the values on which this work is inevitably based. It would be disingenuous to pretend that in undertaking a study of ethnic stability in the Soviet Union, I am concerned solely with illuminating an interesting example of conflict management in the contemporary world. In this respect, Soviet propagandists betray a rare capacity for insight: they realize that critical attitudes necessarily underlie Western scholarly interest in Soviet problem areas. Does scholarship thereby lose in value? Of course not. Rather, by being rigorous and political, it continues in the best traditions of classical political science.

I used to regard with skepticism the gratitude that authors traditionally express to their spouses. This book, in the making for several years, has convinced me of the errors of my ways. Many, many thanks to my wife, whose support, understanding, and patience border on the sublime.

Many thanks, also, to the W. Averell Harriman Institute for Advanced Study of the Soviet Union for its generous financial support, and to Seweryn Bialer, Mark Kesselman, Joseph Rothschild, Glenn Adler, Linda Cook, Ainslie Embree, Stuart Fagan, Charles Gati, Lubomyr Hajda, Vera Kaczmarskyj, Philip Oldenburg, Myroslaw Prokop, Dennis Quinn, Jonathan Sanders, Irwin Selnick, Jack Snyder, and Stanislaw Wellisz for their encouragement, comments, and criticisms.

Finally, owing to the wonder of word processing—something I still don't understand—I have, alas, no typists, proofreaders, or secretaries to thank.

ALEXANDER J. MOTYL

New York, New York

**Will the
Non-Russians Rebel?**

CHAPTER 1

Stability and
the State

The concept of stability, so central to contemporary political science, enjoys a dubious distinction. Most scholars use the term without specifying what they mean by it; those who attempt to do so have yet to agree on a common definition.[1] For better or for worse, its meaning remains elusive. Despite (or perhaps because of) this elusiveness, many scholars continue to disregard Thomas Hobbes's advice that concepts should be defined before syllogisms are formed.[2] Instead, there is a pronounced tendency to put the cart before the

1. For a sampling of some recent views of stability, see Francis G. Castles, "Political Stability and the Dominant Image of Society," *Political Studies*, no. 3 (September 1974), pp. 289–98; B. J. Dudley, *Instability* (Ibadan: Ibadan University Press, 1973); Wolf-Dieter Eberwein, ed., "Politische Stabilität und Konflikt: Neue Ergebnisse der makroquantitativen Politikforschung," *Politische Vierteljahresschrift*, no. 14 (1983); Ted Robert Gurr, "Persistence and Change in Political Systems, 1800–1971," *American Political Science Review*, no. 4 (December 1974), pp. 1482–1504; Leon Hurwitz, "An Index of Democratic Political Stability: A Methodological Note," *Comparative Political Studies*, no. 1 (April 1971), pp. 41–67; Leon Hurwitz, "Democratic Political Stability: Some Traditional Hypotheses Reexamined," *Comparative Political Studies*, no. 4 (January 1972), pp. 476–89; Ian Lustick, "Stability in Deeply Divided Societies: Consociationalism versus Control," *World Politics*, no. 3 (April 1979), pp. 324–44; Uriel Rosenthal, *Political Order: Rewards, Punishments, and Political Stability* (Alphen aan den Rijn: Sijthoff & Noordhoff, 1978); Svante Ersson and Jan-Erik Lane, "Political Stability in European Democracies," *European Journal of Political Research*, no. 3 (September 1983), pp. 245–64.

2. Thomas Hobbes, *Leviathan* (Harmondsworth: Penguin, 1976), p. 115.

horse and plunge immediately into explanation. "Writers have tended simply to preface their work on the causes of stability or instability with a few remarks about what they mean by the terms," note two British political scientists, "but have signally failed to analyse the concepts with the same thoroughness that they have devoted to the discovery of their causes."[3] Confusion reigns, for although all political scientists appear to have a gut feeling about stability, few can describe that sentiment with any degree of precision.

Compounding these difficulties is the fact that existing definitions of stability are theoretically unsatisfactory for two related reasons. First, they tend to lapse into the essentialist definitional mode, viewing stability as an essence—indeed, almost as a Platonic form—that can be uncovered and dissected. And second, they tend to reify the abstractions by which stability is defined, thus implying that concepts are actually existing things and not just referents. While this is hardly the place to resolve the long-standing philosophical controversies at the root of these distinctions, a practical political science must opt for nominalism and eschew reification. Otherwise, it will lapse into mystification, become thoroughly incomprehensible, and cease to be a viable pursuit.

The essentialist perspective is evident in the "differing views and approaches to political stability" distilled from the literature by Leon Hurwitz. The "essence" of stability, according to these views, consists of a variety of attributes—the "absence of violence," "governmental longevity/duration," the "existence of a legitimate constitutional regime," the "absence of structural change."[4] Since the only important research question concerns the existence or nonexistence (or presence or absence) of these attributes, an essentialist inquiry inevitably results in arbitrariness and one-dimensionality. With stability defined in terms of an either/or proposition, there is ultimately no way of knowing whether or not the correct essence has been isolated (Socrates, naturally, would object). Worse still, the search for essences reduces stability to a lifeless property with no capacity for capturing the dynamism, relativeness, and subtlety of politics. And politics, presumably, is what political science concepts such as stability are about.

The pitfalls of reification are illustrated by Samuel P. Huntington's

3. Keith M. Dowding and Richard Kimber, "The Meaning and Use of 'Political Stability,'" *European Journal of Political Research*, no. 3 (1983), p. 229.

4. Leon Hurwitz, "Contemporary Approaches to Political Stability," *Comparative Politics*, no. 3 (April 1973), p. 449.

approach to stability. Huntington correctly realizes that the only alternative to essentialism is to treat stability in terms of a relation, since only relations can convey the ambiguity and dynamism at the heart of politics. According to his widely quoted formula, stability exists when "institutionalization" exceeds "participation"; instability results when the relationship is reversed.[5] The intellectual attractiveness of Huntington's conceptualization is obvious; its flaws are no less so. By defining stability in terms of a relation between two abstractions, Huntington commits the sin of reification. "Institutionalization" and "participation" cannot interact—even in the sense of one's exceeding the other—because they are not actually existing entities. Relations require human actors, the real institutions and participants who actually can become involved in an interaction. To paraphrase Seweryn Bialer's point, if "stability is an outcome of relations," then they must be "between social items, groups, and institutions."[6]

A focus on actors rather than on abstractions has two related consequences. The first is that it forces us to be concrete and specific—qualities that are frequently in short supply in political science analysis. For example: the accusation of essentialism aside, the presence or absence of, say, violence says little about stability, unless one first determines who is directing it against whom and why (or "*Kto kogo?*" as Lenin put it). By the same token, Claude Ake's suggestion that stability be measured by the ratio of infractions of the law to law-abiding actions is inadequate because it fails to identify the actors involved while making stability so diffuse a phenomenon as to include all human activity.[7]

5. Samuel P. Huntington, *Political Order in Changing Societies* (New Haven: Yale University Press, 1968), pp. 55, 78–79.

6. Seweryn Bialer, *Stalin's Successors: Leadership, Stability, and Change in the Soviet Union* (Cambridge: Cambridge University Press, 1980), p. 132.

7. Claude Ake, "A Definition of Political Stability," *Comparative Politics*, no. 2 (January 1975), p. 277. Another instance of excessive diffuseness is Huntington's later conclusion that "political stability can be most meaningfully conceived in terms of historical patterns of change peculiar to individual societies" ("Remarks on the Meanings of Political Stability in the Modern Era," in *Radicalism in the Contemporary Age*, ed. Seweryn Bialer [Boulder, Colo.: Westview, 1977], III, 282. The idea that the study of stability must involve the study of history is a welcome and long-overdue corrective to a widespread tendency among social scientists to ignore the past. But to argue, as Huntington does, that the study of stability is equivalent to the study of history is not only to exaggerate the case but to offer a guideline that is singularly unhelpful, even for historians. "Historical patterns of change" encompass all human experience, and analyzing them is too large a task, both for political scientists and for historians.

The second consequence of this approach is that it helps us unravel the tangled conceptual relationship between legitimacy and stability. Political scientists commonly claim that no government can survive without the active consent of the governed, that is, without legitimacy.[8] But what, specifically, does this statement mean? Is the active consent of *all* the governed at *all* times the requirement? If it were, most states would have collapsed a long time ago. Clearly, the legitimacy of *some* "items, groups, and institutions" at most or even some times is the prerequisite. Theda Skocpol emphasizes that "what matters most is always the support or acquiescence not of the popular majority of society but of the politically powerful and mobilized groups, invariably including the regime's own cadres."[9] Walker Connor has made this point with even greater force, going so far as to argue that "legitimacy is not needed for a state to function," as the "durability of the multinational state well into the national era" seems to prove. Especially insightful is Connor's remark that "legitimacy cannot be inferred from a peaceful situation," since docility can be explained by fear, habit, apathy, inertia, apoliticalness, political and cultural isolation, and lack of organization.[10] Docility or, more generally, acquiescence may therefore be more crucial to system maintenance than legitimacy—a point we shall return to later. Implicitly, Connor has also underscored the importance of coercion and manipulation to the maintenance of stability in both the short and the ever-elusive long run—particularly with regard to the social units considered unimportant by the system or state.

Provisionally, we may define stability as a relation between human actors. The inadequacy of so vague a definition is obvious, since it

8. For discussions of this issue, see Joseph Rothschild, "Observations on Political Legitimacy in Contemporary Europe," *Political Science Quarterly*, no. 3 (Fall 1977), pp. 487–501; Peter G. Stillman, "The Concept of Legitimacy," *Polity*, no. 1 (Fall 1974), pp. 32–56.

9. Theda Skocpol, *States and Social Revolutions* (Cambridge: Cambridge University Press, 1979), p. 32. Bialer also emphasizes that "the absolutely essential distinction . . . concerns the process of formation and sustenance and the extent of legitimization of the political regime among societal elites on the one hand and among large social strata, the 'publics,' on the other hand" (*Stalin's Successors*, p. 185).

10. Walker Connor, "Nationalism and Political Illegitimacy," *Canadian Review of Studies in Nationalism*, no. 2 (Fall 1981), pp. 218–22. See also Renate Mayntz, "Legitimacy and the Directive Capacity of the Political System," in *Stress and Contradiction in Modern Capitalism*, ed. Leon N. Lindberg et al. (Lexington, Mass.: Lexington Books, 1975). In particular, Mayntz writes that "the main argument for a distinction between general support and legitimacy is that general support can derive from other factors and does not depend only on the political system's legitimacy" (p. 264).

leaves unanswered two questions: What kind of relation and between whom? Yet to pose these questions in this manner is almost to answer them. Since our preliminary definition refers to units of analysis that are capable of functioning as actual actors engaged in a relation, one of them, surely, cannot be the concept that is generally associated with stability—the political system. Systems are almost definitionally incapable of initiative and willful action. As faceless black boxes, they process inputs into outputs in an excessively reactive, almost automatic manner. Put another way, the type of politics practiced by systems tends to be a dependent variable, whereas we need a politics that is, at least sometimes, an independent variable. We need a politically active unit of analysis—one that is not, in Skocpol's words, a "mere arena in which socioeconomic struggles are fought out."[11] That unit, as Alfred Stepan has argued, is the state—the "continuous administrative, legal, bureaucratic, and coercive systems that attempt not only to structure relations between civil society and public authority in a polity but also to structure many crucial relationships within civil society as well."[12]

Associating stability with the state leads us to another set of conclusions. First, the other actors involved in a relation with the state must also be active entities concerned with transforming political and social relations—groups variously identified as insurgents, contenders, and disloyal oppositions.[13] Nonopponents are either neutral toward or allied with the state, in which case they are either passive or, for all practical purposes, merged with it. Either way, such actors are analytically irrelevant to the relational quality embodied by stability. Obviously enough, these antistate forces may be located within the state itself, in the society associated with the state, or in the international environment (i.e., they may be other states). Second, since the relation to which stability refers involves the state and its opponents, it is by definition adversarial and may be best characterized as one of political struggle. And third, since stability involves a relation of struggle, it

11. Skocpol, *States and Social Revolutions*, p. 29.

12. Alfred Stepan, *The State and Society: Peru in Comparative Perspective* (Princeton: Princeton University Press, 1978), p. xii. According to Skocpol, the state is "a set of administrative, policing, and military organizations headed, and more or less well coordinated by, an executive authority" (*States and Social Revolutions*, p. 29).

13. Harry Eckstein, "On the Etiology of Internal Wars," in *Why Revolution?* ed. Clifford T. Paynton and Robert Blackey (Cambridge, Mass.: Schenkman, 1971), pp. 132–33; Juan Linz, *The Breakdown of Democratic Regimes* (Baltimore: Johns Hopkins University Press, 1978), p. 15; Charles Tilly, "Does Modernization Breed Revolution?" *Comparative Politics*, no. 3 (April 1973), pp. 437–39.

must in some way involve the efforts of all actors to win; exactly how is discussed below.

What kind of political struggle is it? States and their opponents conflict over a variety of issues, but the one that towers over the rest is state survival. Antistate forces mount challenges, which the state attempts either to prevent or to contain. They seek both to undermine the state's survival and to reduce the effectiveness of its pursuit of survival. In turn, states aspire and struggle to remain states. They want both to survive and to be able effectively to manage challenges to their survival. The two sides are involved in a perpetual tug-of-war: they push and pull, lose ground, and gain it back continually. Although Harry Eckstein resorts to reified abstractions, he is not incorrect to identify effectiveness and survival as two components of stability.[14] How do we retain Eckstein's insights while interpreting them in terms of a contentious and dynamic relation between real political actors? By defining stability as the state's effective pursuit of survival vis-à-vis antistate forces.[15]

Are all antistate challenges relevant to stability? If so, then we are back in Ake's nebulous conceptual world, which draws no distinctions between significant and insignificant acts of opposition. We can establish boundaries by following Charles Tilly's recommendation that genuine assaults on a state involve "collective action"—"people's acting together in pursuit of common interests."[16] Only the vio-

14. Harry Eckstein, *Division and Cohesion in Democracy: A Study of Norway* (Princeton: Princeton University Press, 1966), p. 229; Bialer, *Stalin's Successors*, p. 133.

15. The utility of this approach is apparent when it is contrasted to the static conceptualization of stability developed by Keith M. Dowding and Richard Kimber. "Political stability," they write, "is the state [*sic*] in which a political object exists when it possesses the capacity to prevent contingencies from forcing its nonsurvival." More specifically, "a government has the property of being unstable in relation to a given contingency, *C*, over the whole period in which it lacks the capacity to cope with *C*. If *C* actually occurs, and the government falls, this proves to the analyst that the government lacks the requisite capacity" ("Meaning and Use of 'Political Stability,'" pp. 238–39). Premised on systemic passivity, this conceptualization is fundamentally uninterested in anything less than fatal contingencies. If, to use Dowding and Kimber's example, we somehow know that a system will collapse at a level of violence, *R*, any level below *R*— and there can be thousands—represents a contingency in relation to which the system is stable. Inevitably, it follows that even a .99 *R* level is meaningless with regard to instability. But why divorce system breakdown from the chain of events that may precede it by arguing that there is no such chain and that the .99 *R* level is conceptually and practically unrelated to breakdown? In a word, why drain stability of the conflict and dynamism that are at the core of politics?

16. Charles Tilly, *From Mobilization to Revolution* (Reading, Mass.: Addison-Wesley, 1978), p. 7.

lent and nonviolent challenges of *groups* can threaten a state, since groups of like-minded individuals pursuing common goals can mobilize far more resources, engage in far more extensive activity, and therefore pose a much greater threat than isolated individuals.[17] Stability, or the effective pursuit of survival, thus consists of a state's prevention and containment of antistate collective actions by antistate forces. It follows that the larger the number of such actions and the greater their concentration in some period of time, the more daunting is the tug-of-war and the more imperative that prevention be timely and containment effective. In other words, the greater the accumulation of antistate challenges, the greater the cumulative challenge.

This argument is central to my conceptualization. Since such scholars as David Sanders consider it both "fallacious" and "ethnocentric"—charges that, I suspect, Ferdinand Marcos, Corazon Aquino, Jean-Claude Duvalier, the Ayatollah Khomeini, Bishop Desmond Tutu, and Kim Dae Jung would reject—his own challenge will have to be met before we can proceed any further. Sanders's alternative is to treat stability and instability in terms of "the extent to which the occurrence or non-occurrence of changes in and challenges to the government, regime or community deviates from the previous system specific 'normal' pattern of regime/government/community changes or challenges."[18] The key to his approach is, of course, the historically

---

17. The Russian émigré organization NTS (*Narodno-Trudovoi Soiuz*) currently espouses what one of its leaders has termed "molecular" opposition to the Soviet state. According to the plan, isolated anti-Soviets in the USSR declare themselves members of the organization and, as individual "molecules," carry on the antistate struggle. Although the KGB assiduously pursues NTS adherents, it must realize, as does no doubt the NTS leadership in Frankfurt, that an atomized organization is a contradiction in terms.

18. David Sanders, *Patterns of Political Instability* (London: Macmillan, 1981), p. 66. Sanders's conceptualization immediately founders on the fact that the point at which one begins to measure some pattern must be chosen arbitrarily. Thus the initial "normal pattern," which will serve as the basis of all future comparisons, is inevitably also arbitrary. Starting the pattern at year X may produce an initial pattern Z; starting the measurement at years $X - Y$ or $X + Y$, however, may produce a totally different result, pattern Z' or Z''. Where, then, should a researcher begin? Sanders can give no answer, because the choice of a starting point cannot be his. Relatedly, in order to determine the "normal pattern" one must choose certain time segments as units of comparison. Sanders suggests that months be used; presumably they provide greater accuracy than years. Still, why stop at months? Why not weeks, days, or, for that matter, even hours, minutes, and seconds? I am, of course, purposely resorting to *reductio ad absurdum* argumentation, because it highlights the insurmountable and—again—ultimately arbitrary choices Sanders and his methodology face (pp. 66–72).

determined "system specific normal patterns"—if they fall, so does Sanders's conceptualization.

And fall they do. Since these patterns act as a point of reference, any deviation from them must be symptomatic of instability. If one is to be logically rigorous, however, this means that even a sudden downward dip in a "normal pattern" is indicative of instability. For example, a system that normally experiences twelve assassinations a year (say, one a month) over several years would have to be deemed less stable if its quota were suddenly and unexpectedly to drop to eleven, ten, or even zero annual assassinations![19] Furthermore, Sanders would have to agree that a system-specific normal pattern exists whenever the slope of the "change or challenge events" line is constant. In addition to zero-sloped lines, positively and negatively sloped lines are "normal" in that they indicate perfectly regular and quite predictable upward or downward climbs in the number of change or challenge events. But if a positive slope does not represent increasing instability, what does? Implicit in Sanders's argument is a rejection of upper limits on challenges that systems dare not cross—a conclusion that is, in effect, a denial of relatively common types of upheavals. Some Third World revolutions—such as those in China, Cuba, Vietnam, and Nicaragua—arguably have occurred as the result of an ever-increasing pattern of regular and predictable violence, which at some point proved to be the proverbial straw that broke the camel's back. For Sanders, no last straw is possible, as long as the accumulation of straws is steady and predictable.

Although his own approach does not stand up to scrutiny, Sanders is not quite unjustified in his dissatisfaction with mere numbers. After all, not all challenges are alike, and not all challenges evoke the same response from the state. In this sense, to say that more challenges represent a greater challenge is to state a general truth that conceals as much as it reveals. But if we expand the focus of our inquiry from the number of collective actions (or challenges) per se to their qualitative dimensions and to the manner in which states prevent and contain them, we can transcend raw numbers (and perhaps even witness the

---

19. Dowding and Kimber argue against Sanders's "pattern of behavior" approach in similar fashion: "If in a particular system governments are overthrown weekly over a long period, a lack of deviations from the trend produces a norm in which there is no . . . instability at time *t*. Yet most people would want to say that in this system, whatever else was stable, the government that fell at time *t* was not" ("Meaning and Use of 'Political Stability,'" p. 235).

transformation of quantity into quality!) and examine the actual contours of the state's confrontation with antistate forces.

Collective actions can be dissected along four dimensions: frequency, size, intensity, and duration.[20] *Frequency* refers to the number of antistate actions in a certain period of time; *size* refers to the number of contenders involved; *intensity*, to the damage in, say, lives lost which was inflicted on the state; and *duration*, to the length of time in, say, days during which the collective actions lasted. Since frequency is associated with the initiation of collective actions, it is a consequence of the breakdown of prevention. The lower the frequency of antistate actions, the greater their prevention, while the higher the frequency, the lesser their prevention. The frequency curve, therefore, is a measure of the state's capacity for survival. Size, intensity, and duration, however, presuppose already existing collective actions and are associated with their containment—with the state's ability to set things right. The size, intensity, and duration curves, which need not have the same slopes, are therefore measures of the state's capacity for effective management of challenges to its survival. From a state's perspective, the ideal combination would involve a high level of survival capacity (low frequency) and a high level of management effectiveness (low size, intensity, and duration). Antistate forces, of course, ideally aspire to the opposite combination. A large and chronologically concentrated set of sizable, intense, and protracted antistate collective actions represents a confluence of low survival capacity and low management effectiveness and amounts to a rebellion.

Normally, we would expect the frequency curve to be inversely related to the size, intensity, and duration curves, so that, say, a high level of survival capacity should be associated with a high level of management effectiveness. But low frequency may also be associated with great size, intensity, and duration. This is a case of a simultaneously high level of prevention and a low level of containment, indicative of a precarious and volatile situation for both the state and its opponents. Surely, this is what is meant by a political situation that "can go either way." In contrast to states that occupy this or other intermediate positions on the stability scale, high-stability states are characterized by high levels of prevention and containment, low-stability states have low prevention and containment levels, while unstable states possess no capacity for prevention and containment. Quite simply, they are powerless and on the verge of collapse.

20. Tilly, *From Mobilization to Revolution*, pp. 96–97.

The above remarks assume that we can successfully identify certain collective actions as somehow being antistate. But how do we know whether or not an action is opposed to the state? Since opposition is a relative concept (i.e., one cannot just be opposed, one must be opposed to something), isolating its characteristics requires a closer look at that which is being opposed—the state. Fortunately, existing definitions of the state, unlike those of stability, avoid essentialism and reification and are more than adequate for our needs.

Max Weber calls the state a "relation of men dominating men"; Alfred Stepan speaks of it as a "mechanism of domination and control"; Ralf Dahrendorf calls it an "imperatively coordinated association."[21] Implicitly if not explicitly, the key idea in all these definitions is control—just what we would expect from a willful human community, a policy-making and policy-implementing organization with a logic, structure, and interests of its own. The state embodies two different kinds of control, however. Externally, the state aspires to control the individuals, classes, and ethnic groups that comprise the society inhabiting the territory under its jurisdiction. Internally, the state represents a set of institutions organized along hierarchical lines. One or more institutions lead the state as a whole; in turn, the leading institution or institutions are guided by a strategic elite. Although these entities set the tone for the state, neither the leading institution(s) nor the elite at the apex is omnipotent, so that political jockeying for power and a constant tug-and-pull among state agencies are always the order of the day.[22]

As an asymmetrically arranged collection of offices, the state is based on a distribution of authority both among and within its constituent parts.[23] Such patterns of authority are thus of two kinds—inter- and intrainstitutional.[24] The former are characteristic of complex or-

21. Max Weber, "Politics as a Vocation," in *From Max Weber: Essays in Sociology*, ed. H. H. Gerth and C. Wright Mills (New York: Oxford University Press, 1958), p. 78; Stepan, *State and Society*, p. xii; Ralf Dahrendorf, *Class and Class Conflict in Industrial Society* (Stanford: Stanford University Press, 1959), pp. 289–90.

22. Stepan, *State and Society*, p. xii.

23. According to Dahrendorf, "authority can be described as legitimate power" (*Class and Class Conflict*, p. 166). I speak of authority rather than power because authority is intrinsic to the very notion of a state. Dahrendorf unnecessarily restricts the "structure of authority relations" to "positions and persons endowed with the right to issue authoritative commands," so that "in the state . . . authority is exercised by certain persons by virtue of their positions" (p. 290). Clearly, relations between institutions can also be marked by a structure of authority.

24. Harry Eckstein and Ted Robert Gurr, *Patterns of Authority: A Structural Basis for Political Inquiry* (New York: Wiley, 1975), p. 22.

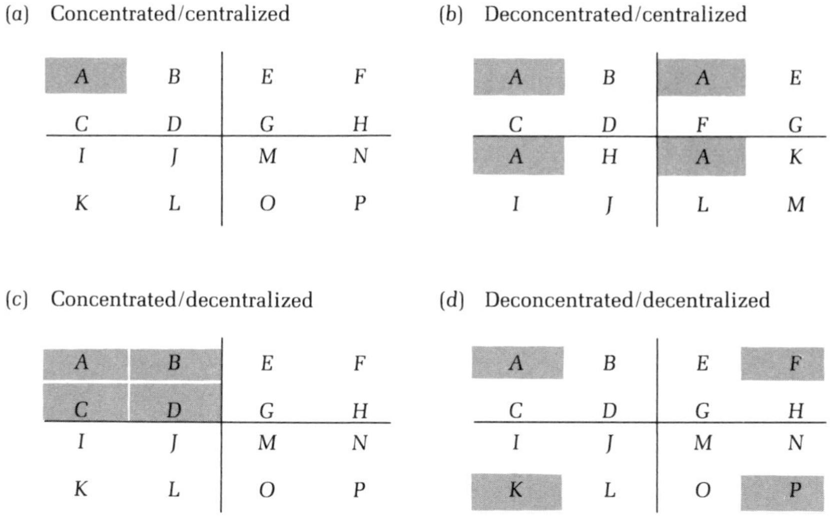

(a) Concentrated/centralized

A	B	E	F
C	D	G	H
I	J	M	N
K	L	O	P

(b) Deconcentrated/centralized

A	B	A	E
C	D	F	G
A	H	A	K
I	J	L	M

(c) Concentrated/decentralized

A	B	E	F
C	D	G	H
I	J	M	N
K	L	O	P

(d) Deconcentrated/decentralized

A	B	E	F
C	D	G	H
I	J	M	N
K	L	O	P

Capital letters represent institutions; quadrants represent regions.

Figure 1. Types of political authority structure

ganizations; the latter are characteristic of the simple interpersonal hierarchical relationships that can be found even in mom-and-pop stores. Interinstitutional patterns are of immensely greater conceptual interest than the intrainstitutional variety, especially because they offer an approach to the conceptualization and categorization of states. Since authority may be distributed among institutions, which in turn may be distributed throughout the territory of the state, we may plot the interinstitutional distribution of authority in a state along two axes—centralization and concentration. A state's bundle of authority may be centralized in one leading institution or it may be decentralized, that is, distributed among several. Authority may also be concentrated in some particular region or deconcentrated throughout the area under state control. Four types of political authority structure are possible (see Figure 1):

(a) *Concentrated/centralized*: one leading institution, located in one region, holds most available authority.
(b) *Deconcentrated/centralized*: one leading institution, dispersed throughout several regions, holds most available authority.

(c) *Concentrated/decentralized:* several leading institutions, all located in one region, share most available authority.
(d) *Deconcentrated/decentralized:* several leading institutions, dispersed throughout several regions, share most available authority.

We now embark on the kind of ahistorical heuristic experiment performed by Hobbes, Locke, and other classical theorists. In the state of nature we construct, political authority patterns describe "pure" states. As unadulterated crystallizations of political authority, such states are suspended, cloudlike, in conceptual mid-air. Clearly, pure states are fully autonomous entities. Divorced from all reality, they could not be anything but completely independent of their environment. Once such states are—conceptually—brought down to earth, however, this primary autonomy inevitably erodes. Once states are conceived of as willful human communities embedded in a social and international environment, a state–society and state–world exchange must take place. States will still aspire to do what they want to do— pursue their own interests as they see them—but they will be constrained by their environment. Conceptually, therefore, states may be termed perpetual autonomy maximizers, while societies and other states are autonomy encroachers. Since no real states are pure, their independence of the environment is always, at best, limited.

In their collision with pure states, societal and international actors impinge on state autonomy in three ways.[25] First, societal forces penetrate a state and curtail its autonomy directly. Second, societal and international forces constrain its independence by means of specific actions vis-à-vis the state. And third, social and international actors create an environment whose structure and logic demand particular forms of state behavior. The last two points appear obvious enough; the first one, however, requires additional explanation, since it involves externally generated pressure on the state from *within.* How does this paradoxical condition come about, and what are its implications for the state?

As societal forces collide with the pristine state, they inevitably occupy strategic junctures within its authority structure (a process discussed in greater detail in Chapter 2). As they become holders of inter- and intrainstitutional authority, societally generated authority

25. Ralph Miliband, *Marxism and Politics* (Oxford: Oxford University Press, 1977), pp. 66–117.

patterns are formed and come to be inscribed on the state's political authority structure. Although, as autonomy maximizers, states resist all constraints on their independence of action, as self-maintainers committed to the effective pursuit of survival they are also vitally interested in preserving the authority patterns inscribed within them and in reproducing the environmental conditions that account for these patterns. The result is a condition of permanent tension between state autonomy and state stability. Forced to walk an endless tightrope between autonomy maximization and self-maintenance, states continually face the possibility that these goals may conflict with or actually contradict each other. Consequently, the state's relations with society are not only permanently tense but also perpetually fluid.

Analysts of the state traditionally have focused only on its relationship with and possible independence of class forces in society. This is an unfortunate oversight, since ethnic forces are an equally important social category (a point developed in Chapter 2). For the time being, let us take it for granted that the societally generated authority patterns mentioned above can be of both a class and an ethnic variety: both classes and ethnic groups may collide with the pure state, penetrate it, and come to inscribe their presence upon the state's political patterns of authority. If identical ethnic patterns are inscribed in the distribution of authority both among and within state institutions, then ethnic patterns of domination exist. Where there are no such patterns, states qualify as ethnic "terrains of struggle."[26] It need not follow from the existence of an ethnic pattern of domination that the dominant ethnic group either fully supports the state or uniformly benefits from its policies. Indeed, the state's political or class authority patterns may be seen as repugnant by elements within the group.

How do we know whether or not a state's loci of authority have become the property of some ethnic group? Intrainstitutional authority holding is self-evident: if members of an ethnic group occupy the leading positions of an institution's hierarchical structure, then that group may be said to hold its commanding heights. Interinstitutional authority holding is obviously more complex, since it involves the leading institution or institutions. But how do we determine the eth-

---

26. Clearly, I disagree with Nicos Poulantzas's conceptualization of the state as intrinsically a "terrain of class struggle," within which societal class relations are "crystallized" or "condensed," because it assumes an automatic mirroring within the state of societal relations (Nicos Poulantzas, *State, Power, Socialism* [London: Verso, 1980], pp. 123–45). See also Göran Therborn, *What Does the Ruling Class Do When It Rules?* (London: Verso, 1980).

nic character of an institution? In three ways. The first and most obvious one involves the explicit possession by the leading institution of a specific ethnic label: the NSDAP, for example, was an explicitly German institution. Preferring to adopt an internationalist veneer, few states care to follow this practice today. Even so, we may discern an ethnic slant if the leading institution has a purportedly supra-ethnic designation, while ethnically labeled subordinate institutions are assigned to all ethnic groups but one—the ethnic dominant. As I argue in Chapter 3, the Communist Party of the Soviet Union, which consists of republican Party organizations in all republics save one—the Russian Soviet Federated Socialist Republic—illustrates this tendency. The third variation is an outgrowth of intra-institutional dominance. If members of an ethnic group literally saturate the leading institution, whatever its designation, then the inter-institutional distribution of authority is clearly in that group's favor. White domination of the United States' governmental structure is an example of this variation.

Stability thus involves three aspects of a state's effective pursuit of survival. Since state survival is tantamount to the survival of political, class, and ethnic authority patterns, stability in general may be disaggregated into three substabilities: political, class, and ethnic. As long as the state maintains all of its patterns of authority, it maintains itself as the state it is and therefore is stable to a greater or lesser degree. If any pattern of authority is, for whatever reason, replaced by another, then the original state has in fact ceased to exist. (Mere changes in state personnel—such as changes in or of government—are unrelated to stability.) We now know what *antistate* means. Since *stability* refers to the tug-of-war between a state, for which the maintenance of the existing patterns of authority inscribed within it is a policy goal, and forces in the state, society, and the world, which aspire to undermine these patterns, the term *antistate* refers to opposition to a state's political, class, and ethnic patterns of authority.

So far, so good, but why and how does antistate opposition arise? Although the literature on conflict is enormous, the question as to its causes has not been settled, and probably never will be.[27] I prefer to think that conflict is inherent in human relationships. This Hobbesian premise, like its Rousseauian opposite, is a matter more of faith than

---

27. Eckstein, *Division and Cohesion*, pp. 134–38. See especially Harry Eckstein, "Theoretical Approaches to Explaining Collective Political Violence," in *Handbook of Political Conflict*, ed. Ted Robert Gurr (New York: Free Press, 1980), pp. 135–66.

of science and cannot be demonstrated, although the pervasiveness of conflict, at all times, in all places, and involving all kinds of individuals, does appear to lend some persuasiveness to this view. With this as our point of departure, our task is to explain not the presence of conflict—that would be too obvious—but its absence. Especially in conditions where authority relations, such as those between society and state, exist, we expect antistate collective activity to be endemic and unavoidable.

More specifically, opposition to the state is inherent in the very notion of the state as an imperatively coordinated association and a mechanism of domination and control. Conflict, as Dahrendorf has convincingly argued, is the inevitable concomitant of authority relations: "the distribution of authority in associations is the ultimate 'cause' of the formation of conflict groups."[28] Thus the differential distribution of authority means that latent conflict tendencies suffuse every relationship involving authority. If we extend Dahrendorf's insight beyond the authority relations between a state's institutions to those between the state and society and between the state and other states, we can posit structurally determined conflict relationships at all three levels. (Obviously, this does not mean that conflicts will be based only on authority patterns, a caveat that applies most to international actors.) As noted above, state institutions are directly involved in authority relations with other institutions in general and with the leading institution in particular: if the state is an ethnic terrain of struggle, state subunits will be engaged in a kind of ethnic free-for-all; if it is marked by an ethnic pattern of domination, certain units will tend to be more or less permanently subordinate to others. Societal and world actors, meanwhile, be they ethnic groups or states, will always be involved in an inherently conflictual political relationship with the authority-wielding state, regardless of its particular authority configuration. If the state is marked by a pattern of ethnic domination, however, its relationship with societal ethnic subordinates will differ markedly from that with societal ethnic dominants. The former will be involved in a relationship that is inherently conflictual on both the political and ethnic levels; the latter will experience the state only as a source of political authority, whose weight may be mitigated by its ethnic propinquity.

While necessary, latent structural conflict tendencies are not sufficient to produce antistate collective activity. (Locke was right: the

28. Dahrendorf, *Class and Class Conflict*, p. 172.

state of nature is not equivalent to the state of war.) Minimally, four behavioral conditions must be met for such activity to occur. First, antistate activity presupposes at least some willingness to engage in it: the requisite *attitudes* must exist.[29] Since conflict is innate in authority relations, the absence of oppositional inclinations under conditions of authority is due, therefore, not to the nature of the relationship between citizen and state, but to state intervention and interference in the attitudinal and behavioral life of society and the individuals, classes, and ethnic groups that compose it.

Second, people must be able to communicate their opposition before they can actually oppose the state in deed. Antistate attitudes per se, therefore, are only the starting point, since it is the public airing or *deprivatization* of such attitudes that really counts. It is necessary to persuade oneself and others of the correctness of one's views, and persuading others presupposes the existence of sufficient political autonomy free of state control and interference within which deprivatization can take place.[30] Without political autonomy the oppositional inclinations of elites and masses simply cannot be acted upon, no matter how burdensome the authority relations with the state. Fortunately for rebels, political autonomy is built into most state–society relationships, since few states are able or willing to deny it completely.

Third, there must be a *collectivity*, a group of some kind sharing deprivatized antistate attitudes and willing and able to engage in antistate activity.[31] An antistate collectivity can arise only if there is sufficient space for it in that conceptually distinct sphere of life within which collective undertakings occur. Located between the individuals comprising society, or the private sphere, and the state, the

29. Ted Robert Gurr, *Why Men Rebel* (Princeton: Princeton University Press, 1970); Eckstein, "On the Etiology of Internal Wars," pp. 134–38; Ivo K. Feierabend and Rosalind L. Feierabend, "The Comparative Study of Revolution and Violence," *Comparative Politics*, no. 3 (April 1973), pp. 393–424.

30. According to Barrington Moore, "to overcome the moral authority of suffering and oppression means to persuade oneself and others that it is time to change the social contract. Specifically, people come to believe that a new and different set of criteria ought to go into effect for the choice of those in authority and the manner of its exercise, for the division of labor, and for the allocation of goods and services" (*Injustice: The Social Bases of Obedience and Revolt* [White Plains, N.Y.: M. E. Sharpe, 1978], p. 81).

31. Theda Skocpol, "What Makes Peasants Revolutionary?" *Comparative Politics*, no. 3 (April 1983), pp. 351–75; Roy Hofheinz, "The Ecology of Chinese Communist Success," in *Chinese Communist Politics in Action*, ed. A. Doak Barnett (Seattle: University of Washington Press, 1969), pp. 3–77; Joel Migdal, *Peasants, Politics, and Revolution* (Princeton: Princeton University Press, 1974).

public sphere is the site of organized public activity and discourse. If the state occupies all the space available in the public sphere, then collective activities of the sort on which autonomous groups are premised become impossible.

Finally, *leaders* are necessary. A variety of scholars have correctly emphasized that collective activity without leadership is either infeasible or, at most, ineffective.[32] "It is always an activist minority that promotes and promulgates new standards of condemnation," according to Barrington Moore. "They are an indispensable if insufficient cause of major social transformations, peaceful and gradualist as well as violent or revolutionary."[33] The task of elites is threefold: to exploit the available political autonomy, to mobilize constituencies, and to guide them in their activity within the public sphere.

The causal chain connecting these variables is as follows. Latent conflict tendencies between a state and its subunits, society, and the world, if acted upon by relatively autonomous collectivities mobilized around deprivatized antistate attitudes and led by adversarial elites, may translate into antistate collective activity, which in turn may produce declining levels of stability or even instability. Obviously, the process is neither that simple nor that automatic, since each of the steps is contingent on what the state does or does not do. Indeed, the state and its actions are critical to the entire scheme. Having recourse to a variety of instrumental, normative, and coercive organizational means,[34] the state may attempt to make the asymmetrical features of its authority structure materially advantageous and therefore tolerable, it may conceal them, or it may seek to prevent the deprivatization of antistate attitudes and the emergence of collectivities and elites capable of mobilizing them and generating antistate actions. An astute state will presumably keep its finger on the pulse of change in order to respond to it effectively, channel it into desirable directions, and prevent antistate attitudes from deprivatizing and collectivities and elites from forming. Thus, while environmental condi-

---

32. These arguments are not, of course, new, having been articulated by Plato, Aristotle, Machiavelli, and, obviously, Mosca, Pareto, and Michels. See also Moore, *Injustice*; Joseph Rothschild, *Ethnopolitics* (New York: Columbia University Press, 1981); Skocpol, *States and Social Revolutions*; Eric A. Nordlinger, *Conflict Regulation in Divided Societies* (Cambridge, Mass.: Center for International Affairs, 1972).

33. Moore, *Injustice*, p. 472.

34. Amitai Etzioni, *A Comparative Analysis of Complex Organizations* (New York: Free Press, 1975), pp. 3–23. See also Alex Simirenko, "A Paradigm for the Study of Social Control in a Socialist Society," *Annals of the Ukrainian Academy of Arts and Sciences in the United States*, nos. 37–38 (1978–80), pp. 68–86.

tions may constrain states, it is state policies (or, more precisely, inadequate policies or the lack of policies) that directly permit anti-state attitudes, collectivities, and elites to arise and antistate collective activity to threaten state stability.

An important conceptual consequence of this proposition is that environmental conditions—except for immense natural catastrophes and similar externally generated, uncontrolled, and uncontrollable conditions of "fate" and "acts of God"—are *intrinsically* neither stabilizing nor destabilizing: they become so only in relation to states and to what states make (or fail to make) of them. This, surely, is the lesson of Tilly's observation that "population growth, industrialization, urbanization, and other large-scale structural changes do, to be sure, affect the probability of revolution. But they do so indirectly, by shaping the potential contenders for power, transforming the techniques of governmental control, and shifting the resources available to contenders and governments."[35] Economic, social, cultural, and international conditions affect a state's tug-of-war with contenders only insofar as they are used by either of the two sides. Conditions neither create the tug-of-war—the differential distribution of authority does that—nor decide its outcome.

These considerations have important implications for the process by which stable states become unstable. The obvious, and correct, explanation of why states lose the tug-of-war is that defeat stems from their inability to prevent or contain certain kinds of antistate collective actions. But why do states fail at this task? As Juan Linz suggests with respect to some democratic regimes, their failure may be due to shortsightedness and incompetence.[36] More significant for our purposes, they may fail because the policy measures required are a cure that is worse than the disease. That is, they are even more immediately subversive of the state than the antistate collective activity to be prevented or contained. Certain policy measures are fundamentally incompatible with the patterns of authority inscribed in a state and, in that sense, are antistate policies that no stability-seeking state is likely to implement. Socialism, as Marxists argue, may indeed be the answer to the "crisis of the capitalist state," but no self-respecting capitalist state is going to dig its own grave in order to mollify its critics. Dismembering the Soviet Union might just solve its ethnic problems, but the Soviet state can hardly be expected to initiate this action.

35. Tilly, *From Mobilization to Revolution*, p. 447.
36. Linz, *Breakdown of Democratic Regimes*, pp. 50–55.

Otto Kirchheimer's notion of "confining conditions" is helpful in explaining this point. Kirchheimer has argued that the choices open to postrevolutionary regimes are limited by the "particular social and intellectual conditions present at [their] birth." Specifically, the "social and economic frame of the particular society . . . lays down a conditioning parameter within which . . . [a] choice has to be made and solutions have to be sought." In the end, these "confining conditions," defined as "chiefly those of social structure," must be "overcome if the new regime is to continue."[37]

Kirchheimer gives primacy to environmental conditions. Let us place him on his head and broaden the perspective. External conditions are confining only in relation to the internal conditions that characterize a state, postrevolutionary or not. These internal conditions—a state's patterns of authority—both delimit the possible range of a state's policies and demand the implementation of certain of these policies. In this sense, the state itself is its own primary confining condition. Paradoxically, the logic of survival may, under certain circumstances, fatally circumscribe state autonomy and thus prove to be the major obstacle to self-maintenance. Unable to prevent or contain those forms of collective activity that are both supportive of and detrimental to them, unable to act autonomously, states may freeze, ineffectively pursue survival, and perhaps cease to exist. Quite simply, they will have lost the tug-of-war.

37. Otto Kirchheimer, "Confining Conditions and Revolutionary Breakthroughs," *American Political Science Review*, no. 4 (December 1965), pp. 964, 966.

CHAPTER 2

Ethnicity and
the State

All scholars agree that the bundle of objective markers and subjective values called ethnicity is real. Such unanimity is a symptom of topical banality: there is no denying the existential reality of so obvious a fact of life. Far more interesting and divisive is the question of ethnicity's sociopolitical significance. Is it a basic datum of human existence, or is it only an acquired characteristic? Is ethnicity an independent variable or a dependent one? Primordialists ascribe fundamental social importance to ethnicity qua ethnicity. They argue that ethnicity is a real and tangible quality with a real and tangible existence of its own. Contextualists regard it as an epiphenomenon reducible "in the last analysis" to something else, generally class.

Harold Isaacs and Orlando Patterson occupy the extreme positions in this debate. For a primordialist such as Isaacs, "basic group identity consists of the ready-made set of endowments and identifications which every individual shares with others from the moment of birth by the chance of the family into which he is born at that given time in that given place."[1] Patterson disagrees; he contends that "ethnicity is

1. Harold R. Isaacs, "Basic Group Identity: The Idols of the Tribe," in *Ethnicity*, ed. Nathan Glazer and Daniel P. Moynihan (Cambridge: Harvard University Press, 1975), p. 31. In addition, argues Isaacs, "the baby acquires a name, an individual name, a family name, a group name. He acquires the history and origins of the group into which he is born. The group's culture-past automatically endows him, among other things, with his nationality or condition of national, religious, or tribal affiliation, his language, re-

a chosen form of identification." How are such choices made? According to Patterson, "ethnic loyalties reflect, and are maintained by, the underlying socioeconomic interests of group members."[2] *Ubi bene, ibi patria.*

Which position is more valid? Boyd C. Shafer's slightly cryptic remarks on nationalism offer a good approach to our problem: "We know a great deal about nationalism. We do not know a great deal about nationalism. Both statements are true. Though we have much more to learn than we have learned, we do . . . know enough to have some idea—at least, inkling—of our ignorance."[3] In view of the epistemological arrogance involved in claiming perfect knowledge about any social phenomenon, it is not unreasonable to acknowledge the sociopolitical importance of both ethnicity and class. Indeed, it simply makes more analytical sense to say that ethnicity can, under certain circumstances and at certain times, have a salience all its own. Joseph Rothschild is surely right to argue that "ethnicity is not simply primordial and that ethnic groups and ethnic conflict are not mere masks for socioeconomic classes and class conflict."[4] To insist, instead, that class alone really matters and that ethnic interests are ultimately reducible to class interests is, first, to engage in semantic games (after all, when exactly does the "last analysis" occur?); second, to be guilty of monocausality and reductionism; third, to flirt with the genetic fallacy by "arguing that the origin of something [ethnicity] is identical with that from which it originates [class]";[5] and fourth, to ignore the available empirical evidence to the contrary.[6] "When you examine at close quarters the colonial context," wrote Frantz Fanon, "it is evident that what parcels out the world is to begin with the fact of belonging to or not belonging to a given race, a given

ligion, and value system—the inherited clusters of mores, ethics, aesthetics that come out of the geography or topography of the birthplace itself, all shaping the outlook and way of life upon which the new individual enters from his first day" (p. 32).

2. Orlando Patterson, "Context and Choice in Ethnic Allegiance: A Theoretical Framework and Caribbean Case Study," in *Ethnicity*, ed. Glazer and Moynihan, pp. 309, 305.

3. Boyd C. Shafer, "If We Only Knew More about Nationalism," *Canadian Review of Studies in Nationalism*, no. 2 (Fall 1980), p. 176.

4. Joseph Rothschild, *Ethnopolitics* (New York: Columbia University Press, 1981), p. 33.

5. Peter A. Angeles, *A Dictionary of Philosophy* (London: Harper & Row, 1981), p. 100.

6. H. Hoetink, *Two Variants in Caribbean Race Relations* (London: Oxford University Press, 1967); Leo Kuper, *Race, Class, and Power* (Chicago: Aldine, 1975).

species."[7] Even Soviet scholars admit that nationalism is not exclusively the product of socioeconomic conditions. A. I. Kholmogorov, for example, has written that "survivals of nationalism and chauvinism do not disappear by themselves" in Soviet society, although it allegedly knows no socioeconomic inequality.[8] And a collective of Soviet Ukrainian scholars flatly claim that "the nation does not disappear with a change in production relations."[9]

Political émigrés, whom we may define as individuals who left their homelands for political reasons, provide a convincing illustration of the potential existential autonomy of ethnicity. Why, to take a specific example, have so many post–World War II Ukrainian political émigrés remained Ukrainian, even as émigrés? (The same question, with many of the same answers, could be addressed to pre-revolutionary Russian Marxists in Europe, who, despite claims of internationalism, decidedly remained Russians.) Why did so many of them retain their objective markers and subjective values in foreign environments? Contextualists such as Patterson would have difficulty accounting for this persistence. To remain Ukrainian in the United States, Canada, and Western Europe was not and is not a profitable enterprise, as Ukrainian émigrés have found very few persuasive socioeconomic reasons for sustaining their ethnic ties for more than the first few years after their arrival. At the beginning of their immigrant experience, their fellow countrymen and the various associations, clubs, and groups that they had founded did serve to lessen the pains of culture shock. Moreover, once the initial adjustment period was over, many acted in line with Patterson's expectations and consciously chose to "pass." Nevertheless, an equally large, if not larger, number—as energetic, ambitious, and successful as their assimilated fellows in the outside world—continued to live in their ethnic ghettoes and maintain their ethnic identity. Why did these émigrés choose to remain Ukrainian? The answer is obvious: Because they were political. Their commitment to the Ukrainian cause, to Ukrainian nationalism, was of such a strong and enduring character that it continued to exist, indeed to thrive, and involved them in a variety of political activities and conflicts despite the contextual illogic of such a commitment. Why do so many hyphenated Ukrainians still remain

7. Frantz Fanon, The Wretched of the Earth (New York: Grove Press, 1968), p. 40.

8. A. I. Kholmogorov, "Deiatel'nost' partii v oblasti natsional'nykh otnoshenii," Voprosy istorii KPSS, no. 12 (December 1984), p. 36.

9. Mova i protsesy suspil'noho rozvytku (Kiev: Naukova Dumka, 1980), p. 21.

devoted to a seemingly hopeless cause—Ukrainian statehood—almost completely divorced from the day-to-day political, social, and economic concerns of living in a new country? Because ethnicity, once it is politicized, becomes a fact of life as real as any material concern: it assumes a psychological, almost primordial reality that ceases to be contextual.

This analysis suggests a conceptual device for refining our understanding of ethnicity. Just as Paul Brass differentiates among "ethnic categories," "communities," and "nationalities,"[10] we may categorize individuals according to their position on an ethnic ladder. The analytically distinct rungs on this ladder may be said to correspond to different levels of ethnic consciousness. The lowest rung corresponds to the mere possession of ethnic markers with no awareness of what they mean. Empirically, such a level, which is similar to the state of nature depicted by Rousseau, probably could not persist for long because interaction among individuals who share certain markers and others without them would ineluctably raise one to the second level on the ethnic ladder—ethnic awareness. An individual or group of individuals at this stage is aware of the commonality of ethnic markers. The next rung may be designated national identity; it signifies that the individual now identifies as a nation all those who possess certain ethnic markers and share in ethnic awareness. Higher up on the ladder is national fealty—a condition of mind in which an individual pledges loyalty to his nation and none other. National fealty is the simplest form of nationalism. Following fealty is a sense of national primacy: at this more developed nationalist stage, an individual believes that his nation requires a political state. The last rung is self-explanatory: it corresponds to national exclusivity or chauvinism.

Once an ethnic group is examined in light of this scheme, it becomes immediately obvious that generalizations regarding the group's actions, feelings, opinions, and the like are necessarily inaccurate because the consciousness levels (the reader will forgive me this terminological throwback to the 1960s) of individual group members can and will differ so very widely. By the same token, what is true in the aggregate need not apply to every individual member of that aggregate. Although most members of an ethnic group may consider themselves members of a nation, not all have to do so for that category justifiably to be called a nation. Likewise, not all members of a nation

10. Paul R. Brass, "Ethnicity and Nationality Formation," *Ethnicity*, no. 3 (September 1976), pp. 233–39.

have to be nationalists for that nation to be highly positioned on the ethnic ladder. Why some individuals rush ahead and why others lag behind with regard to ethnic consciousness are complex questions that, fortunately, our purposes do not require us to answer.

Similar reasoning may be applied to individuals who possess objective class characteristics. Like ethnicity, class is fluid and variable, so that all objective members of a class can be positioned on a class ladder. Some workers, for example, simply labor in factories and have no particular sympathy with their class or understanding of its purported goals; others are class militants; still others dutifully pay their union dues. To put it differently, some workers embody class-in-itself positions, while others represent class-for-itself positions. Marxists and nationalists are not unaware of such distinctions in consciousness. Rather than speak of "true" and "false" consciousness, however, I prefer the more value-neutral term "levels of consciousness." No rung on the ethnic (or class) ladder is inherently preferable to any other; none is superior.

Three questions follow from these considerations. First, is progress up the ethnic ladder inevitable, both for individuals and for groups? Second, is it reversible? And third, are the rungs associated with particular socioeconomic classes and levels of socioeconomic development?

Ethnicity *qua* ethnicity can propel groups and individuals up the ethnic ladder, but only at its ends. The first encounter with the "other" will push an individual or group to the level of awareness. At the acutely politicized stage of national primacy, repeated encounters with ethnic others should suffice to raise the subject to the level of exclusivity. In between, however, ethnicity's propellent force is contingent on outside variables. Radical nationalist interpretations to the contrary, the histories of contemporary nations reveal that a variety of objective and subjective ethnic and nonethnic factors—events, personalities, ideas, outside forces, and so on—have been responsible for the transformation of ethnic categories into particular nations. Indeed, John Breuilly has made a convincing case for viewing nationalism itself "as a form of politics" and for holding "that that form of politics makes sense only in terms of the particular political context and objectives of nationalism"—that is, the state.[11]

Although ascent up the ethnic ladder may not be inevitable, is it at

---

11. John Breuilly, *Nationalism and the State* (Manchester: Manchester University Press, 1985), p. 352.

least irreversible? Can an individual or group, having reached a certain level, descend to a lower one? It should surely be possible to do so in theory, as it is evidently possible in practice. The same complex of objective and subjective factors that produce ascent can, perhaps in different combinations, also result in descent. Minimally, states can either foster or forbid nationalism and thereby affect the behavior of most citizens and the attitudes of some. History is full of examples of how extreme nationalism has been defused—if only by outside force—and reduced to simple national identity: the transformation of Nazi chauvinism into West German nationalism is an obvious case in point. The complete or partial assimilation of nations is also quite possible, though by no means easy. Nations may even disappear altogether as ethnic categories, but, as Joshua Fishman argues, usually only as a result of massive doses of coercion.[12]

Are the rungs of an ethnic ladder associated with particular classes or social strata? A variety of analysts have suggested that nationalists are derived from elites whose professional lives are closely intertwined with national-cultural concerns.[13] Workers, on the other hand, should be subjectively indifferent to issues that are objectively irrelevant to their occupations. My view of this approach has already been outlined above: ethnicity is not just a smoke screen for class or material interests. To insist that certain classes have a direct connection to nationalism is to commit the genetic fallacy and claim that nationalism is invariably bourgeois nationalism—even if its exponents happen to be workers, peasants, and just plain ol' folk. Polish workers, according to such schemes, should not be nationalists; neither should American rednecks.[14] Alas, they are, and extremely so. Perhaps their nationalism is due to some intervening variable, say, religion or culture? To argue in this manner, however, is to lapse into tautology: the only true workers are those who stick to the definition and act as true workers; those who do not are not true workers. Such reasoning might have appealed to Thrasymachus, but, as Socrates recognized, it is not very illuminating.[15]

Finally, is ascent up the ethnic ladder in some way related to levels

12. Joshua A. Fishman, "Language Maintenance and Ethnicity," *Canadian Review of Studies in Nationalism*, no. 2 (Fall 1981), pp. 238–39.

13. Victor Zaslavsky, "The Ethnic Question in the USSR," *Telos*, no. 45 (Fall 1980), pp. 45–76; Mary McAuley, "Nationalism and the Soviet Multi-ethnic State," in *The State in Socialist Society*, ed. Neil Harding (Albany: SUNY Press, 1984), pp. 179–210.

14. See Seymour Martin Lipset, *Political Man* (Garden City, N.Y.: Anchor, 1963).

15. *Plato's Republic* (Indianapolis: Hackett, 1974), pp. 14–15.

of socioeconomic development? To argue, as some scholars do, that modernization can play a decisive role here is unhelpful for three reasons.[16] On purely conceptual grounds, modernization is too imprecise a variable; as it encompasses all of contemporary reality, it may be employed to prove or disprove just about anything. More important, mere socioeconomic conditions have no innate and necessary political overtones. As we noted in Chapter 1, conditions just exist, as it were, waiting to be molded by particular actors: the intervention of human beings is necessary to convert the impulses of the base into impulses of the superstructure. Finally, by focusing exclusively on developmentally acquired attributes, modernization ignores innate ones, such as size and presence, both of which are fundamental to ethnic relations.

Despite its unsatisfactory nature, the concept of modernization need not be thrown overboard. It does instruct us to focus on certain characteristics that may not be irrelevant to our concerns. We can easily imagine a set of interrelated social and economic factors that will provide an ethnic elite (assuming one exists, of course) with the resources and rationale to push its co-nationals up the ethnic ladder. In this sense, socioeconomic factors may facilitate, though not cause, ascent up the ethnic ladder. Specifically, if a politically subordinate ethnic group, whether modernized or not, comes to dominate everything but politics in the region it inhabits, then it is likely that its elite will begin to voice increasingly political demands—but only if allowed to by the dominant state. If a nation attains hegemony (a concept to be discussed below), it is necessary for the state only to give the ethnic elite the political autonomy to express itself for it to begin clamoring for political control as well. Although regional hegemony

---

16. Other Soviet authors implicitly and explicitly support this view. Iu. V. Bromlei openly speaks of the "growth of national self-consciousness" as the result of the "economic, social, and cultural progress of Soviet nations" ("K izucheniia natsional'nykh protsessov sotsialisticheskogo obshchestva v kontekste etnicheskoi istorii," *Istoriia SSSR*, no. 6 [November–December 1984], p. 41). A Turkmen Party functionary has made the following remarkable confession: "The accelerated development of the Union republics and the all-round economic and cultural progress of all the nations and nationalities of our country . . . were accompanied by a stormy growth in their national self-consciousness. A feeling of national pride developed in people, and love of one's own nation, language, values, and heroic past grew stronger, all of which in and of itself is natural and positive. However, in some cases this process was accompanied by several negative phenomena and the animation of national prejudices. In people with a backward, socially immature consciousness, natural pride in the successes of national development turned into national conceit, presumptuousness, and a disrespectful attitude toward other peoples" (M. G. Gapurov, "V bratskoi sem'e narodov po puti sotsial'nogo progressa," *Voprosy filosofii*, no. 10 [1984], p. 30).

does not cause conflict, it strengthens the hand of local elites while simultaneously weakening or complicating the state's management of the hegemon. For a regionally hegemonic nation, the political authority of foreigners can—in time and via the mediation of their elites—appear as foreign authority. This is not to say that elites and masses will immediately perceive this latent conflict tendency, conclude that it is unbearable, and therefore rebel, but that such an attitudinal and behavioral chain will be likely unless it is prevented or, minimally, contained by the political authorities. Consequently, the holders of foreign authority—the state—must perform a very careful balancing act in order to keep the regionally hegemonic nation's perceptions and actions at a benign level.

At this point of our argument, the state still appears bereft of any ethnic characteristics—a shortcoming I shall remedy presently. Moreover, the concept of ethnic hegemony needs to be developed in greater detail. We still have to specify the kinds of resources it refers to; more important, we must analyze how ethnicity in general and hegemony in particular interacts with and affects the state—a relationship that has received relatively little attention in the political science literature. This oversight is understandable, if unfortunate, since most mainstream political scientists still prefer the concept of the political system to that of the state, while those scholars who use the state as their unit of analysis tend to be neo-Marxists and therefore treat ethnic relations as an epiphenomenon of class.

Rothschild's "typology of patterns of ethnic stratification" suggests the direction in which we should proceed. According to Rothschild, "societies may stratify their ethnic groups according to models of vertical hierarchy, of parallel segmentation, or of cross-patterned reticulation." Only the vertical hierarchical model experiences a "categorical correspondence among all dimensions—political, social, economic, and cultural—of ethnic superordination and subordination." Parallel segmentation implies that "each ethnic community is internally stratified by socioeconomic criteria and each has a political elite to represent its interests vis-à-vis the corresponding elites of the other ethnic segments." In the reticulate model, meanwhile, "ethnic groups and social classes cross-populate each other" so that a "certain amount of overrepresentation and underrepresentation of ethnic groups within economic classes and political-power clusters is possible—indeed, likely."[17] Although my terminology differs from Rothschild's, I fully agree with his insight that political, social, economic,

17. Rothschild, *Ethnopolitics*, pp. 79–82.

and cultural dimensions must be regarded as analytically discrete properties that can be distributed among ethnic groups in a variety of ways.

It will now be useful to develop a notion whose inspiration is as much pluralist as it is Marxist. Just as Marxists speak of "class power," pluralists speak of "resources." We may infuse Marxist terminology with non-Marxist content and speak of "ethnic power." What, exactly, is ethnic power? Unlike class, ethnicity per se carries no connotation of power. As such earlier champions of nationalism as Mazzini and Herder recognized, all ethnicities are equivalent. What gives an ethnic group its power is not its ethnicity, its ethnic markers and values as such, but its possession of certain qualities and characteristics of a nonethnic nature. That is, the power of ethnic groups is grounded in the concrete contexts in which they live and interact. Thus ethnic power subsumes but is not coterminous with class power.

Ethnic power refers to the combination of resources that position a given group in the ethnic hierarchy of a given society or region.[18] We can compare ethnic groups along several power dimensions—demographic size, economic modernization, social development, cultural vitality, communications capacity, and organizational capacity. (Naturally, my choice of dimensions need not be the final word on the matter.) In each of these categories, as Rothschild tells us, some groups will be dominant and others will be subordinate, or a rough balance may exist among them. For our purposes, possession of a majority of *total available* resources (e.g., more than 50 percent of total population) qualifies a group as dominant in that resource. I insist on a majority, and not a plurality, of resources, so that resource dominance will be both a relative and an absolute concept. (If it were only the former, we would have to accept the conceptually unsatisfactory possibility that a plurality of, say, 10 percent in some resource makes that group dominant, in spite of the 90 percent shared equally by ten others and arrayed against it.)

An ethnic group that is dominant in five or six categories may be termed hegemonic; one that dominates in three or four is dominant; where no one ethnic group is hegemonic or dominant, ethnic balance may be said to exist. (For our present purposes, we may assume—not

---

18. For an excellent discussion of collective resources as the bases of power, see Dennis H. Wrong, *Power: Its Forms, Bases, and Uses* (New York: Harper & Row, 1979), pp. 125–45.

quite correctly—that all categories are of equal weight.) According to this logic, a hegemonic ethnic group—which does not necessarily enjoy the highest standard of living—possesses more ethnic power than a dominant group, and much more than a balanced one. Why ethnic groups vary along these six power coordinates need not concern us here.[19] Clearly, historical development, the uneven spread of modernization, political contingencies, and various internal dynamics are involved. At any point in time, however, the relationship among the ethnic groups of a given country presumably can be disaggregated into these six dimensions and a power hierarchy can be established.[20]

Operationalizing these variables is a historically contingent procedure. In most (but not necessarily all) *contemporary* contexts, the following rough indexes will, I suggest, apply. Demographic size is self-evident; economic modernization may be measured by the size of an ethnic group's working class; social development, by the number of urban dwellers; cultural vitality, by the size of the ethnic intelligentsia; communications capacity, by the number of books and/or newspapers published; and organizational capacity, by the number of ethnic sociopolitical organizations and/or activists. To be sure, some degree of arbitrariness is necessarily involved here, but this problem is unavoidable in even the most behavioristically inclined studies and is unlikely to undermine the value of this approach. Indeed, in many cases, measurable indexes will for all practical purposes be irrelevant, since hegemony, dominance, and balance will be intuitively clear to informed observers.

Our concepts clarified, we follow again in the footsteps of classical theorists and engage in a series of thought experiments. First, we hold constant the state's political authority pattern. All things being equal (which, of course, they never are), which constellations of ethnic power may be imagined as providing their holders with the greatest opportunity of penetrating the state and generating ethnic patterns of domination? Naturally, we expect hegemonic ethnic groups to be

19. On the other hand, it is precisely such questions that interest Michael Hechter. See his *Internal Colonialism: The Celtic Fringe in British National Development, 1536–1966* (Berkeley: University of California Press, 1975).

20. Using somewhat different categories, Zev Katz attempts to develop a hierarchy of Soviet nationalities. See Zev Katz, ed., *Handbook of Major Soviet Nationalities* (New York: Free Press, 1975), pp. 440–65. Teresa Rakowska-Harmstone engages in a similar endeavor in "The Dialectics of Nationalism in the USSR," *Problems of Communism*, no. 3 (May–June 1974), pp. 1–22.

most successful. Their unchallengeable control of a society's ethnic resources, and particularly their control of organizational and leadership resources, guarantee them the greatest access to the state's loci of authority. We need look no further than pluralist theory to find convincing explanations of why this should be so.[21] Presumably, dominant ethnic groups will be somewhat less successful than hegemonic ones in generating patterns of domination, while a situation involving balanced groups should be least likely to produce such patterns. Ethnic balance, meanwhile, will be most likely, and ethnic hegemony least likely, to transform the state into an ethnic terrain of struggle.

We now hold ethnic power constant, and ask how political authority patterns affect the formation of an ethnic pattern of domination. All things being equal once again, we expect concentrated/centralized states least to permit societal penetration and the concomitant formation of an ethnic pattern of domination. Being most susceptible to some penetration by all ethnic groups, deconcentrated/decentralized authority patterns will be most inclined to evolve into ethnic terrains of struggle. Should one of the contending groups be hegemonic, however, the terrain of struggle is likely to develop quickly into a pattern of domination. Relatedly, deconcentrated/centralized and concentrated/decentralized patterns of authority, although less open to penetration by all ethnic groups, could probably be captured by a hegemon with sufficient ethnic power to overcome all other contenders.

The above two exercises leave us with expected results: the stronger the societal force, the greater its capacity to penetrate the state; the stronger the state, the greater its capacity to withstand societal pressure. Hegemonic ethnic groups, it may be hypothesized, will have least difficulty in penetrating deconcentrated/decentralized states, while balanced ethnic groups will have most difficulty penetrating concentrated/centralized states. These conclusions, as Descartes might have argued, appear to be eminently reasonable and therefore true, and we will leave them at that.

A far more important question interests us: How will concentrated/centralized states interact with hegemonic ethnic groups? As I suggested, this particular political authority pattern discourages societal penetration and the formation of ethnic patterns of domination,

21. Harry Eckstein, "The Determinants of Pressure Group Politics," in *Comparative Politics: A Reader*, ed. Harry Eckstein and David E. Apter (New York: Free Press, 1963), pp. 408–18.

while hegemonic ethnic power tends to produce the opposite effect. What happens when the irresistible force of ethnic hegemony meets the immovable object of concentrated centralization?

A hegemon is likely to be the only ethnic group with extensive access to the state. Indeed, it will probably be overrepresented in the state's personnel, since it enjoys a near-monopoly on organizational and leadership resources within society, and even concentrated/ centralized states must draw their personnel from somewhere. The distribution of authority within institutions, therefore, is likely to be heavily slanted in favor of the hegemonic group. But will ethnic hegemony also manifest itself in the form of an ethnic authority pattern *among* state institutions? An ethnic group's control of state personnel would surely facilitate the emergence of an interinstitutional ethnic pattern. Ethnic personnel might regard the state as theirs and structure it accordingly. More important, with so many societal resources concentrated in the hands of only one ethnic group, the strategic elite may adjust the state's institutional set-up to the logic and structure of the ethnic environment in order to be able better to manage societal relations and thus pursue survival effectively. The emergent state structure is likely to skew the interinstitutional distribution of authority in favor of the hegemon, so that an ethnic pattern of domination does indeed appear to emerge. I stress the apparent nature of the pattern under this scenario, because the state itself generates *autonomously* the interinstitutional component, which then complements the intrainstitutional pattern produced by the hegemon. Although the state's action represents a concession to the force of external circumstances and is tantamount to a diminution of autonomy, its loss is only partial since at least half of the overall authority pattern is self-imposed. The result is a paradox: the "naturally" autonomous concentrated/centralized state will, when confronted with ethnic hegemony, probably adopt a nonautonomous ethnic authority structure.

Such a state will experience with particular intensity the inevitable conflict between autonomy maximization and survival. The drive for self-maintenance impels all states to reinforce the societal sources of their patterns of authority; their concern for autonomy maximization repels them from the same forces to which they are beholden. This dilemma is particularly acute for such self-contained, strong entities, which, as the most effective autonomy maximizers, will never quite fully succumb to or fully overcome societal hegemons. Instead, their relationship with such groups will be characterized by constant tensions, a perpetual push and pull between two reluctant partners. We may expect their policies toward ethnic hegemons to be fraught with contradictory impulses, as such states act to reinforce simultaneously both their autonomy and their ethnic patterns. Locked in this embrace, concentrated/centralized states will face their greatest difficulties when survival requires that, at least momentarily, they give priority either to autonomy maximization (and thus embark on self-transformation) or to pattern reinforcement (and thereby retrench). A possible consequence of their confrontation with such confining conditions could be immobility—the incapacity to push through effective policies with respect to stability. It is at such points—within the vacuum that develops as a result of a state's vacillation and indecision—that antistate ethnic forces are likely to find their greatest opportunities for collective action.

Regionally hegemonic groups also present a problem for states with ethnic patterns of domination. Although such hegemons possess far less total ethnic power than the group that managed to penetrate the state, regionally they are capable of challenging, if not necessarily undermining, the state's ethnic authority patterns. Thus regional hegemons in general and their elites in particular represent a constant potential threat to the ethnic stability of the state. Clearly, the greater the regional hegemony of some ethnic group, the greater its potential for antistate activity. Politically subordinate groups with a regional ethnic power that is almost equal to or, indeed, greater than that of the overall hegemon will pose the greatest challenge to the state's effective pursuit of survival.

Three more thought experiments remain to be performed. First, how do class patterns of authority (either as patterns of domination or as class terrains of struggle) further or hinder the formation of an ethnic pattern of domination? Second, how does an already inscribed ethnic pattern of domination influence the formation of a class pattern of authority? And third, how do already inscribed class/ethnic authority patterns affect changes in a state's political authority patterns?

Since both class and ethnic authority patterns apply to *holders* of authority, the greater the identity between a hegemonic class and some ethnic group (as well as, conversely, between a hegemonic ethnic group and some class), the more the two patterns will tend to reinforce each other. If the intrainstitutional authority holders within a class pattern of domination all belong to a certain nation, that nation will clearly enjoy a head start on others in the race to penetrate the state. The same reasoning holds if the intrainstitutional authority holders within an ethnic pattern of domination all belong to a certain class. If, on the other hand, the authority pattern we start with is a class/ethnic terrain of struggle, its influence on the formation of ethnic/class patterns of domination will probably be negligible. Naturally, if the ethnically homogeneous holders of authority within a class pattern of domination do *not* belong to the hegemonic ethnic group, the hegemon's penetration of the state will be impeded. Again, similar reasoning holds if the class-homogeneous authority holders within an ethnic pattern of domination do not belong to the hegemonic class.

As to a state's political authority patterns, class/ethnic patterns of *domination* will reinforce existing political patterns and thus act as an obstacle to change, while class/ethnic terrains of struggle will facilitate, or at least not obstruct, political change. Stated more simply, since such patterns of domination represent highly entrenched interests, bureaucrats are unlikely to want to rock the boat by supporting change in a sphere of authority that at least partly affects their own position of dominance. As Zbigniew Brzezinski put it in a different context, the "nationality question in the Soviet Union has a profoundly conservative influence upon the prospects of political evolution in the Soviet Union."[22]

We can now suggest how the interaction of political patterns of authority, class patterns of domination, and hegemonic ethnic power will affect the formation of ethnic patterns of domination. We can better visualize this dynamic with the help of Figure 2. Injecting ethnic hegemony into quadrant *A* will produce an ethnic pattern of domination that is externally generated (by ethnic hegemony's penetration of deconcentrated decentralization) though internally encouraged (by ethnically hegemonic class authority holders). Injecting ethnic hegemony into quadrant *B* will lead to the formation of an ethnic pattern of domination that is generated both externally (for reasons outlined above) and internally (by state adaptation to an ethnically hegemonic environment) and is internally encouraged as well. Quadrants *C* and *D* are more problematic. In both cases, the ethnically different holders of class authority will impede state penetration by the ethnic hegemon. The degree of impeding, however, will be far smaller in quadrant *C*, where a deconcentrated/decentralized political pattern

22. Zbigniew Brzezinski, "Political Implications of Soviet Nationality Problems," in *Soviet Nationality Problems*, ed. Edward Allworth (New York: Columbia University Press, 1968), p. 76.

Political authority pattern

		Deconcentrated/ decentralized	Concentrated/ centralized
Class authority holders	Members of hegemonic ethnic group	A	B
	Nonmembers of hegemonic ethnic group	C	D

Figure 2. Sources of ethnic patterns of domination

encourages penetration, than in quadrant *D*, where a concentrated/
centralized pattern does not. Unlike the impenetrable political science jargon of these last few paragraphs, quadrant *A* will be most susceptible to penetration, quadrants *B* and *C* less so, and *D* least of all.
Impressionistic evidence supports this proposition. In such quadrant
B states as the USSR and China, and in such quadrant *A* states as Great
Britain, France, and West Germany, the ethnic hegemony of, respectively, the Russians, Han, English, French, and Germans has indeed
been converted into particularly entrenched ethnic patterns of domination.

As I hinted above, these thought experiments are not infallible for-
mulas for predicting state–ethnicity outcomes, if only because of their
complete ahistoricity. As heuristic devices, they can only illuminate
certain features of this dynamic. In the rarefied conceptual atmo-
sphere that we have just left, such intellectual experiments may make
a great deal of sense. In reality, of course, they serve only to point out
possible tendencies and probable tensions—in the same manner that
the states of nature of Hobbes, Locke, and Rousseau served, not as
accurate descriptions of the world *wie es eigentlich gewesen sei*, but
as methods of isolating relevant variables and examining their con-
nections without reference to the messiness of reality. Nevertheless,
an immediate benefit of our ruminations is that they complicate our
analytically simple distinctions among class, ethnic, and political patterns of authority. In reality, the three are symbiotically related, so
that separating one from the others is admittedly a facile solution to a
complicated practical problem. Since there really are no purely economic or political issues for a state desirous of maintaining the ethnic
authority pattern inscribed within it, any problem is potentially capa-

ble of affecting an existing ethnic pattern. By the same token, the distinction among ethnic, class, and political substability is an artifice not fully reflective of the complex underlying realities.

Although I am aware of these problems, conceptual clarity and analytical precision demand that we take this risky step. We must make somewhat strained distinctions if we hope to resolve the conceptual tangle involving the state, ethnicity, and stability. The alternative is to do what is generally done in the literature: compress these different notions and recognize no analytical and conceptual boundaries between them, with the result that no meaningful conceptualizations, not to speak of hypotheses, can be made. For most of this study, therefore, I will insist on the validity of the conceptual distinctions among class, ethnic, and political patterns of authority and among class, ethnic, and political substability, while fully cognizant of the fact that, in reality, their relationship is quite problematic.

CHAPTER 3

Ethnic Hegemony and the Soviet State

Far too often, conceptualizations of state–ethnicity relations in the USSR tend toward one of three interpretive extremes. The first divorces state (or system, Party, or elite) from society.[1] Nationality issues, it argues, are in essence no different from other problems (the economy, youth, disarmament, etc.) confronting the ethnically neutral Soviet state. The second tendency collapses state and society. A not untypical argument from this perspective might suggest, as Zbigniew Brzezinski does, that the "Soviet Union is the political expression of Russian nationalism," since "from time immemorial Russian society expressed itself politically through a state."[2] The third extreme, the most lamentable one, is to ignore the nationality question altogether.[3]

A better way of addressing the state–ethnicity dynamic might be to step outside the Sovietological ghetto and consult broader social science approaches. Internal colonialism, dependency, and imperialism

1. See Michael Voslensky, *Nomenklatura: The Soviet Ruling Class*, trans. Eric Mosbacher (New York: Doubleday, 1984); Jerry F. Hough and Merle Fainsod, *How the Soviet Union is Governed* (Cambridge: Harvard University Press, 1979); Basile Kerblay, *Modern Soviet Society* (New York: Pantheon, 1983).

2. Zbigniew Brzezinski, "Tragic Dilemmas of Soviet World Power," *Encounter*, December 1983, p. 10.

3. For example, Mary McAuley, *Politics and the Soviet Union* (Harmondsworth: Penguin, 1977).

immediately come to mind. All three are sophisticated attempts at conceptualizing center–periphery and dominant–subordinate relations. Although suggestive, how applicable are they to the Soviet context? Answering this question will set the stage nicely for a discussion of my own approach.

Alas, the internal colonialism perspective is disqualified on the basis of its initial premise, that the unequal relationship being analyzed deals with the regions of a unitary state.[4] The Union of Soviet Socialist Republics is, after all, a conglomeration of countries—a fact that Lenin's preference for a federal structure and Stalin's option for a unitary state recognized, albeit in different ways. (The slogan of "socialism in one country" is as a result decidedly misleading.) Internal colonialism also posits a radical division of the country in question into a rich, industrial, exploiting core and a poor, agricultural, exploited periphery—a distinction that may have been applicable to core–periphery relations in tsarist Russia but that does not hold for the Soviet republics today. Except for the period of forced collectivization from 1929 to 1933, it is virtually impossible to argue that the republics were or are exploited regions of the sort internal colonialism theorists have in mind.[5]

Dependency theory, which appears to be of greater applicability to the Soviet context, also involves substantial problems. Although the republics are unquestionably dependent on Moscow—in the sense that their development is a function of Moscow's priorities—their dependence is qualitatively different from the kind that *dependencia* theorists talk about. Raymond D. Duvall has cogently argued that *de-*

4. Michael Hechter, *Internal Colonialism: The Celtic Fringe in British National Development, 1536–1966* (Berkeley: University of California Press, 1975); Pablo Gonzalez Casanova, "Internal Colonialism and National Development," *Studies in Comparative International Development*, no. 4 (1965), pp. 27–37; Rodolfo Stavenhagen, "Seven Fallacies about Latin America," in *Latin America: Reform or Revolution?*, ed. James Petras and Maurice Zeitlin (Greenwich, Conn.: Fawcett, 1968). See also A. Eugene Havens and William L. Flinn, eds., *Internal Colonialism and Structural Change in Colombia* (New York: Praeger, 1970).

5. Alvin Gouldner's characterization of collectivization as an example of internal colonialism vis-à-vis the peasantry is also inaccurate, since it ignores the fact that collectivization's most intensely colonialist features were, perhaps not accidentally, revealed in the non-Russian regions of the USSR—Kazakhstan, the Ukraine, the Kuban, and the middle Volga area (Alvin Gouldner, "Stalinism: A Study of Internal Colonialism," *Telos*, no. 34 [Winter 1977], pp. 5–48). See Dana G. Dalrymple, "The Soviet Famine of 1932–1934," *Soviet Studies*, no. 3 (January 1964), pp. 250–84; James E. Mace, "Famine and Nationalism in Soviet Ukraine," *Problems of Communism*, no. 3 (May–June 1984), pp. 37–50.

pendence refers to "a context of differentially or asymmetrically structured reflections of the processes of capitalist production and reproduction at the international level." In other words, dependency theory deals with capitalist relationships among politically independent states—but neither of these conditions holds for interrepublican relations in the USSR. This is not to say that asymmetrical or exploitive relations may not exist among variably autonomous socialist systems, but only that such relations should be characterized and conceptualized differently—which is Duvall's point precisely: "The often waged criticism that dependencia theorists pay insufficient attention to Soviet imperialism and the dependence of Eastern Europe on the Soviet Union is fundamentally irrelevant and misdirected. The referential context is different, and hence, according to dependencia theorists, a different set of processes is apt to be involved and a different set of knowledge claims is apt to be validly applicable."[6]

The third approach, imperialism, involves what Wolfgang J. Mommsen calls the "expansion of a nation-state beyond its own borders for the purpose of acquiring overseas dependencies and if possible uniting them in a world-wide empire."[7] Despite his unnecessary reference to "overseas dependencies," Mommsen's definition correctly implies that Soviet Russia's original expansion into the formerly tsarist borderlands in 1918–21 and the USSR's current relations with Eastern Europe and other members of the Council for Mutual Economic Assistance (CMEA) may deserve the imperialist label. However, the approach falters with respect to interrepublican, center–periphery relations in the USSR today. Although, as I shall later argue, the Soviet state is decidedly Russian (i.e., it possesses a Russian pattern of domination), it is a crass oversimplification to assert that the USSR is actually ruled by a Russian nation-state. The straightforward imperialist paradigm does injustice to the complex, integrated nature of Soviet state and society by reducing them to "Russia and her colonies."[8] The non-Russian republics are certainly subordinate to

6. Raymond D. Duvall, "Dependence and Dependencia Theory: Notes toward Precision of Concept and Argument," *International Organization*, no. 1 (Winter 1978), pp. 57–58. For an excellent synthesis and bibliography of dependency theory, see James A. Caporaso, "Dependence, Dependency, and Power in the Global System: A Structural and Behavioral Analysis," *International Organization*, no. 1 (Winter 1978), pp. 13–50.

7. Wolfgang J. Mommsen, *Theories of Imperialism* (New York: Random House, 1980), p. 4.

8. For similar interpretations, see Walter Kolarz, *Russia and Her Colonies* (New York: Praeger, 1952); Roman Smal-Stocki, *The Nationality Problem of the Soviet Union and Russian Communist Imperialism* (Milwaukee: Bruce, 1952); Dmytro Solovei, *Polityka*

Moscow and their presence in the Union may not be as voluntary as Soviet propagandists insist, but they are anything but mere colonies. Even Abdurakhman Avtorkhanov, who argues in this mode, is aware that "a direct comparison between Soviet colonialism, that is, treatment of the non-Russian national minorities, and 'classic' Western colonialism is invalid."[9] But, if so, then why call Soviet treatment of the non-Russians "colonialism"?

I hope to provide a more sensible approach to state–ethnicity relations in the USSR by concentrating on the distribution of authority rather than on economic exploitation, and by viewing the Soviet state's relationship with Russian hegemony as the key to understanding the subordinate position of the non-Russians. This approach has three principal conceptual advantages: it encapsulates all the important elements of ethnic relations in the USSR; it manages to combine them in a manner that is isomorphic, analytically suggestive, and nonextreme; and it remains true to its concepts and eschews "stretching" them.[10] Analytically, the task this approach sets before us is also threefold. First, the conceptualization enjoins us to focus on and define the Soviet state. Second, it directs our attention to the distribution of ethnic power within Soviet society and to the Soviet state's ethnic authority patterns. Finally, it suggests where to look for potential ethnic challenges to state stability.

Most interpretations of the Soviet state confine it to the multi-layered system of ministries and councils extending throughout the USSR. Although the Communist Party is acknowledged to play a leading role in state institutions, it is said to fall outside the confines of the state, since it formally lacks coercive power and thus exerts only influence. Naturally, this division into Party and state is grossly mis-

---

TsK KPSS u plianuvanni rozvytku promyslovosty ta promyslovykh kadriv na Ukraini (New York: Proloh, 1960); Dmytro Solovei, *Ukrains'ka nauka v koloniial'nykh putakh* (New York: Proloh, 1963).

    9. Abdurakhman Avtorkhanov, *The Communist Party Apparatus* (Chicago: Henry Regnery, 1966), p. 319. Michael Rywkin and Martin Spechler also refer to Soviet economic policy in Central Asia as "welfare colonialism" (Michael Rywkin, *Moscow's Muslim Challenge* [Armonk, N.Y.: M. E. Sharpe, 1982], pp. 57, 117–19; Martin C. Spechler, "Regional Development in the USSR, 1958–1978," in *Soviet Economy in a Time of Change: A Compendium of Papers Submitted to the Joint Economic Committee of the Congress of the United States* [Washington, D.C.: Government Printing Office, 1979], I, 145).

    10. On conceptual stretching, see Giovanni Sartori, "Concept Misformation in Comparative Politics," *American Political Science Review*, no. 4 (December 1970), pp. 1033–53.

leading. V. Chkhikvadze is instinctively aware of this when he splits hairs by arguing that, while one may speak

> of the unity of Party directives and legal enactments, they should not be identified [with each other]. In the same way that the Party is the nucleus of state power but cannot be identified with this power, so a Party directive is the nucleus of a law but is not identical with it. Party directives assume the legal force after they have been expressed in the form of laws or other legal enactments promulgated by organs of the state.[11]

These distinctions, like scholastic arguments about angels on a pin, are absurd. If the Party sets the tune for the sovereign state and acts as its core for over sixty years, then it is high time to acknowledge it to be as much a part of the state as any formal-legal state agency. To their credit, Soviet scholars and policy makers appear recently to have understood that the traditional distinction between Party and state is conceptually weak and intellectually dishonest. Fedor Burlatskii, for example, prefers the broader notion of the "political system," since that permits him to include the Party within the USSR's political process.[12] More important, the 1977 constitution devotes its first chapter to the Soviet "political system," thus testifying to the fact that Burlatskii's views have acquired official sanction.[13]

The consequences of expanding the Soviet state to include the Party are twofold. First, since the Party is the leading institution, the state's strategic elite must be the members of the Politburo and the Secretariat, which stand at the CPSU's apex and guide both the formal state and the apparatus. And second, expanding the state puts seriously into question its purported multinationality. Formally-legally, Soviet theorists are right to claim that the USSR truly is a union of free and equal Soviet socialist republics. Although one may quibble about the rationale for dividing ministries into the Union, Union-republican, and republican varieties, on the whole the state structure of the USSR does approximate an equitable formal solution to the nationality question. Merging the Party with the state disrupts this happy arrangement. Although Soviet theorists like to depict the Communist Party

11. V. Chkhikvadze, *The State, Democracy, and Legality in the USSR* (Moscow: Progress, 1972), p. 49.

12. Fyodor Burlatsky, *The Modern State and Politics* (Moscow: Progress, 1978), pp. 47–52.

13. *Konstitutsiia (Osnovnoi Zakon) Soiuza Sovetskikh Sotsialisticheskikh Respublik* (Moscow, 1977), pp. 7–8.

only as a collection of individual proletarians, it is much more than that; the CPSU is also an institution. Party members may and do belong to all of the Soviet Union's ethnic groups, but, institutionally, the CPSU belongs to one group only—the Russians. Since the Communist Party of the Soviet Union has a branch in every republic except the RSFSR, all titular nations, except the Russians, belong to ethnically labeled subordinate institutions. By the process of identification proposed in Chapter 2, the purportedly supra-ethnic leading institution, the CPSU as a whole, must be considered the property of the Russians. And just as the CPSU is a Russian institution, so, too, the Politburo-Secretariat shares in the Party's institutionally Russian character. Seweryn Bialer confirms this view: "The Russians do not need a separate party organization, as do other Soviet nations, because they run the all-union party and its central establishment as their own fief."[14]

The enlarged state of which the Party is so important a part can have no claims to genuine multinationality because both the Party and the strategic elite skew state authority toward institutionally Russian agencies. The character of this imbalance was somewhat different under Stalin, but not so that the state ceased to be Russian. Stalin's personal dictatorship was tantamount to a radical contraction of the strategic elite and a massive expansion of state autonomy, and in both senses it represented a diminution of the institutionally Russian factor. However, the secret police, which was promoted to a leading role, was (and still is) structured along the same institutionally Russian lines as the CPSU. Under Stalin, therefore, the locus of Russian institutionality expanded, from the original core of the state, the Party, to include its avenging arm, the secret police, while the strategic elite, in the person of the dictator, hovered above both Russian agencies while playing off one against the other. The Stalinist state was shapeless, with no one leading institution; nevertheless, it remained institutionally Russian.

The Soviet state is Russian in another, more commonly recognized sense as well. The distribution of authority *within* institutions, among state personnel, has traditionally been and still is slanted in the Russians' favor, especially in central institutions such as the Politburo, the Secretariat, the Central Committee and its apparatus, ministries of all-Union importance, and second secretaryships of republican par-

14. Seweryn Bialer, *Stalin's Successors: Leadership, Stability, and Change in the Soviet Union* (Cambridge: Cambridge University Press, 1980), p. 220.

ties.[15] Admittedly, their dominance is no longer so overwhelming as it once was. Ukrainians and Belorussians have been co-opted into the central state in large numbers, while affirmative action has expanded non-Russian representation at the republican, or substate, level. In Uzbekistan, for example, elite recruitment patterns are a complex procedure that permits Russians to continue to hold on to some established key positions while allowing Uzbeks and other Central Asians to make substantial inroads into others, generally those that arose from an expansion of the Uzbek substate.[16] Despite these important gains, Russians still do rule by controlling the strategic elite and its affiliated central institutions, while non-Russians primarily only govern.[17]

A Russian pattern of domination, based on a Russian slant in both the inter- and intrainstitutional distribution of authority, has been inscribed—with varying degrees of depth—on all Soviet state formations since the 1920s. Indeed, we may refer to them in the singular, as the Soviet Russian state. Such nomenclature does not mean that the Soviet Russian state is a Russian national state. The Soviet state is Russian primarily in the sense that the holders of most of its inter- and intrainstitutional authority are Russian. The national state is Russian because it explicitly pursues Russian national goals, however defined. The root difference between the two types of states involves autonomy. While a Russian national state is beholden to the Russians, the Soviet Russian state is a highly autonomous entity capable of pursuing a variety of policies toward them—including, as Frederick Barghoorn has shown, Russian nationalism.[18] Stalin chose to identify himself with Russian hegemony, Khrushchev played down the Russian connection, Brezhnev played it up. These zigs and zags notwithstanding, no Soviet leader has ever turned his back on Russian hegemony, and in this sense the Soviet Russian state is not unlike its nationally minded cousin.

Why *is* the Soviet state a Russian state? According to our conceptual framework, the answer we seek lies in the distribution of ethnic

15. See Yaroslav Bilinsky, "The Rulers and the Ruled," *Problems of Communism*, no. 5 (September–October 1967), pp. 16–26; Seweryn Bialer, "How Russians Rule Russia," *Problems of Communism*, no. 5 (September–October 1964), pp. 45–52.

16. Irwin Steven Selnick, "The Ethnic and Political Determinants of Elite Recruitment in the Soviet National Republics: The Uzbek Soviet Elite, 1952–1981," Ph.D. dissertation, Columbia University, 1984.

17. Bialer, *Stalin's Successors*, p. 213.

18. Frederick C. Barghoorn, *Soviet Russian Nationalism* (New York: Oxford University Press, 1956).

TABLE 1

Ethnic resources in the USSR controlled by Russians, 1922–1980 (percent)

Resource	1922	1940	1965	1970	1975	1980
Population (Russians)	53%[a]	58%[b]	55%[c]	53%	n.a.	52%[d]
Workers (RSFSR)	71	67	62	60	59	58
Urbanites (RSFSR)	60	60	52[c]	60	n.a.	58[d]
Scientific workers (RSFSR)	n.a.	63	69	68	69	68
Books and brochures (Russian)	n.a.	75	76	76	77	78[e]
CP members (Russians)	65[f]	68[g]	64[h]	62[i]	61[j]	60[k]

n.a. = not available.

[a] 1926.	[d] 1979.	[g] 1946.
[b] 1939.	[e] 1981.	[h] 1961.
[c] 1959.	[f] 1927.	[i] 1967.

[i] 1973.
[k] 1983.

Sources: *Narodnoe khoziastvo SSSR, 1922–1982* (Moscow: Finansy i Statistika, 1982), pp. 12–13, 126, 403, 530, 532; *Partiinaia zhizn'*, no. 15 (1983), p. 23; Paul S. Shoup, *The East European and Soviet Data Handbook: Political, Social, and Developmental Indicators, 1945–1975* (New York: Columbia University Press, 1981), pp. 130, 140.

power in Soviet society. With regard to the "question of Russian dominance within the USSR," I agree fully with Bialer that "there is no doubt about the domination, without even going into it. This is an obvious fact that anybody who studies the Soviet Union knows."[19] As Table 1 illustrates, albeit somewhat crudely, the Russians have traditionally controlled and continue to control a major share of each of the resources that constitute ethnic power—demographic size, economic modernization (size of working class), social development (number of urban dwellers), cultural vitality (number of scientific workers as a substitute for size of intelligentsia), communications capacity (number of books published), and organizational capacity (number of sociopolitical activists or organizations). Simply put, the Russians are hegemonic societally.

Our conceptual framework also suggests that, irrespective of the Soviet state's political and class patterns of authority, Russian ethnic hegemony should suffice to produce a significant imprint on the "pure" Soviet state. As I have argued, a hegemonic nation can dominate a state's personnel—as the Russians have indeed done in the Soviet case—while its societal weight may so constrain the state as to induce it to adapt its interinstitutional authority patterns to the ethnic environment within which it is embedded. The theory may or may

19. Seweryn Bialer, "Comment—The Impact of Common RSFSR/USSR Institutions," in *Ethnic Russia in the USSR*, ed. Edward Allworth (New York: Pergamon, 1980), pp. 197–98.

not be persuasive, but it is not, of course, a proof of anything at all. Logic is no substitute for an empirically demonstrated connection, and it is at this point that our framework is revealed as just that—a theoretical construct that is helpful for analyzing reality but not necessarily for describing it.

The problem revolves about the notion of a "pure" Soviet state. If, as we know, such an entity has never existed, how can we determine the effect upon it of Russian hegemony? We resolve this theoretical and practical conundrum by embarking on an interpretive foray into the past. Since we have identified the Communist Party as the agency that invests the Soviet state with an institutionally Russian character, it will be helpful to focus our inquiry on the Party's origins and pre-revolutionary development and attempt to discover the sources of its Russian institutionality. If we can succeed in demonstrating that the Party's emergence in a hegemonically Russian environment accounts for its own ethnic character, we can claim to have established a connection, although not as direct as we would like, between Russian societal hegemony and the Soviet state's institutionally Russian profile.

The first point of importance is that the distribution of ethnic power in late-nineteenth- and early-twentieth-century Russia was over-whelmingly in favor of the Great Russians. Several hundred years of tsarist rule had led to the assimilation of borderland nobilities, the centralization of intellectual and cultural pursuits in St. Petersburg and Moscow, the transformation of many cities into largely Russian outposts, and the confinement of most non-Russian populations to the countryside. Only the Russian share of the population—44.32 percent in 1897—detracted from the magnitude of Russian hegemony. Perhaps most critical from the viewpoint of the emergent Marxist movement, the working class, although small, was solidly Russian. Second and equally important, the late tsarist state pursued policies that were openly intended to promote Great Russian political, economic, and cultural interests. As Richard Pipes has pointed out, "the period from the accession of Alexander III (1881) to the outbreak of the 1905 Revolution was that in which persecution of the minorities culminated. The Russian government perhaps for the first time in its entire history adopted a systematic policy of Russification and minority repression."[20]

20. Richard Pipes, The Formation of the Soviet Union (New York: Atheneum, 1974), pp. 6–7.

The stirrings of non-Russians in tsarist times were just that—incipient calls for a variety of rights with little mass resonance and uncertain appeal. The development of the Ukrainian movement is a case in point, clearly illustrating the prewar weakness of what, in 1917–21, turned out to be one of the strongest non-Russian political currents. Until the turn of the century, the Ukrainian national movement was almost exclusively cultural in its orientation. The pattern was broken in 1900 with the creation of the Revolutionary Ukrainian Party. Thereafter, a variety of parties came into being, but all were centered on the tiny Ukrainian intelligentsia.[21] Indeed, with the possible exception of such incipient right-wingers as Dmytro Dontsov and Viacheslav Lypyns'kyi, virtually no prerevolutionary Ukrainian activists had clear-cut separatist goals in mind.[22] Independence was generally viewed as unrealistic, and some form of autonomy was usually the maximal political aspiration. Even after the tsar's abdication in February 1917, the Ukrainian Central Rada, which consisted of the country's most astute leaders, demanded only autonomous status for the Ukraine. Just as telling is the fact that the Ukrainian Revolution's foremost actors—Volodymyr Vynnychenko, Mykhailo Hrushevs'kyi, and Symon Petliura—were not politicians, but a writer, a historian, and a journalist, respectively. And what held for the Ukrainians was equally true of most other non-Russians. In the words of Emanuel Sarkisyanz, "until the dissolution of Russia in 1918 the Poles and Finns were the only two subject nations to demand separation from the Russian state. All the other non-Russian peoples . . . , even those anti-Russian Muslims of Daghestan and Uzbek Kokand who had been most recently conquered by tsarist imperialism, demanded only autonomy within a federalized Russian democracy."[23]

Russia's Marxist movement took shape within this suffocatingly Russian societal and state environment. It would have been well-nigh impossible for a political party claiming the urban, largely Russian proletariat as its base of support and professing an ideological prefer-

21. See Jurij Borys, *The Sovietization of Ukraine, 1917–1923* (Edmonton: Canadian Institute of Ukrainian Studies, 1980), pp. 73–97.

22. See Alexander J. Motyl, *The Turn to the Right: The Ideological Origins and Development of Ukrainian Nationalism, 1919–1929* (Boulder, Colo.: East European Monographs, 1980), pp. 25–27, 62, and "Viacheslav Lypyns'kyi and the Ideology and Politics of Ukrainian Monarchism," *Canadian Slavonic Papers,* no. 1 (March 1985), pp. 31–48.

23. Emanuel Sarkisyanz, "Russian Imperialism Reconsidered," in *Russian Imperialism from Ivan the Great to the Revolution,* ed. Taras Hunczak (New Brunswick: Rutgers University Press, 1974), p. 71.

ence for centralized political orders and large states not to have been a reflection of the concrete social and political reality within which it functioned. There is, moreover, no way that a party aspiring to lead the working masses of the Russian Empire, overthrow the tsarist state, and establish its own order could have been anything but Russian, since a personnel and structure based on the non-Russians would have been self-defeating for a group with such large ambitions. From this perspective, the difference between a party that calls itself *rossiiskaia* and one that calls itself *russkaia* is purely semantic. Indeed, although opposed to the tsarist socioeconomic order and dedicated to smashing the state it generated, the Bolsheviks accepted fully the territorial integrity of Russia. The nationality question could be used, as Lenin astutely realized, for the attainment of particular political ends, but national self-determination was decidedly not supposed to be on the agenda of the emancipated non-Russian working classes. Thus the Bolsheviks' starting point in dealing with the recalcitrant nationalities was Russia and their attitude toward the nationality problem was by and large the attitude of the ruling party of a great power. From their viewpoint, the nationality question was essentially a nuisance that threatened to break up their preferred state unit— Russia—and their preferred party unit—the unitary Bolshevik wing of the Social Democratic Party.

In response to these environmental and ideological constraints, the Bolsheviks adopted an institutionally Russian structure. From the start, as Merle Fainsod has observed, they rejected "any division of working-class organizations on national lines," and they pursued this policy assiduously.[24] Vehemently opposed to the Austro-Marxist slogan of "national-cultural autonomy," they believed that all Social Democrats, whatever their nationality, should submerge their differences through joint work in the party organization of their territory[25]—one of the many reasons for their unsettled relations with the supraterritorial Bund. Territorial subunits of the party were encouraged—not as entities of equal value to the Russian party, but as regional parts of the Russian whole. Given this institutional bias, it was no wonder that many non-Russians identified the Bolsheviks with Russia, for the two were indeed inextricably related. Pipes ex-

24. Merle Fainsod, *How Russia Is Ruled* (Cambridge: Harvard University Press, 1953), p. 58.

25. Robert C. Tucker, "Stalin's Revolutionary Career before 1917," in *Revolution and Politics in Russia*, ed. Alexander and Janet Rabinowitch (Bloomington: Indiana University Press, 1972), p. 168.

plains just how close this relation was: "To the overwhelming majority of Communists and Communist sympathizers, the goals of the movement—the 'dictatorship of the proletariat,' the 'unity of the anticapitalist front,' or the 'destruction of counterrevolutionary forces'—were synonymous with the establishment of Great Russian hegemony."[26] Small wonder that Lenin found his postrevolutionary party teeming with Great Russian chauvinists. Nothing in the party's structure or personnel, after all, dispelled such tendencies. Even the mercurial Ukrainian national Communist Volodymyr Vynnychenko, a man who was subject to a certain political blindness, recognized the objectively Russian character of the Russian Communist Party after his unsuccessful attempt at reconciliation with the Bolsheviks in 1920.[27]

The party that emerged victorious from the Russian Revolution was, therefore, an institutionally Russian party. Together with its creation, the Cheka, it occupied, if not monopolized, the core of all the USSR's subsequent state formations, inevitably skewing the state's ethnic authority patterns in a Russian direction. The continued existence of Russian societal hegemony has thus served to support, although mediately, the Russian institutionality of the Soviet state. Not unjustifiably, we may consider Russian societal hegemony as both the ultimate source and immediate prop of the Soviet Russian state's ethnic patterns of domination.

Unlike ethnic patterns, which have remained more or less constant since the early 1920s, the Soviet state's political and class patterns of authority have experienced some variation. What kind of variation and why? The answer to this question tells us a great deal about why the state has been so effective in pursuing survival and why its opponents have been so ineffective in mounting serious antistate challenges.

Nineteen-twenty-one was a year of crisis for the Bolshevik state. War Communism had inevitably called forth opposition at all levels and among all sectors of the former tsarist empire, especially among peasants, nationalities, and sailors. The extreme, though unavoidable, centralization and concentration of authority it involved greatly sharpened inherent conflict tendencies between society and the state, while the chaos of civil-war conditions ensured that the political autonomy available for opposition was sufficiently large to permit antistate collective activities to occur on a massive scale. The state's re-

26. Pipes, *Formation of the Soviet Union*, p. 277.
27. Motyl, *Turn to the Right*, p. 55.

sponse to these threats to its political, class, and ethnic substabilities, as embodied in *korenizatsiia* and the New Economic Policy (NEP), was to retain control of the "commanding heights" while embarking on a "temporary retreat" and devolving authority to republican and local levels. A deconcentrated/centralized state largely independent of the various classes sprouting under the semimarket conditions of the NEP and a temporary defusion of the crisis were the result. Although a partial answer to the original crisis of overcentralization and overconcentration, deconcentration bore within itself the seeds of a new crisis, this time resulting from underconcentration. Encouraged by the devolution of authority and still enjoying substantial political autonomy, local elites and masses ventured boldly into the public sphere. There they began to engage in a variety of increasingly dysfunctional political, economic, and national-cultural activities—dysfunctional, that is, from the perspective of the still-centralized state. Since decentralization, the logical response to the crisis of the mid- to late 1920s, would have been tantamount to the Party's breakup and the state's dissolution, the crisis of underconcentration had to be resolved by the only means possible—reconcentration, and of no less extreme a kind than under war communism. The resulting Stalinist state eventually came to embody extraordinarily high centralization and concentration of authority; and by ending the NEP, it marked the emergence of a state-generated "new class" that controlled, if not owned, the means of production.

Since Stalin held so large a part of state authority, his death in 1953 inevitably produced another crisis—at first only within the state, since the political autonomy available to society was virtually nil. A Stalinist state without Stalin was a contradiction in terms, and Stalin's death ensured that an intense power struggle over the vast amount of state authority he bequeathed would necessarily ensue among his successors. In time the Party wrested supremacy from the secret police, and the strategic elite expanded to include Khrushchev and the entire collective leadership. In the process of reasserting the Party's leading role, the strategic elite revitalized the emasculated republican Party organizations and deconcentrated authority via the Sovnarkhoz reform. Additionally, the curbing of the secret police implied a massive and rapid expansion in political autonomy. Ironically, though not unexpectedly, the scenario of the 1920s repeated itself, and the combination of deconcentration plus autonomy again proved dysfunctional for the centralized Soviet state. The deconcentration of authority threatened to undermine the political stability of the state, since growing localism meant that the "social surplus" was being kept within the republics. By expanding political autonomy, meanwhile, Khrushchev unintentionally gave a filip to local political and cultural elites. Although very few ethnically based antistate collective actions took place in the early 1960s, the increasing volume of non-Russian elite assertiveness was perceived as an incipient threat to ethnic stability. Khrushchev's decision to split the Party in two was the final blow. As in the 1920s, the centralized status of the leading institution was being undermined. Countermeasures were called for: the strategic elite ousted the "harebrained" Khrushchev, while the Brezhnev-Kosygin leadership resolved the crisis of underconcentration by reconcentrating authority. The Sovnarkhozes were abolished, the Party's unitary structure was reestablished, autonomy was contracted, and opposition was crushed by a revived KGB. Class, ethnic, and political patterns have persisted to the present, although there are indications that Mikhail Gorbachev is responding to the crisis-laden legacy bestowed upon him by Brezhnev with Khrushchev-like attempts to deconcentrate authority and expand autonomy. If my analysis is correct, we should expect a new crisis of underconcentration and another crackdown in the near future.

Notably, in maintaining high levels of state stability, Lenin, Khrushchev, and perhaps Gorbachev have responded to cyclical crises of over- and underconcentration by tinkering only with the degree of concentration of the state's political authority patterns, thus expanding or contracting the political autonomy necessary for antistate activity. The currently existing class, ethnic, and centralized political patterns, which have remained unchallenged and unchanged since the late 1920s, thus appear as the bedrock of the strategic elites of all Soviet states. Elite power is derived from their dominance over the "new class," their symbiotic relationship with a hegemonically Russian societal environment, and, most important, their hold on centralized institutional authority. In practice, these theoretically disparate dimensions of state authority have become interconnected and mutually reinforcing. Class privileges, Russian institutionality, and bureaucratic power have fused into a whole. The limits to change are formidable, since an assault on one substability is likely to call forth a defensive reaction from the guardians of the others. Attempts at "revolution from above" will meet with the determined opposition of entrenched state interests and be confined to a secondary aspect, such as concentration of authority. Barring a truly enormous systemic crisis, societal forces will be as unsuccessful in launching antistate actions in the future as they have been in the past.[28]

Although subversion of state ethnic stability continues to be unlikely, regional challenges are not. As I argued in Chapter 2, regional hegemony greatly facilitates the elite impulse to use inherent conflict tendencies to make political demands. If a politically subordinate group becomes near-hegemonic in relation to a superordinate group, the state may eventually be transformed into an ethnic terrain of fierce struggle. The example of Lebanon suggests that country-wide civil war could then be the outcome. If, on the other hand, a subordinate group achieves full hegemony in a particular region only, political tensions will probably be confined to that area, thus necessitating heightened ethnic management by the central state. The Ukraine and other non-Russian republics that either already possess or approach regional hegemony are examples of this latter tendency.

The Soviet Russian state faces two potential threats to its ethnic stability. First, the non-Russian nations represent at least fourteen possible sources of ethnic discontent—a fact that demands of Moscow an especially sensitive nationality policy. Should the non-Russians be regarded as a collective threat to ethnic stability? As I argue in greater detail in Chapter 9, a non-Russian front is doubtful, since the differences among them appear to be as great as those between them and the Russians. Second, although Russians outpace Ukrainians in every category of ethnic power, Ukrainians—alone of all the non-Russians—have the absolute strength to pose a serious threat to the Soviet Russian state on their own. Ukrainians may not be as intractable as the Poles, but they possess as many, if not more, political, economic, social, and cultural resources. Indeed, the Ukraine could become the USSR's Poland—a comparison that says as much about the republic's capacity for trouble as it does about the likelihood of its success.

Statistical evidence underscores Ukrainian regional hegemony. At present, Ukrainians constitute 73.6 percent of their republic's population, 62.9 percent of its urban dwellers, 73.6 percent of the working class, 59.9 percent of white-collar workers, and 66 percent of the Communist Party of the Ukraine; book publishing, as Chapter 6 shows at greater length, is the only sphere of ethnic power in which Ukrainians lag behind. Table 2 points out that things were not always so. In

28. See [Alexander J. Motyl], "Gorbachev, Systemic Change, and the Nationality Question," *Soviet Nationality Survey*, no. 5 (May 1985), pp. 1–3.

TABLE 2

Ethnic resources in the Ukraine controlled by Ukrainians, 1922–1979 (percent)

	1922	1927	1939	1959	1970	1979
Population						
passport Ukrainians	n.a.	80.0%[a]	73.5%	76.8%	74.9%	73.6%
political Ukrainians	n.a.	n.a.	n.a.	72.7	69.0	66.0
Workers	n.a.	n.a.	65.8	69.5	73.6	n.a.
Urbanites	44.4%[b]	47.3[a]	n.a.	61.5	62.9	n.a.
White-collar workers	n.a.	n.a.	56.2	58.7	59.9	n.a.
Books and brochures	16.3[b]	55.9	42.0[c]	59.4	38.2	26.7
CP members	23.0	52.0	63.0[c]	64.0	65.0[d]	66.0[e]

n.a. = not available.
[a]1926.   [c]1940.   [e]1976.
[b]1923.   [d]1971.

Sources: Narodnoe khoziastvo Ukrainskoi SSR (Kiev: Tekhnika, 1977), p. 14; Bohdan Krawchenko, "Changes in the National and Social Composition of the Communist Party of Ukraine from the Revolution to 1976," *Journal of Ukrainian Studies*, no. 16 (Summer 1984), pp. 33–54; Bohdan Krawchenko, *Social Change and National Consciousness in Twentieth-Century Ukraine* (New York: St. Martin's Press, 1985), p. 206; George Liber, "Language, Literacy, and Book Publishing in the Ukrainian SSR, 1923–1928," *Slavic Review*, no. 4 (Winter 1982), pp. 679, 681; Steven L. Guthier, "Ukrainian Cities during the Revolution and the Interwar Era," and Roman Szporluk, "Urbanization in Ukraine since the Second World War," both in *Rethinking Ukrainian History*, ed. Ivan L. Rudnytsky (Edmonton: Canadian Institute of Ukrainian Studies, 1981), pp. 165, 190; Myroslav Shkandrij, "Literary Politics and Literary Debates in Ukraine, 1971–81," in *Ukraine after Shelest*, ed. Bohdan Krawchenko (Edmonton: Canadian Institute of Ukrainian Studies, 1983), p. 64; Yaroslav Bilinsky, "Shcherbytskyi, Ukraine, and Kremlin Politics," *Problems of Communism*, no. 4 (July–August 1983), p. 7; Borys Lewytzkyj, *Politics and Society in Soviet Ukraine, 1953–1980* (Edmonton: Canadian Institute of Ukrainian Studies, 1984), p. 171.

the early 1920s, for example, the Ukrainian share of ethnic power was much smaller. Since then, Ukrainians have progressively approached republican hegemony, and indeed they achieved that condition by approximately the late 1950s.

How hegemonic are the Ukrainians in reality? Our previous discussion of the ethnic ladder suggests that Soviet nationality statistics are not nearly so meaningful as we would like them to be. Statistics on the Ukrainians—and other nationalities—are actually only a measure of the socioeconomic and political characteristics of individuals who possess Ukrainian passports. Several samizdat writers differentiate between "true" Ukrainians and "paper" or "abstract" Ukrainians, whom they accuse of representing non-Ukrainian interests.[29] We do not have to share their negative assessment, but the question they raise is valid: Do all holders of Ukrainian passports occupy politically

29. *The Ukrainian Herald, Issue 7–8: Ethnocide of Ukrainians in the U.S.S.R.* (Baltimore: Smoloskyp, 1976), p. 72.

important positions on the Ukrainian ethnic ladder, that is, those
located somewhere above ethnic awareness and perhaps even above
national identity? The question is of more than academic interest,
since the way we—and the Soviet state—answer it will determine the
real extent of Ukrainian republican hegemony.

As unsatisfactory as it is, the census question regarding *rodnoi
iazyk* (native tongue) is the only way of addressing this problem.
Since the question is so formulated as to imply some ethnic allegiance, the percentage of holders of Ukrainian passports who identify
Ukrainian as their native language—93.5 percent in 1959, 91.4 percent in 1970, and 89.1 percent in 1979—may be considered a more
exact measure of the number of political Ukrainians, those individuals positioned on politically significant rungs of the Ukrainian
ethnic ladder. By the same logic, holders of non-Ukrainian passports
who declare Ukrainian to be their native language should be considered Ukrainian. Only 489,914 holders of non-Ukrainian passports, or
1.2 percent of the population, held that distinction in 1959, 444,604
(0.9%) in 1970, and 423,890 (0.9%) in 1979.[30] The true number of
occupants of politically significant rungs was, therefore, 72.7 percent
of the total republican population in 1959, 69 percent in 1970, and 66
percent in 1979. Even with the ethnic power statistics adjusted across
the board, Ukrainians still retain ethnic hegemony in their republic,
but it is clearly not so overwhelming as it was before.

How has the post-Stalin state managed to suppress the antistate
collective activity of the ethnically hegemonic Ukrainians? We shall
see shortly that some state techniques have a decidedly ethnic bent
and unquestionably belong to the realm of nationality policy alone;
others cover a wide range of possible antistate collective actions and
have relevance to ethnic, class, and political substability. We noted in
Chapter 2 that the four necessary conditions of conflict were antistate
attitudes, their deprivatization, antistate collectivities, and antistate
leaders. Preventing and containing these troublesome phenomena are
the state's ends; instrumental, normative, and coercive organizational
techniques are its means; the public sphere is where its highly successful struggle with adversaries takes place.

30. *Itogi Vsesoiuznoi perepisi naseleniia 1959 goda: Ukrainskaia SSR* (Moscow:
Gosstatizdat, 1963), p. 168; *Itogi Vsesoiuznoi perepisi naseleniia 1970 goda* (Moscow:
Statistika, 1973), IV, 153; *Chislennost' i sostav naseleniia SSSR: Po dannym Vsesoiuz-
noi perepisi naseleniia 1979 goda* (Moscow: Finansy i Statistika, 1984), pp. 102–3;
Narodnoe khoziastvo Ukrainskoi SSR (Kiev: Tekhnika, 1977), p. 14.

CHAPTER 4

Prosperity and Passivity

At least since Aristotle, theorists and practitioners of politics have believed that economic well-being is conducive to acceptance of the status quo. The Roman emperors who distributed free bread acted on this principle; so did Machiavelli, who encouraged princes to "reassure people and win them over by benefiting them."[1] At present, left-wing critics of capitalist society charge that consumerism lulls the working class into accepting a basically exploitive system,[2] Janos Kadar is persuaded that "goulash communism" is largely responsible for Hungary's current quiescence, while most non-Marxists would probably concur with Samuel P. Huntington's statement that "modernity breeds stability" while "modernization breeds instability."[3]

That economic well-being *should* inculcate acceptance of the system appears intuitively obvious. Materially satisfied people may be less inclined to risk their wealth by engaging in political or economic adventures, while a certain degree of wealth may function as the spark

1. Niccolò Machiavelli, *"The Prince" and "The Discourses"* (New York: Modern Library, 1950), p. 35.
2. See, for example, John Alt, "Beyond Class: The Decline of Industrial Labor and Leisure," *Telos*, no. 28 (Summer 1976), pp. 56–81; Herbert Marcuse, *One Dimensional Man* (Boston: Beacon, 1964).
3. Samuel P. Huntington, *Political Order in Changing Societies* (New Haven: Yale University Press, 1968), p. 41.

that kindles moderation in them. The causal chain, according to Seymour Martin Lipset, could go like this:

> Economic development, producing increased income, greater economic security, and widespread higher education, largely determines the form of the "class struggle," by permitting those in the lower strata to develop longer time perspectives and more complex and gradualist views of politics. A belief in secular reformist gradualism can be the ideology of only a relatively well-to-do lower class.[4]

Although the evidence and logic supporting the well-being/stability correlation is not unpersuasive, the connection is not so simple as it appears to be. After all, if expectations outstrip capacities for their fulfillment—something that is most likely in conditions of some prosperity—relative deprivation, frustration, and perhaps aggression may result.[5] Sudden fluctuations in an otherwise high level of prosperity may also encourage people to engage in political dissent.[6] In addition, as Ekkart Zimmermann points out, "political protest, as distinct from rebellion, does *not* tend to level off as a polity becomes economically more developed." Indeed, "since the economically most developed countries are democracies and since political protest is tolerated in democracies, economic development might have a positive net impact on the man-days of political protest in spite of the inhibiting conditions of economic development."[7] Finally, it would be foolhardy and ethnocentric to view contemporary developed countries as having entered upon an era of prosperity and stability. Golden ages tend always to end, and one does not have to be a Spenglerian pessimist to realize that unbounded optimism is historically and intellectually of dubious value.

These caveats aside, it is not unreasonable to adopt the prosperity/stability connection as a starting point for discussing the state of economic well-being in the Soviet Union in general and the Ukrainian SSR in particular. Post–World War II Soviet economic growth has been sizable, and the rise in the population's standard of living has been no less so. I suspect that these advances have contributed

4. Seymour Martin Lipset, *Political Man* (Garden City, N.Y.: Anchor, 1963), p. 45.
5. Ted Robert Gurr, *Why Men Rebel* (Princeton: Princeton University Press, 1970).
6. James C. Davies, "The J-Curve and Power Struggle Theories of Collective Violence," *American Sociological Review*, no. 4 (August 1974), pp. 601–13.
7. Ekkart Zimmermann, "Macro-comparative Research on Political Protest," in *Handbook of Political Conflict*, ed. Ted Robert Gurr (New York: Free Press, 1980), p. 177.

substantially both to the persuasiveness of the Soviet Russian state's ideological self-depiction as a benevolent organ of all-people's rule and to popular acquiescence in a materially advantageous situation. Whether or not rising living standards have actually produced greater political legitimacy for the Soviet state is another question altogether—one that cannot and need not be answered conclusively.

Let us begin with Soviet economic growth after World War II. It is generally recognized, both in the Soviet Union and in the West, that postwar reconstruction and subsequent economic expansion were fueled by massive injections of additional factors of production— labor, capital, and land. The work force grew rapidly; the state was committed to a vigorous investment policy; and an abundance of land, especially in Kazakhstan and Central Asia, served as the basis for agricultural expansion. Economic growth was extensive, not intensive.

Following the devastation of World War II, in which the Soviet Union lost an estimated 20 million men and women, its population grew most rapidly in the decade of the 1950s, increasing by 19 percent, from 178.5 million in 1950 to 212.4 million in 1960.[8] The 1960s registered a 14 percent growth, while the 1970s saw a 9 percent rise.[9] Although population growth manifested a long-term decline, the implications of which will be discussed in Chapter 10, the postwar take-off supplied the Soviet economy with the massive infusions of labor that its effective functioning demanded. The working-age population, defined as consisting of 16- to 59-year-old males and 16- to 54-year-old females, grew by approximately 17 million in the 1950s, 11 million in the 1960s, and 24 million in the 1970s.[10]

Population and labor force growth was matched by continued heavy investment in the economy along the lines of the Stalin growth model. Total gross investment increased by 89 percent in 1951–55, 87 percent in 1956–60, 45 percent in 1961–65, and 43 percent in 1966–70.[11] Most important for the Soviet population, an increasing share of

8. Frederick A. Leedy, "Demographic Trends in the U.S.S.R.," in *Soviet Economic Prospects for the Seventies* (Washington, D.C.: Government Printing Office, 1973), p. 431.

9. Murray Feshbach, "Population and Labor Force," in *The Soviet Economy: Toward the Year 2000*, ed. Abram Bergson and Herbert S. Levine (London: Allen & Unwin, 1983), p. 82.

10. Ibid., p. 87.

11. Keith Bush, "Resource Allocation Policy: Capital Investment," in *Soviet Economic Prospects*, p. 42.

the investment budget went to agriculture, with the result that gross fixed capital in agriculture increased 4.4 times between 1960 and 1980,[12] rising from 16 percent of gross fixed investment in the early 1960s to over 25 percent by the late 1970s.[13] The consequences of such solicitude, together with the equivalent of a guaranteed wage and a bona fide pension plan for collective farmers, are well known: a marked advance in the standard of living of the rural population and substantial improvements in the Soviet population's diet.

Finally, Soviet leaders greatly expanded the amount of acreage available to Soviet farmers both directly, by increasing the amount of arable land under cultivation, and indirectly, by means of a variety of land reclamation projects. Khrushchev in particular expanded sown acreage by more than 60 million hectares between 1954 and 1962. Total sown acreage in the 1960s exceeded that of the 1949–53 period by 39 percent and accounted for about 30 percent of the increase in Soviet agricultural production.[14] Output also grew respectably, at an average of 3.4 percent annually between 1951 and 1979. This aggregate figure conceals a secular decline—from 4.8 percent in the 1950s to 1.8 percent in the 1970s—but, when seen in comparison with agriculture's performance under Stalin, it provides some idea of the changes for the better experienced by Soviet citizens. For all its inefficiencies, Leonid Brezhnev's food program represents the state's continued commitment to developing the agricultural sector.

The results of what Soviet economists call "extensive growth" were undeniably impressive. The average annual percentage growth in net material product (NMP; roughly, gross national product [GNP] minus services) was 11.1 in 1951–55, 9.1 in 1956–60, 6.5 in 1961–65, 7.7 in 1966–70, 5.7 in 1971–75, and 4.2 in 1976–80. According to Central Intelligence Agency estimates, Soviet GNP (or, roughly, NMP plus services) grew by 5.5 percent in 1951–55, 5.9 percent in 1959–60, 5.0 percent in 1961–65, 5.2 percent in 1966–70, 3.7 percent in 1971–75, and 2.7 percent in 1976–80. Both sets of measures reveal secular declines in economic growth, but, just as clearly, both also show that

---

12. Robert Leggett, "Soviet Investment Policy in the 11th Five-Year Plan," in *Soviet Economy in the 1980's: Problems and Prospects* (Washington, D.C.: Government Printing Office, 1983), I, 131.

13. Bush, "Resource Allocation Policy," p. 41; James R. Millar, "The Prospects for Soviet Agriculture," in *The Soviet Economy*, ed. Morris Bornstein (Boulder, Colo.: Westview, 1982), p. 281.

14. Douglas B. Diamond et al., "Agricultural Production," in *Soviet Economy*, ed. Bergson and Levine, pp. 147–48.

the Soviet economy has been doing quite well, especially by world standards. "For the entire 1951–79 period, the [GNP] figure for the Soviet Union is roughly in the middle of the OECD range. Japan, West Germany, Spain and Turkey clearly achieved faster growth than the Soviet Union, and several other nations achieved rates close to the Soviet figure." Until the late 1970s the Soviet Union consistently enjoyed a higher growth rate than the United States.[15]

More important than growth per se is the degree to which economic largess has been distributed among the population. After all, the Soviet economy also grew rapidly in the 1930s, but few of the material advantages of industrialization and urbanization trickled down to the general population. As Gertrude E. Schroeder puts it, "consumers fared poorly under Stalin." Indeed, in 1950, "real household consumption per capita, after large declines during the early 1930s and during the war, had reached a level only about one-tenth above that in 1928." The 1950s, however, marked a major watershed in the life of the Soviet consumer. While "combined household and communal consumption per capita increased at an average annual rate of 1.1 percent during 1928–50," it grew by 4.3 percent in the 1950s, 3.8 percent in the 1960s, and 2.5 percent in the 1970s, for a 1951–79 annual average of 3.5 percent. Not unexpectedly, growth in consumption was erratic. In general, household services, along with public transportation and communications, fared best; the goods category, especially durables, followed close behind. Housing stock, the USSR's perennial soft spot, grew most slowly, while food consumption grew by a respectable, if unspectacular, 3.4 percent in 1951–60, 3.0 percent in 1961–70, and 1.4 percent in 1971–79.[16] We may assume that Soviet consumers, inured to rather low expectations by decades of Stalin's neglect, greeted this sizable upturn in their fortunes with some enthusiasm. Although they may or may not have invested the state with a greater degree of legitimacy, consumers surely had less reason to complain and indulge in antistate attitudes after 1950 than before.

In addition to improvements in aggregate levels of well-being, Soviet citizens have also experienced marked, if erratic, reductions in income differentials. Since 1950, for instance, the earnings of produc-

15. *USSR: Measures of Economic Growth and Development, 1950–80* (Washington, D.C.: Government Printing Office, 1982), pp. 25, 15, 19.

16. Gertrude E. Schroeder, "Consumption," in *Soviet Economy*, ed. Bergson and Levine, pp. 311–13.

tion workers in industry, construction, and state agriculture have risen dramatically in comparison with those of engineering-technical personnel and clerical workers.[17] So rapid a rise in working-class income, when coupled with a decline in the status of white-collar employees (which, incidentally, is not unlike that detected by Harry Braverman in capitalist societies),[18] is especially significant because workers are the Soviet economy's strategic class and the Soviet state's alleged proletarian base. Schroeder reports that "earnings differentials have also contracted among sectors of the economy, and most especially within the industrial sector." Most important perhaps, agricultural wages have literally zoomed upward. Collective farmers, a truly impoverished class under Stalin, used to earn a mere 13 percent of what state farmers did in 1950; by 1976, their share had jumped to 75 percent. In general, in the same time period, "average money wages of agricultural workers rose three times as fast as those of non-agricultural workers," with the result that agricultural wages equaled 70 percent of wages in other sectors in 1976 (as opposed to 11 percent in 1950).[19]

The question of regional, interrepublican differences is far more difficult to resolve. While Soviet spokesmen say that the problem is nonexistent, Western scholars claim that the Baltic republics and the RSFSR are still in the lead, while Central Asia and Moldavia continue to be least developed. At the same time, Western analysts generally do acknowledge that all Soviet nations have experienced some forward movement. What they disagree about is the size of interrepublican differences: Are they large or small? And are they getting larger or smaller, or are they staying the same? After considering the often contradictory evidence, Donna Bahry and Carol Nechemias offer a judicious evaluation worth quoting at some length:

> The most pessimistic assessments of Soviet efforts and successes in promoting regional equality are too pessimistic. In the case of urbanization, industrial development, economic and educational appropriations, and educational access, the most negative findings overstate the degree of inequality, primarily because of the particular choice of definitions, data, and methods used to assess regional conditions.
>
> This is not to proclaim the Soviet promise of equality an unques-

17. Ibid., p. 336.

18. Harry Braverman, *Labor and Monopoly Capital* (New York: Monthly Review Press, 1974), pp. 293–359.

19. Schroeder, "Consumption," pp. 336, 339.

tioned success: there are still disparities in virtually every aspect of regional development. . . . In sum, there is clear evidence of Soviet redistribution to the poorest republics and some evidence that the subsidies help to improve the lot of less developed regions (albeit slowly). But there is far less proof that equalization always has the intended results.[20]

The dilemma facing the Soviet state is not much different from that confronting the Yugoslav or any other leadership of a multinational state. While return per investment is higher in Croatia and Slovenia, the imperatives of ethnic equalization demand investment in Macedonia and the Kosovo. A rapidly expanding economy can afford some inefficient investments; a contracting economy can usually not permit itself this luxury. Of course, as interesting as Soviet equalization difficulties are, they beg the question "So what?" As Bahry and Nechemias put it, "the problem is to determine which of [the disparities] are significant and to decide what implications they hold for the Soviet system."[21] Pinpointing implications is the major problem, since it inevitably involves consideration of how the nations involved perceive or fail to perceive the disparities—a well-nigh impossible assignment in Soviet studies. Do Uzbeks compare themselves with Balts? Probably not. Do they compare their nation's living standards with those they enjoyed several decades ago? Presumably. (But what of intergenerational differences?) Do they compare themselves with Russians living in Uzbekistan? Nancy Lubin suggests that cultural predilections and the flourishing rural second economy lead Uzbeks actually to perceive themselves as more fortunate than local Russians.[22] If they do, Uzbekistan's statistical lagging behind may have very little importance for Uzbeks. Further complicating the picture is the fact that popular perceptions of material prosperity and the implications of regional disparities will vary from republic to republic; they will be functions of cultural traditions, ethnic power, historical past, and so on. What is true of the Uzbeks may not hold for the Georgians or the Ukrainians. Unfortunately, objective indexes of the sort used in equalization studies are of little help in determining perceptions. In a recent study of the correlation between material

20. Donna Bahry and Carol Nechemias, "Half Full or Half Empty?: The Debate over Soviet Regional Equality," *Slavic Review*, no. 3 (Fall 1981), p. 383.
21. Ibid.
22. Nancy Lubin, *Labour and Nationality in Soviet Central Asia* (Princeton: Princeton University Press, 1984), pp. 225–42.

prosperity and a "sense of social well-being," three wise Soviet scholars ask, "Why is the level of contentment with life much higher than
the all-Union level among representatives of all social groups of Azerbaidzhan, while the indexes for the Ukraine are lower [than the all-
Union average], even though the real [material] prosperity in these
regions is virtually identical? . . . To that question," they conclude,
"we can give no definite answer." Clearly, the "connection between
the subjective sphere of life activity and the social structure of society
is acquiring an ever more complex and indirect character."[23]

Subjective perceptions aside, there is no denying that the Ukraine
has been the beneficiary of real prosperity. Ihor Gordijew and I. S.
Koropeckyj estimate that the Ukraine is currently at about the same
developmental level as Italy—quite an achievement for a country that
sixty years ago was populated by peasants, most of them illiterate.[24]
Indeed, the average annual growth of the Ukrainian net material product outpaced that of the USSR as a whole in the 1950s (10.3% for the
USSR, 10.5% for the Ukraine) and in the first half of the 1960s (6.6%
USSR, 6.9% the Ukraine).[25] Thereafter, in 1965–70 and in 1970–77,
the Ukrainian growth rate slowed to a respectable annual average of
6.8 and 4.8 percent, respectively. Overall, the republic's NMP grew
3.9 times between 1956 and 1978.[26] The post-1965 slowdown in the
Ukrainian economy will be addressed in a later chapter, but, although
it is more severe than that afflicting the Soviet economy as a whole,
economic growth, at 4.8 percent in 1970–77, was hardly insignificant.

Although the Ukraine's growth was slightly lower than that of the
USSR in 1956–78, its starting point—the incredible destruction
wrought by the German occupation during World War II—makes the
Ukrainian statistics all the more significant. Seven hundred fourteen
cities and 28,000 villages had been destroyed, most livestock had
been "killed or removed," and an estimated 11 million persons lost
their lives in the war.[27] The point of comparison for most Ukrainians,
unlike that for most non-Ukrainians in the USSR, was virtually zero.

23. V. Kh. Bigulov et al., "Material'noe blagosostoianie i sotsial'noe blagopoluchie,"
Sotsiologicheskie issledovaniia, no. 4 (1984), p. 92.

24. Ihor Gordijew and I. S. Koropeckyj, "Ukraine," in *Economics of Soviet Regions*,
ed. I. S. Koropeckyj and Gertrude E. Schroeder (New York: Praeger, 1981), pp. 286–87.

25. Stanley H. Cohn, "Economic Growth," in *The Ukraine within the USSR*, ed. I. S.
Koropeckyj (New York: Praeger, 1971), p. 70. Note the slight difference between Cohn's
NMP figures for the USSR and those of the CIA (see n. 15).

26. Gordijew and Koropeckyj, "Ukraine," pp. 280, 279.

27. Ibid., pp. 278–79.

Any improvement, however small, is likely to have been magnified several times in the eyes of the indigenous population.

Just as in the USSR as a whole, economic growth has resulted in increased material well-being for the Ukraine's inhabitants. "On balance," writes Schroeder, "the evidence assembled suggests that consumers in the Ukraine improved their lot substantially during 1960–74. Judging from indirect evidence, the level of living in the Ukraine must have risen even more rapidly during the 1950s."[28] Ukrainian émigrés, with relatives back home to whom they mail occasional packages, probably know best the degree to which Soviet Ukrainian material needs and tastes have changed in the last four decades. Scarves, once used as a quasi-currency, are no longer in great demand; jeans (but only Wranglers!), Rubik's Cubes, and Sony Walkman tape recorders are. As even the Soviet press reluctantly admits, most Ukrainians (as well as most other Soviet citizens, regardless of nationality) have joyfully embraced consumerism. The recent discussion in Soviet specialized journals of "reasonable needs" and of the popular tendency to aspire to unreasonable ones is testimony to widespread materialism, especially among young people. One unusually truthful Soviet Ukrainian scholar analyzes the reasons for these tendencies as follows:

> The formation of young people's needs in the 1950s and 1960s was affected, on the one hand, by the economic difficulties of the reconstruction period and, on the other, by the desire of a segment of older-generation parents to shield the growing generation from these difficulties. ("We've had it hard, at least our children will have it easier.") It was then that one could notice a certain gap between a young person's needs and his personal participation in labor activity. This gap grew in the 1970s, when the opportunities to satisfy needs grew significantly as a result of a significant improvement in welfare. The results of parents' work were directed at the satisfaction of the needs of children, who were still not working. . . . The social-psychological consequence was that youth did not make the connection between the satisfaction of its needs and its own labor. . . . In this segment of youth there arose a one-sided development of needs primarily directed at "articles of prestige."[29]

28. Gertrude E. Schroeder, "Consumption and Personal Incomes," in *Ukraine within the USSR*, ed. Koropeckyj, p. 106.

29. "Formuvannia rozumnykh potreb liudyny," *Filosofs'ka dumka*, no. 3 (1984), p. 14.

Another scholar provides a fascinating profile of the Soviet young person with "unreasonable needs":

> On the basis of our research we developed a social-psychological profile of the young specialist disposed to accumulate articles of prestige. This is how it looks. This category of young people has an excessively developed "need for leisure." They are active and energetic, but not in the productive sphere. Frequently they do not like their work and therefore have unsatisfactory relations with their bosses and colleagues. Naturally, they are also dissatisfied with the size of their pay. The striving for accumulation produces within them a distorted sense of all other human needs and, in the end, amorality and philistinism. Goodness is not a character trait of accumulators. Quite the contrary, the successes of friends generally provoke their dissatisfaction and envy.[30]

Needless to say, societies that display such tendencies have long since ceased to be needy.

Official Soviet statistics confirm these impressions (see Tables 3 and 4). Ukrainians can now indulge in a variety of modern appliances; an increasing minority can even afford the greatest of Soviet luxuries, an automobile. Though still insufficient to meet demand, the supply of housing has expanded rapidly, as the figures for housing construction indicate (in thousands of square feet):[31]

1946–50	1951–55	1956–60	1961–65	1966–70	1971–75	1976–80	1981–83
45,981	42,122	87,429	94,994	96,090	97,706	90,818	54,678

Fewer families each year are sharing kitchens and bathrooms. Despite certain zigs and zags, consumption of eggs, meat, and vegetables has generally risen, while that of bread and potatoes has fallen. In the case of the Soviet Ukrainian elite, exotic Western appliances, country dachas, and occasional trips to the decadent West act as an added incentive not to rock the boat.[32] Naturally, this rather rosy picture has to be tempered with the caveat that "despite notable quantitative progress," in Schroeder's words, "consumers in the Ukraine, as in all republics, continue to suffer from poor-quality consumer goods, spo-

---

30. Ibid., p. 15.

31. *URSR u tsyfrakh u 1979 rotsi* (Kiev: Tekhnika, 1980), pp. 99–100; *Narodnoe khoziastvo Ukrainskoi SSR v 1983 godu* (Kiev: Tekhnika, 1984), p. 249.

32. See Mervyn Matthews, *Privilege in the Soviet Union: A Study of Elite Life-Styles under Communism* (London: Allen & Unwin, 1978).

TABLE 3

Number of household appliances sold in the Ukraine, 1965–1983
(per 1,000 people)

Appliance	1965	1970	1975	1979	1983
Clocks and watches	805	1,206	1,360	1,516	1,596
Radios	144	172	198	220	254
TVs	61	151	224	245	315
Cameras	52	71	75	87	99
Sewing machines	120	140	156	167	177
Refrigerators	23	82	170	227	283
Washing machines	54	137	187	204	192
Vacuum cleaners	14	32	56	80	112
Motorcycles, mopeds	16	18	22	26	40

Sources: *Ukrains'ka RSR u tsyfrakh u 1979 rotsi* (Kiev: Tekhnika, 1980), p. 99; *Ukraina za p'iatdesiat rokiv (1917–1967)* (Kiev: Politvydav, 1967), p. 202; *Narodnoe khoziastvo Ukrainskoi SSR v 1983 godu* (Kiev: Tekhnika, 1984), p. 275; *Narodnoe khoziastvo Ukrainskoi SSR: Iubileinyi statisticheskii ezhegodnik* (Kiev: Tekhnika, 1977), p. 327.

radic shortages of desired products, a deplorably low level of everyday service facilities, inadequate and poorly built housing, and limited ability to influence consumption pattern[s]."[33] Whether Mikhail Gorbachev's promise to improve product quality and galvanize the consumer and service sectors will produce tangible results is still impossible to tell.

Although few data are available, income differentials in the Ukraine appear to have narrowed along overall Soviet lines. In 1960–70, for example, the average annual pay rose 182 percent for the republic's collective farmers, 85 percent for state-farm workers, and 38 percent for industrial workers. Collective farmers' annual income was 45.7 percent of that enjoyed by state farmers in 1960 and 69.6 percent in 1970.[34] In Schroeder's estimate, "even though these figures omit earnings from private plots, it is evident that a dramatic reduction in income differentials between agricultural and nonagricultural workers took place in the Ukraine."[35] Just as striking is the progressive convergence in levels of economic development among the Ukraine's oblasts. According to a formula developed by a Soviet Ukrainian economist, the index of economic development of the republic's most

33. Schroeder, "Consumption and Personal Incomes," p. 106.

34. Ibid., pp. 93, 94.

35. Ibid., p. 94.

TABLE 4

Food consumption per person per year, Ukraine, 1955–1983, by category
(kilograms)

Category	1955	1960	1966	1970	1975	1979	1983
Meat and meat products	30	42	45	49	60	61	61
Milk and milk products	174	230	258	311	335	336	323
Eggs (units)	92	137	132	156	210	229	229
Bread products	184	163	156	155	151	143	140
Potatoes	162	174	158	156	143	146	140
Vegetables and melons	n.a.	89	102	103	118	116	116

n.a. = not available.

Sources: *Ukrains'ka RSR u tsyfrakh u 1979 rotsi* (Kiev: Tekhnika, 1980), p. 98; *Ukraina za p'iatdesiat rokiv (1917–1967)* (Kiev: Politvydav, 1967), p. 200; *Narodnoe khoziastvo Ukrainskoi SSR v 1983 godu* (Kiev: Tekhnika, 1983), p. 274.

developed oblasts fell by a factor of 1.16 between 1960 and 1980, while that of the least developed provinces rose by a factor of 1.14.[36] Most telling are the declining differences between highest and lowest oblast indexes: 1960, Donets'k with 1.67 vs. Ternopil' with 0.55; 1970, Dnipropetrovs'k with 1.58 vs. Zakarpattia with 0.56; and 1980, Dnipropetrovs'k with 1.43 vs. Zakarpattia with 0.62 (see Table 5). Significantly, the highly developed oblasts with declining indexes of economic development—Donets'k, Zaporizhzhia, Dnipropetrovs'k, Voroshylovhrad, and Kharkiv—are the ones in which most of the Ukraine's Russians live.

Most scholars agree that, in quantifiable terms, the Ukraine compares favorably with the other republics. The evidence provided by Stanley H. Cohn, Ellen Jones and Fred W. Grupp, and Gordijew and Koropeckyj supports Schroeder's view that, "broadly speaking, on most measures the Ukraine tends to rank behind the RSFSR and the Baltic republics, and ahead of the other republics."[37] True, the Ukrai-

36. D. N. Stechenko and O. A. Liubitseva, "Predplanovoe obosnovanie urovnei ekonomicheskogo razvitiia oblastei Ukrainskoi SSR," *Ekonomicheskaia geografiia*, no. 36 (1984), p. 71.

37. Schroeder, "Consumption and Personal Incomes," p. 106. See also Vsevolod Holubnychy, "Some Economic Aspects of Relations among the Soviet Republics," in *Ethnic Minorities in the Soviet Union*, ed. Erich Goldhagen (New York: Praeger, 1968), pp. 50–120; Ralph S. Clem, "Economic Development of the Russian Homeland: Regional Growth in the Soviet Union," in *Ethnic Russia in the USSR*, ed. Edward Allworth (New York: Pergamon, 1980), pp. 205–13; Jan Ake Dellenbrant, *Soviet Regional Policy* (Stockholm: Almqvist & Wiksell, 1980); Ellen Jones and Fred W. Grupp, "Modernisation and Ethnic Equalisation in the USSR," *Soviet Studies*, no. 2 (April 1984), pp. 159–84.

TABLE 5

Indexes of economic development and ranks of Ukrainian oblasts, 1960–1980

Oblast	Index of economic development			Rank		
	1960	1970	1980	1960	1970	1980
Donets'k	1.67	1.38	1.24	1	3	4
Zaporizhzhia	1.50	1.40	1.33	2	2	2
Dnipropetrovs'k	1.49	1.58	1.43	3	1	1
Voroshylovhrad	1.43	1.32	1.25	4	4	3
Kharkiv	1.24	1.17	1.11	5	5	5
Kherson	1.02	1.02	0.99	6	6	8
Kiev	0.98	0.92	0.93	7	10	12
Mykolaiv	0.96	0.94	0.97	8	8	9
Odessa	0.96	0.86	0.81	9	13	17
Crimea	0.91	0.93	0.83	10	9	15
L'viv	0.79	0.84	0.89	11	14	14
Sumy	0.79	0.90	1.00	12	12	7
Kirovohrad	0.79	0.91	0.96	13	11	11
Poltava	0.73	0.97	1.06	14	7	6
Cherkasy	0.69	0.82	0.93	15	16	13
Zhytomyr	0.68	0.71	0.80	16	18	18
Vinnytsia	0.68	0.73	0.82	17	17	16
Chernihiv	0.68	0.84	0.96	18	15	10
Chernivtsi	0.67	0.66	0.72	19	20	22
Volyn'	0.65	0.62	0.71	20	23	23
Khmel'nyts'kyi	0.59	0.65	0.80	21	21	19
Rovno	0.57	0.65	0.74	22	22	21
Ivano-Frankivs'k	0.57	0.70	0.76	23	19	20
Zakarpattia	0.56	0.56	0.62	24	25	25
Ternopil'	0.55	0.62	0.70	25	24	24

Source: D. N. Stechenko and O. A. Liubitseva, "Predplanovoe obosnovanie urovnei ekonomicheskogo razvitiia oblastei Ukrainskoi SSR," *Ekonomicheskaia geografiia*, no. 36 (1984), p. 71.

nian level of contentment with life may be lower than that of Azerbaidzhan and perhaps of other republics, but is it accompanied by resentment of non-Ukrainians in general and of Russians in particular? As suggested above, there really is no way of answering a question like this with a simple yes or no. Expressions of discontent with Soviet investment policy, such as those made in the early to mid-1960s, may reflect the conviction that the Russians—or, just as possibly, the Central Asians—are the prime beneficiaries of Ukrainian capital.[38] On the other hand, while the residents of Kiev, L'viv, Odessa, and Kharkiv

38. I. S. Koropeckyj, "Economic Prerogatives," in *Ukraine*, ed. Koropeckyj, pp. 34–35.

may be awed by what Moscow, Riga, Vilnius, and Tallinn have to offer, they are unlikely to be impressed by such provincial backwaters as Omsk, Tomsk, Minsk, Pinsk, and scores of other cities in the RSFSR, Central Asia, Siberia, and the Caucasus. In addition, as Roy Medvedev argues, Ukrainian peasants have no reason to be envious of most Russian peasants,[39] especially those living in the materially impoverished Non-Chernozem zone. The point, finally, is that no clear-cut, across-the-board comparison can be made, on the order of that between, say, the Ukraine and Hungary, and it remains to be proven that most Ukrainians feel compelled to make one.

With respect to Russians living in the Ukraine, the existing evidence is more conclusive. I noted above that oblast equalization statistics reveal decelerating development in the provinces most inhabited by Russians. This trend may or may not be economically desirable, but it is surely no cause for alarm for comparison-minded Ukrainians. The Ukraine's class structure also suggests that Ukrainians are making large gains with respect to the republic's Russians. Data on Ukrainian representation in the republic's working class, white-collar staff, and collective farmers, for example, indicate that passport Ukrainians increased their share of the former from 65.8 percent in 1939 to 69.5 percent in 1959 to 73.6 percent in 1970, while remaining more or less constant among the latter two categories—56.2, 58.7, and 59.9 percent of white-collar personnel and 85.3, 95.5, and 93.3 percent of the collective farm peasantry. While these figures testify to a somewhat skewed Ukrainian class structure, they do not indicate that passport Ukrainians have been relegated to the bottom half of a cultural division of labor.[40] In light of white-collar personnel's low prestige and relatively declining income, apparent Russian overrepresentation in this stratum points not to an ascendant Russian minority but to a vigorous Ukrainian majority.[41] Moreover, given the working class's high prestige *and* relatively growing income and the enormous socioeconomic strides made by the Ukraine's almost exclusively Ukrainian collective-farm peasantry, it becomes amply obvious that there are few grounds for considering passport Ukrainians an economically exploited nation. Finally, although most of the Ukraine's collective

39. Roy Medvedev, "What Lies Ahead for Us?" New Left Review (September–December 1974), p. 62.

40. Bohdan Krawchenko, Social Change and National Consciousness in Twentieth-Century Ukraine (New York: St. Martin's Press, 1985), p. 206.

41. Alex Pravda, "Is There a Soviet Working Class?" Problems of Communism, no. 6 (November–December 1982), pp. 1–24.

farmers are Ukrainian, most Ukrainians are no longer *kolkhozniki*. The latter's share among Ukrainians in the USSR as a whole (which is probably very close to their percentage in the Ukraine) has fallen quite drastically, from 52.6 percent in 1939 to 52 percent in 1959 to 33.4 percent in 1970 to as low as 19 percent in 1979.[42]

But how do the Ukrainians actually perceive the Russians living in their republic? Their real gains notwithstanding, do Ukrainians view Russians as a privileged economic elite? The Ukrainian dissident Ivan Dziuba, for example, has written that on the construction crew that built the Kiev hydroelectric station in the early 1960s, "almost all the top posts . . . (construction chief, chief engineer, most sectional and divisional managers) were occupied by Russians. They also constituted the majority among the rank-and-file engineers and technicians. Among the Russian workers a much higher percentage are highly skilled than among the Ukrainians."[43] Was Dziuba more or less alone in pointing to this differential distribution of positions, or do most Ukrainians share his view? It is hard to see how they can. As I argue in Chapter 8, socioeconomic differences between Russians and Ukrainians appear to have figured very little, if at all, in the motivation of young Ukrainian dissenters in the 1960s. In absolute terms, Ukrainians outrank and outnumber Russians across the board and have been making substantial socioeconomic advances in the last three decades. It is not at all evident, therefore, why objective disparities, which are not necessarily visible to the average Ukrainian untrained in Western Sovietology, should be so infuriating as they are often assumed to be. Consider also the following mitigating micro-level factors. First, Russians in the Ukraine are highly concentrated in the heavily industrialized oblasts in the east. Second, passport Ukrainians who inhabit these areas appear to occupy some of the lowest rungs of the Ukrainian ethnic ladder. And last, working alongside these and other Russians are just as many, if not more, passport Ukrainians. The first factor reduces overall Russian visibility in the republic; the second makes them more than acceptable to their immediate Ukrainian comrades; and the third undercuts anti-Russian resentment.

Most important, Soviet Ukrainians have experienced—and know they have experienced—an enormous expansion of educational op-

42. Darrell Slider, "A Note on the Class Structure of Soviet Nationalities," *Soviet Studies*, no. 4 (October 1985), pp. 536–38.

43. Ivan Dzyuba, *Internationalism or Russification?* (New York: Monad, 1974), pp. 110–11.

portunities since Dziuba made his comments. According to an authoritative Soviet source, the "number of higher education students
per 1000 population" in 1959–60 in the Ukraine was 9 "among [the]
total population of the republic" and 5 among Ukrainians.[44] By 1969–
70, the figure was 17 for the total population and 15 for Ukrainians.
As the size of the Ukrainian population had increased from 32.2 million in 1959 to 35.3 million in 1970, more than three times as many
Ukrainians were attending colleges (vuzi) in 1969–70 as in 1959–60.
A simple calculation reveals that non-Ukrainians had increased their
representation from 21 per 1,000 in 1959–69 to 23 per 1,000 in 1969–
70. In contrast to the slight increase experienced by—presumably—
Russians and Jews, Ukrainians had enjoyed a veritable educational
boom. Personal impressions and conversations with tourists and émigrés confirm these statistics. Indeed, one Ukrainian traveler explained
her support of the 1984 school reform with the remark that "even
street cleaners now have diplomas."

The implications of these findings are twofold. First, they reveal
that Ukrainians cannot be considered the benighted nation they are
often made out to be. This fact must surely play some role in their
general unwillingness to engage in antistate collective activity. And
second, if a Russified higher educational system is no bar to Ukrainians' educational advancement, then the mechanism of Russification, generally interpreted as a means of keeping Ukrainians out of
particular social and political positions, has to be reconsidered. Indeed, as I shall argue in Chapter 6, its real function may be just the
opposite: to integrate Ukrainians into the system.

It may now be worth asking an unanswerable question: How widespread is the absence of antistate attitudes in the Ukrainian SSR?
There is, of course, no reliable way of knowing. However, if participation in state, civic, and other organizations and activities is any indi-
cation of acceptance of the status quo, then it is evident that as far as
the Ukrainians' relationship with the Soviet Russian state is concerned, overall willingness to live and let live has been and still is on
the rise. The numbers of members and candidate members of the
Communist Party of the Ukraine have increased steadily:[45]

1946	1956	1966	1976	1983
320,307	895,403	1,961,408	2,625,808	3,037,981

44. Present-Day Ethnic Processes in the USSR (Moscow: Progress, 1977), p. 176.
45. Partiinaia zhizn', no. 15 (August 1983), p. 16; Boevoi otriad KPSS (Kiev: Politizdat Ukrainy, 1978), pp. 15–16.

as have the numbers of Komsomol members (in thousands):[46]

1940	1950	1955	1960	1965	1970	1975	1980
1,750	1,449	2,957	3,057	3,859	4,307	5,671	6,468

and workers' deputies:[47]

1947	1957	1967	1977	1982
307,372	336,822	422,576	522,021	525,500

and trade union members (in millions):[48]

1957	1965	1971	1977	1982
8.5	13.6	17.9	21.4	25

and participants in socialist competition (in thousands):

1959	1971	1972	1977	1980
6,149	13,992	20,000	20,488	21,275

and participants in the Movement for a Communist Attitude toward Labor (in thousands):[49]

1959	1961	1965	1971	1973	1977	1980	1982
600	4,000	6,000	8,660	10,000	11,487	12,925	13,400

It might be interjected that participation need not be a measure of legitimacy: after all, participation may be less than voluntary and enthusiastic, as it is often presumed to be in the Soviet case.[50] But this

46. *Narodnoe khoziastvo Ukrainskoi SSR* (Kiev: Tekhnika, 1977), p. 42; *Ukrains'ka Radians'ka Entsyklopediia*, 2d ed., VI, 120.

47. *Ukraina za p'iatdesiat rokiv (1917–1967)* (Kiev: Politvydav, 1967), p. 54; *Narodnoe khoziastvo SSSR, 1922–1982* (Moscow: Finansy i Statistika, 1982), p. 46; *Ukrains'ka Radians'ka Entsyklopediia*, 2d ed., VII, 38.

48. *Narodnoe khoziastvo Ukrainskoi SSR* (Kiev: Tekhnika, 1977), p. 41; *Ukrains'ka Radians'ka Entsyklopediia*, 1st ed., XVII, 230, 232; *Ukrains'ka Radians'ka Entsyklopediia*, 2d ed., IX, 164; *Suspil'no-politychne zhyttia trudiashchykh Ukrains'koi RSR* (Kiev: Naukova Dumka, 1974), II, 110.

49. *Narodnoe khoziastvo Ukrainskoi SSR* (Kiev: Tekhnika, 1977), p. 42; *Ekonomika Radians'koi Ukrainy*, no. 2 (1984), p. 49; *Ukrains'ka Radians'ka Entsyklopediia*, 2d ed., IX, 528; *Suspil'no-politychne zhyttia trudiashchykh Ukrains'koi RSR* (Kiev: Naukova Dumka, 1974), II, 250, 275, 276, 289; A. A. Kondrats'kyi, *Suspil'no-politychna aktyvnist' robitnychoho klasu Ukrains'koi RSR v umovakh rozvynutoho sotsializmu* (Kiev: Naukova Dumka, 1978), p. 93.

50. On participation in the USSR, see Theodore H. Friedgut, *Political Participation in the USSR* (Princeton: Princeton University Press, 1979); Jerry F. Hough, "Political Participation in the Soviet Union," *Soviet Studies*, no. 1 (January 1976), pp. 3–30;

objection misses the point, since participation certainly indicates that, if nothing else, the citizen has accepted the state's expectations and that a *modus vivendi* between citizen and state has been attained.

The Soviet Russian state's continued survival suggests that such a compromise does indeed exist. David Hume recognized that persisting things tend to be accepted and taken for granted.[51] To many Ukrainians, the fact that a Russian pattern of domination has been inscribed in all Soviet states since the early 1920s must be reason enough to accept this pattern as the natural way of things. "Once human beings have learned to take certain social arrangements for granted as part of the way the world works," Barrington Moore notes with a touch of sadness, "it is evidently quite difficult for them to change."[52]

Just how difficult it is to refuse obedience to authority was made chillingly evident by a series of psychological experiments performed in the United States by Stanley Milgram. Asked Milgram: "If an experimenter tells a subject to act with increasing severity against another person, under what conditions will the subject comply, and under what conditions will he disobey?" Milgram's findings were distressing: "A substantial proportion of people do what they are told to do, irrespective of the content of the act and without limitations of conscience, so long as they perceive that the command comes from a legitimate authority."[53] The conditions of Milgram's experiment are qualitatively different from those of Soviet society, where, among other things, the modifier "legitimate" may be somewhat difficult to apply. Even so, his conclusions remain highly suggestive. Not only do people, be they Russians, non-Russian citizens of the Soviet Union, or Americans, tend to submit to existing, time-honored, and therefore legitimate authority, but they are also likely to do its bidding, however much it runs counter to their professed beliefs. We are, alas, probably justified in thinking that most Ukrainian citizens of the Soviet Union accept the authority of a powerful state that goes out of its way to bestow material blessings upon them in return for one thing only—acquiescence in its existence.

Seweryn Bialer, *Stalin's Successors: Leadership, Stability, and Change in the Soviet Union* (Cambridge: Cambridge University Press, 1980), pp. 165–77.

51. Henry D. Aiken, ed., *Hume's Moral and Political Philosophy* (New York: Hafner, 1948), pp. 307–10.

52. Barrington Moore, *Injustice: The Social Bases of Obedience and Revolt* (White Plains, N.Y.: M. E. Sharpe, 1978), p. 43.

53. Stanley Milgram, *Obedience to Authority* (New York: Harper Torchbooks, 1975), pp. xii, 189.

CHAPTER 5

Ideology and Tautology

All states propagate legitimizing mythologies, those "complexes of ideas" that, in Louis Wirth's words, "direct activity toward the maintenance of the existing order."[1] National heroes are created, history is imbued with a message, and the existing state formation is made to appear the culmination of a particularly fortuitous chain of events. The ideologies of democratic states differ from those of authoritarian ones with respect only to content, not to function. American idealization of George Washington may not be so effusive as Soviet exaltation of Lenin, but it serves the same purpose—to provide a time-honored, glorious reference point for the mass of citizens being socialized in the present. By the same token, to a disinterested observer, the virtues of the "American way of life" and the "free-enterprise system" will appear curiously similar to those of the "Soviet way of life" and of "developed socialist society."

Western democracies expend far fewer resources than the USSR on ideological self-justification. Naturally, the Soviet obsession with ideology is due not to some psychological quirk of Soviet leaders but to their appreciation of its indispensable role in the state's effective pursuit of survival. A Russian state with claims to multinationality must devote substantial attention to popular perceptions lest they come to

---

1. Louis Wirth, "Preface," in Karl Mannheim, *Ideology and Utopia* (New York: Harcourt, Brace & World, 1936), p. xxi.

reflect the underlying conflict tendency inherent in the state's ethnic pattern of domination. Thus one function of Soviet ideology—the one that concerns us in this chapter—is to mold perceptions. Soviet ideology does this by enveloping society in a remarkably consistent, coherent, and complex conceptual web. Indeed, it is so seamless that to disentangle its many strands one must begin at the very beginning: the relationship between the Soviet base (classes and economy) and superstructure (Party, state, ethnicity).

The conceptual starting point in addressing this issue is the most fundamental of Marxist-Leninist tenets—that states are the instruments of political domination of ruling classes. As long as classes are struggling with each other, there will always be states to act as the executive committees of the ruling classes. Eliminate class struggle by eliminating classes, and states will necessarily, though not immediately, "wither away." Fundamentally transform classes and class relations and states will inevitably also be transformed.

Of course, the fledgling Soviet Union was a class state, or, as the 1924 constitution specifically says, it was a "dictatorship of the proletariat."[2] One Soviet author puts it more bluntly: "The victory of the socialist revolution in Russia meant the solution of the key issue, that of power—the conversion of the proletariat into a politically ruling class and the establishment of its dictatorship."[3] The main task of the dictatorship of the proletariat was to build socialism. That task required the dictatorship to eliminate the exploiters, to rally all working people to the proletarian cause, and to transform socioeconomic relations in the process. Since the superstructure invariably reflects the base, at least sooner or later, it became manifestly impossible for a socialist society to be ruled by a mere dictatorship of the proletariat. And indeed, by the time of Stalin's 1936 constitution, the "dictatorship of the proletariat" was transformed into a more appropriate superstructural construct—the "socialist state of workers and peasants."[4]

---

2. *USSR: Sixty Years of the Union, 1922–1982* (Moscow: Progress, 1982), p. 176.
    3. A. Lashin, *Socialism and the State* (Moscow: Progress, 1977), p. 72. According to another Soviet author, "the difference between the state of the dictatorship of the proletariat and all previously existing states lies in that its dictatorial aspect vis-à-vis its class opponents is not its most important aspect, in that the main aim of the dictatorship of the proletariat is the radical transformation of political, economic and social relations and the building of socialism" (V. Chkhikvadze, *The State, Democracy, and Legality in the USSR* [Moscow: Progress, 1972], p. 76).
    4. *USSR: Sixty Years of the Union*, p. 229.

As socialist society develops, as it inevitably must, it becomes increasingly socialist and increasingly developed. There is no disputing this tautology, unless one assumes that the transition from socialism to communism takes place in a flash—as Khrushchev mistakenly did by attempting to embark on the "full-scale construction of communism." A variety of profound changes accompany the development of socialism. The economy becomes increasingly socialist, the working class becomes numerically dominant, and the differences between town and country are progressively eradicated. Classes also become socialist formations: their commitment to socialist ideology grows, their love of the Soviet Motherland and all its nations and classes knows no bounds, and their desire to transform the "Land of the Soviets" into a communist country can barely be restrained. Class struggle, which is superfluous among friendly classes, withers away. Indeed, these macro-level changes are so enormous that they begin to affect the individual. Mythic or not, a "Soviet man" begins to emerge. Who is this remarkable comrade? Above all, he is an active builder of communism, and that means that his attitude toward life is premised on selfless participation in the construction of communism. Small wonder that socialist development is accompanied by the transformation of the formerly passive masses into energetic molders of their communist future. Public organizations multiply, worker participation in socialist competition becomes a fact of life, and all social groupings—men and women, young and old, Russian and non-Russian—are integrated into the grand cause of communism.

The upshot of these developments is not unexpected. As classes become increasingly socialist, they inevitably experience a "drawing together" [*sblizhenie*].[5] Classes do not yet disappear—after all, they can do so only under communism—but they become so downright friendly to one another that the social distance separating them becomes progressively smaller. Since class boundaries still remain, occasional problems or "contradictions" between classes may arise, but these contradictions are "nonantagonistic."[6] After all, the antagonistic variety cannot exist in the Soviet Union, because such problems involve fundamental, unresolvable conflicts of interest charac-

---

5. V. V. Kopeichikov, "Sotsialisticheskoe obshchenarodnoe gosudarstvo—glavnoe orudie postroeniia kommunizma," *Sovetskoe gosudarstvo i pravo*, no. 10 (October 1982), p. 114.

6. Ernst Kux, "Contradictions in Soviet Socialism," *Problems of Communism*, no. 6 (November–December 1984), p. 8.

teristic only of warring classes engaged in class struggle. Thanks to Stalin, class warfare disappeared by the mid-1930s.

The state perforce reflects these societal developments. As the people of the Soviet Union become a community of friendly builders of communism, the "socialist state of workers and peasants" becomes an "all-people's state" [*obshchenarodnoe gosudarstvo*].[7] Since classes continue to exist, however, the all-people's state must possess a class character. But if it is not a dictatorship of the proletariat or a state of workers and peasants, what is it? "The all-people's state is not a new type of state, but a qualitatively new and higher stage in the development of a state of the socialist type. The state of the dictatorship of the proletariat and the all-people's state are 'blood' relatives in that they relate to one and the same historical type of state—the socialist [state]."[8] Put another, equally Delphic way, the "socialist all-people's state does not lose its class nature, insofar as classes have still not disappeared and specific class interests continue to exist, although the social uniformity of socialist society has significantly grown and continually develops."[9] Thus, although the all-people's state is "in the last analysis" still based on the working class, it draws its strength from all the nonantagonistic classes grouped about the toilers. The feeling is mutual, of course, and the people's love of their own all-people's state is known as "Soviet patriotism."

All these developments culminate in "developed socialist" society, which, like the all-people's state, is a qualitatively new stage in the development of Soviet society. Indeed, "developed socialist society is a natural stage in the emergence of the communist formation. . . . Developed socialism indicates that the whole system of social relations gradually developing into communist relations has reached a high level of maturity."[10] As befits a transitional society, developed socialism represents the most complex and protracted stage of communist construction, during which simple socialism has to be fully transcended and simple communism has to be attained—no mean

7. Roger E. Kanet, "The Rise and Fall of the 'All-People's State': Recent Changes in the Soviet Theory of the State," *Soviet Studies*, no. 1 (1969), pp. 81–93.

8. N. V. Chernogolovkin, "Sotsialisticheskoe obshchenarodnoe gosudarstvo—vyrazitel' voli i interesov rabochikh, krest'ian i intelligentsii, trudiashchikhsia vsekh natsii i narodnostei strany," *Sovetskoe gosudarstvo i pravo*, no. 11 (November 1982), p. 115.

9. Kopeichikov, "Sotsialisticheskoe obshchenarodnoe gosudarstvo," p. 114.

10. E. Chekharin, *The Soviet Political System under Developed Socialism* (Moscow: Progress, 1977), p. 8.

feat. Cautious, yet full of the promises of the radiant communist future, developed socialism is tailor-made for conservatives, muddlers-
through, and would-be reformers alike. Leonid Brezhnev brought the
concept to life, Konstantin Chernenko defended it till his dying days,
and Mikhail Gorbachev has not abandoned it.[11] His own modifica-
tion, the "perfection of socialism" [*sovershenstvovanie sotsializma*],
takes place during the "stage of developed socialism" and retains all
the features of Brezhnev's formulation while adding a certain measure
of urgency and forward movement. Major breakthroughs in the
USSR's social and productive relations are scheduled to take place as
a result of the "all-round perfection of socialist society," but the process will continue to be complex and protracted.[12] In this sense, Gorbachev's innovation represents a perfectly logical and internally fully
consistent progression in the development of Soviet ideology. (Ironically, by embodying both the caution of Brezhnev and the promise of
Khrushchev, Gorbachev's concept represents even less of a break with
the ideological past than "developed socialism.")

Where does the Party fit into this scheme? Like the state, the Party is
the crystallized superstructural expression of Soviet society. Since it
reflects ongoing social changes, it, too, has undergone a profound
transformation—from a "party of the working class" to a "party of the
entire people." It is, in a word, an all-people's party. Unlike the state,
however, the Party is not a coercive instrument; it does not even share
in state power. Rather, it exerts influence upon the course of socialist
and communist construction by means of the persuasiveness, activism, and *kontrol'* of its members. Who are these high-minded individuals? They are the best and the brightest that Soviet society has to

11. On developed socialism, see Alfred B. Evans, Jr., "Developed Socialism in Soviet
Ideology," *Soviet Studies*, no. 3 (July 1977), p. 427; Robbin F. Laird, " 'Developed'
Socialist Society and the Dialectics of Development and Legitimation in the Soviet
Union," *Soviet Union*, no. 1 (1979), pp. 130–49; Alfred Evans, Jr., "The Decline of
Developed Socialism? Some Trends in Recent Soviet Ideology," *Soviet Studies*, no. 1
(January 1986), pp. 1–23; Oskar Anweiler, "Die 'entwickelte sozialistische Gesell-
schaft' als Lern- und Erziehungsgesellschaft," *Osteuropa*, no. 7 (July 1978), pp. 574–85.
12. See Mikhail Gorbachev, "Bessmertnyi podvig sovetskogo naroda," *Kommunist*,
no. 8 (May 1985), pp. 10–12; V. S. Semenov, "Dialektika sovershenstvovaniia sotsializma i prodvizheniia k kommunizmu," *Voprosy filosofii*, no. 1 (January 1986), pp.
22–36; V. S. Semenov, "Kurs na uskorenie sotsial'no-ekonomicheskogo razvitiia, na
sovershenstvovanie obshchestva razvitogo sotsializma," *Voprosy filosofii*, no. 5 (May
1985), pp. 15–34; O. S. Kapto, "Prohrama planomirnoho i vsebichnoho vdoskonalennia
sotsializmu," *Komunist Ukrainy*, no. 1 (January 1986), pp. 8–20; A. Krukhmalev,
"Kommunisticheskaia formatsiia: Dve fazy razvitiia," *Kommunist vooruzhennykh syl*,
no. 1 (January 1986), pp. 15–23.

offer. No wonder, then, that the CPSU is the "core" of the Soviet political system, of which the state and public organizations are also part.[13]

Given these qualities, it is hardly surprising that the Party was, is, and will continue to be the driving force behind the USSR's march through developed socialism and its more perfect variety toward communism. The hallmark of this stage of communist construction is, after all, complexity. As the number of critical variables grows, societal management becomes increasingly imperative. Whose job will it be to fine-tune socialist society? Only the vanguard is up to the task. And, as systemic complexity grows, so Party leadership must grow. The revised Party program explains the rationale in greater detail:

> In the new historical conditions, when responsible tasks in internal development and in the international arena confront the country, the Party's leading role in the life of Soviet society naturally grows, and higher demands are made on the level of its political, organizational, and ideological activity. This is conditioned by such basic factors as:
> —the growing scale and complexity of the tasks of perfecting socialism and accelerating the country's socioeconomic development. . . .
> —the development of the political system and the deepening of democracy. . . .
> —the need for the further creative development of Marxist-Leninist theory. . . .
> —the interests of deepening the all-round cooperation and strengthening the solidarity of the socialist countries. . . .
> —the complication of foreign policy conditions. . . .[14]

Since the toilers and the Party are becoming increasingly active, is it not incumbent upon the state to begin to wither away? Although Khrushchev did suggest just that, the current answer, for several reasons, is no—and correctly so. First, as an all-people's entity, the Soviet state is not an instrument of class exploitation; consequently, withering away need not be at the top of the agenda of so benign and loving an organism. Second, as the soviets are among the major vehicles for the activization of the masses, their withering away would be inconsistent with the growing participation of the citizenry in the country's political process. Third, the emergence of a "single economic mecha-

---

13. *Konstitutsiia (Osnovnoi Zakon) Soiuza Sovetskikh Sotsialisticheskikh Respublik* (Moscow, 1977), p. 8.

14. *Prohrama Komunistychnoi Partii Radians'koho Soiuzu* (Kiev: Politvydav Ukrainy, 1986), pp. 72–73.

nism," the growing complexity of the USSR's economic tasks, and the imperatives of intensive economic growth necessitate continued central planning and economic management. And fourth, withering away would leave the Party as the only active force in the Soviet political system—but this would be tantamount to Party dictatorship, hardly a feasible option for Soviet ideologists.

We are left, finally, with a remarkable picture: individuals, classes, Party, and state have become mutually reinforcing and mutually supportive. All serious antagonisms have been abolished and unity, harmony, and homogeneity are all that matters. Literally everyone's sociopolitical activity just grows and grows—to the benefit of all concerned. There are no rulers, there are no ruled; no dominants, no subordinates; no elites and no masses. At most, the Party leads, but only because it represents the best of society. Not an elite, it is just the first among equals.

Similar processes take place at the level of nations and national relations. The starting point is the proposition that nations are not immutable, but products of particular historical circumstances, and that national conflicts are in the last analysis epiphenomena of class conflicts. Resolve class conflict by abolishing class contradictions and eventually classes themselves, and the nationality question will also be solved. Marx's teachings must hold: "In proportion as the exploitation of one individual by another is put an end to, the exploitation of one nation by another will also be put an end to. In proportion as the antagonism between classes within nations vanishes, the hostility of one nation to another will come to an end."[15]

The nationality question was a serious problem at the time of the Great October Socialist Revolution. The Russian bourgeoisie exploited the non-Russians and national enmity was rampant; given the capitalist foundations of the tsarist empire, it could not have been otherwise. Thanks to the genius of V. I. Lenin, however, a formula for resolving these tensions was found. It was "socialist federalism," whose "principles" were the "unconditional recognition and realization of the equality of all nations, all peoples and races; the voluntary, equal, and free character of the unification of the Soviet republics; democratic centralism in the order and activity of the Soviet multinational state."[16] The non-Russians' aspirations to independence were

---

15. "Manifesto of the Communist Party," in *The Marx-Engels Reader*, ed. Robert C. Tucker (New York: Norton, 1978), pp. 488–89.
16. I. P. Tsamerian, "Radians'ka bahatonatsional'na derzhava na etapi zriloho sotsializmu," *Filosofs'ka dumka*, no. 4 (July–August 1983), p. 33.

satisfied, and the existence of a just proletarian dictatorship in all the republics guaranteed that their union would be based on class and national equality. Although they have transferred certain of their prerogatives to the all-Union state, the Soviet nations continue to be masters of their own destinies within the sovereign republics they inhabit. They have the right to secede from the Union, and the fact that they have not done so is proof of their satisfaction with Lenin's brilliant arrangement.

Understandably, the Russian nation played a prominent role in the first stages of the new proletarian state. Since the working class was largely Russian, it was inevitable that Russians would assume a high profile. "As a consequence of historical circumstances," writes E. A. Bagramov, "the Russian people were faced after the revolutionary upheaval with an extremely important internationalist mission with regard to the formerly oppressed nations." That mission consisted of selflessly helping the less fortunate non-Russian workers and peasants develop socially, economically, and culturally so that they might rise to the level of the Russians.[17] All these formidable goals were achieved. As the exploiting classes were overcome, as the unity of the working class and peasantry grew, and as the foundations of socialism were built—processes described above—massive transformations also took place within all the Soviet nations. Their industries developed, their cultural levels rose, their languages acquired literary status, and their working classes increased in importance. As the nations of the USSR came increasingly to live in a socialist society, they became transformed into "socialist nations." I. P. Tsamerian encapsulates this lengthy process:

> After the liquidation of class antagonisms, national enmity receded into the past, and the formerly backward national borderlands, where archaic and sometimes even neo-feudal relations to a large degree dominated, attained rapid development. Under the leadership of the Communist Party and thanks to the friendly creative labor of millions of toilers, a single economic complex was created in the USSR, the social structure of the republics qualitatively changed, and socialist multinational culture blossomed in the process of the intensive exchange of spiritual treasures. Socialist nations formed. . . .[18]

17. E. A. Bagramov, "Deistvitel'no proletarskoe otnoshenie k natsional'nomu voprosu i mify antikommunizma," *Voprosy istorii KPSS*, no. 6 (June 1984), pp. 89, 92.

18. Tsamerian, "Radians'ka bahatonatsional'na derzhava," p. 32.

As the nonantagonistic classes underwent *sblizhenie*, so, too, the nonantagonistic socialist nations inevitably drew together. The all-people's state, therefore, is not based merely on the nonantagonistic class relations of the USSR's increasingly friendly classes; it also embodies the growing "friendship of peoples" [*druzhba narodov*] and "proletarian internationalism" [*proletarskii internatsionalizm*] of the Soviet socialist nations. The intensity of their drawing together and friendship is such that, at about the time of the appearance of developed socialist society, the Soviet socialist classes and the Soviet socialist nations attained so great a degree of unity and uniformity as to constitute a "new historical community of people—the Soviet people" [*sovetskii narod*].[19] E. V. Tadevosian describes the critically important relationship between the development of developed socialism and the development of the Soviet people:

> Although definite traits of the future community already appeared in the process of the building of developed socialist society . . . , it is only in conditions of mature socialism that, strictly speaking, the new historical community, as a qualitatively original and integral formation, became a reality. . . . It is not accidental that the Party concludes that the formation of this new community [took place] not in the 30s or 40s but in the 60s, precisely when the country entered into developed, mature socialism. It is fully consistent that the all-people's socialist state replaces the state of the dictatorship of the proletariat, and the CPSU as the party of the working class becomes the party of the entire people in the 60s as well. One can say that the formation of the new historical community of people was an important sociopolitical criterion of the maturity of socialism and the emergence of all-people's socialist statehood.[20]

The process described by Tadevosian was inevitable, given the inevitability of the drawing together of all classes and social groups under

19. For critiques of this concept, see Yaroslav Bilinsky, "The Concept of the Soviet People and Its Implications for Soviet Nationality Policy," *Annals of the Ukrainian Academy of Arts and Sciences in the United States*, nos. 37–38 (1978–80), pp. 87–133; Myroslav Prokop, "Pro t. zv. radians'kyi narod," *Suchasnist'*, nos. 2, 3 (February, March 1976), pp. 70–79, 60–69; Borys Lewytzkyj, *"Sovetskij narod"—"Das Sowjetvolk": Nationalitätenpolitik als Instrument des Sowjetimperialismus* (Hamburg: Hoffmann & Campe, 1983).

20. E. V. Tadevosian, "Sovetskii narod—sotsial'naia osnova Sovetskogo mnogonatsional'nogo obshchenarodnogo gosudarstva," *Sovetskoe gosudarstvo i pravo*, no. 12 (December 1982), p. 15.

conditions of socialism. At present, therefore, the multinational Soviet people, consisting of Soviet socialist classes and Soviet socialist nations, is ruled by a multinational socialist all-people's state and led by a multinational all-people's Communist Party. Individuals, classes, nations, Party, and state are indissolubly united by a commonality not only of modifiers but also of interests.

Although some Soviet theorists have suggested that the Soviet people represent a distinct nation, the present consensus is just what we expect. Since the drawing together of classes and nations lies at the base of the Soviet people, it makes good theoretical sense to call the Soviet people an "interclass and internationality" community.[21] A related controversy concerned the question of whether Soviet socialist nations were undergoing a simple drawing together or an actual "merger" [*sliianie*] and thereby were losing their identities.[22] Although some emphasis was placed on the latter process in the mid-1970s, the current line is that drawing together will continue to intensify during the perfection of socialism, and that final merger will take place only in the "remote historical future."[23] This interpretation makes far more sense, since socialist nations cannot become classless communist nations and then merge so long as classes have not disappeared—and that consummation, obviously, will not come about for quite a while.[24]

Despite the future merger of the Soviet nations, their present drawing together in no way signifies a loss of national identity. Paradoxically, as the socialist nations draw together, they also undergo "blossoming" [*rastsvet*]—a development parallel to the growing activity of Soviet society, Party, and state. The process is more than a trifle dialectical, but it is not at all mysterious if Stalin's dictum regarding "socialist in content and national in form" is kept in mind. Thus the social, political, economic, and other processes at the heart of drawing together are conducted in the national languages and in terms of the national cultures of the socialist nations. The implications of this point appear to make Soviet theorists somewhat uneasy. It hardly requires much ideological perspicacity to suspect that, at some time, the multitude of languages and cultures acting as the vehicles of drawing together may get in the way of the very process they

21. Ibid., p. 16.
22. Bilinsky, "Concept of the Soviet People," pp. 110–18.
23. *Prohrama*, p. 42.
24. Tsamerian, "Radians'ka bahatonatsional'na derzhava," p. 43.

are supposed to encourage. How are the Soviet people supposed to communicate with one another? And how are communist nations supposed to merge if they are still living within their own national boundaries? The Soviet socialist nations need a "language of internationality intercourse" to get them out of this awful impasse.

Enter Russian. The "language of the great Lenin" did not have an "internationalist role" to play in the 1920s and early 1930s, when the non-Russians worked on raising their own cultural and linguistic levels. But in the mid-1930s things changed. "While the social functions of the languages of the many nationalities were expanding in several spheres, including education, there was also a growing necessity for a language of inter-nation communication. Now that the non-Russian peoples had full, equal rights, and had raised their cultural and educational level, there was a greater impetus to learn Russian."[25] An additional impulse to turn to a language of internationality intercourse proceeded from the "objective . . . internationalization of all spheres of social life" and the consolidation of the "single economic complex."[26] As internationality contacts grew and the friendship of peoples bloomed, a lingua franca became a necessity. Perhaps more important, the economic interaction of diverse socialist nations necessitated a common language for conducting the production process. So why Russian? Iu. Desheriev has the answer:

> The vital necessity of the Russian language for the peoples of the USSR is determined by the following exceptionally important social functions: (a) it is the language of the largest people in our country; (b) it is a language of internationality intercourse; (c) it is a language of communication and cooperation of the Soviet peoples with the peoples of other countries of the world; (d) it is one of the main sources of the enrichment and development of the other languages of the peoples of our country.[27]

Despite the fact that Desheriev's second and fourth points betray an inability to differentiate between causes and effects, his message is clear: "The outstanding importance of the Russian language proceeds directly from the role that the Russian people played and continue to

25. *Present-Day Ethnic Processes in the USSR* (Moscow: Progress, 1982), p. 137.

26. L. P. Nahorna, "Partiine kerivnytstvo internatsional'nymy i natsional'nymy protsesamy v suspil'stvi rozvynutoho sotsializmu," *Ukrains'kyi istorychnyi zhurnal*, no. 12 (December 1982), pp. 18, 19.

27. Iu. Desheriev, "Vazhneishii faktor v sblizhenii vsekh natsii i narodnostei strany," *Partiinaia zhizn'*, no. 1 (January 1983), p. 25.

play in the development of Soviet society."[28] The Russians did not just fulfill their internationalist obligations in the 1920s and 1930s and then meekly leave the stage. Although their relations with non-Russians are based on friendship of peoples, proletarian internationalism, and Soviet patriotism, the Russians are still the *primus inter pares* of Soviet socialist nations. Like many other Soviet officials, Deputy Prime Minister G. A. Aliev, an Azeri, has made this point explicitly:

> There has formed among Soviet peoples just the kind of union of which Lenin dreamed—a union that is voluntary, equal, and very intimate. And it is not an exaggeration to say that the Great Russian people are its soul and heart. The Russian people were and remain an example of selflessness in the creation of a new society and in the struggle for the affirmation of Lenin's ideals. Their revolutionary enthusiasm and their disinterested assistance were the basis of the stormy, all-round progress of all the peoples of the country. To them are addressed feelings of love and the very deep esteem and gratitude of Soviet people of all nationalities.[29]

But what is to guarantee that the Russian elder brother will not decide someday to flex his muscles and turn against his younger kin? The existence of the Soviet people precludes even the possibility of this eventuality, Mikhail Kulichenko tells us, since they are "a new historical and socio-political multi-national entity, an unbreakable unity of classes and social groups, nations and nationalities based on a community of goals and interests, of economic and cultural life, of national characters, moral standards, customs and traditions."[30] By definition, the Soviet people's "unbreakable unity" and "community of goals and interests" guarantee that ethnicity will remain the epiphenomenon it is supposed to be. Russian seniority, yes; superiority, no.

At this point the circle is complete. Nations were originally defined in terms of class. Now classes and the perfectibility of their relations are also defined in terms of nations. All variables are equal to one another, as they are all reducible to the same thing—increasingly perfect parts of an increasingly perfect whole that is relentlessly advancing toward complete homogeneity, unity, and equality. Do Soviet

28. Ibid., p. 24.

29. *Pravda*, April 23, 1985.

30. Mikhail Kulichenko, *How the USSR Solved the Nationalities Question* (Moscow: Novosti, 1974), p. 71.

citizens accept this circular interpretation of Soviet reality—one that consigns both the CPSU and the Russians to mere equality? Chapter 6 argues that acceptance is only a part, and a small one at that, of what the state hopes to attain with its ideological bombardment of society. Nevertheless, although there is no way of answering this question conclusively, it would be naive to think that the official world view, which is energetically propagated in every sphere of Soviet life, does not have a substantial number of adherents. Persistent Soviet complaints about the need to "raise the level of ideological work" suggest that many Soviet citizens are still insufficiently friendly, patriotic, and internationalist.[31] Still, there can be no doubt that large numbers must actually believe or at least unthinkingly accept what they are told. The long lines of pilgrims at Lenin's tomb testify to their faith. Interestingly, even many dissidents, who openly claim to reject the official line, continue to think and act in typically Soviet fashion and thus remain "Soviet men and women."

That this should be so is not surprising. Such circular conceptual building blocks permit Soviet ideology to erect a towering barricade between the Soviet world view and the bourgeois one. As a tautology and a totality, Soviet ideology challenges its consumers either to accept it or to reject it in toto. The more circular it becomes, the greater its irrefutability. The more reality it enmeshes in its conceptual webs, the greater the difficulty, if one insists on arguing on its terms, of escaping its entanglements. The only way to refute Soviet ideology is to cast it aside, that is, to seek wholly new premises, develop an entirely new logic, and reach completely different conclusions. But such an alternative is unrealistic for most individuals, who are ideologically indifferent or unsophisticated. Consequently, they remain entangled in its webs.

Ideological acceptance, however, is far more than a question of straightforward indoctrination, as the totalitarian model would have us believe. Contemporary Soviet ideology can be appealing to its consumers because it offers them something as well. Those citizens who accept the ideological message do so because it conveys a complex world view that is supportive of the state without being unduly abhorrent to them. Non-Russians with minimal political ambitions, for ex-

---

31. See Stephen White, "The Effectiveness of Political Propaganda in the USSR," *Soviet Studies*, no. 3 (July 1980), pp. 323–48; Stephen White, "Propagating Communist Values in the USSR," *Problems of Communism*, no. 6 (November–December 1985), pp. 1–17; Gerhard Simon, "Die Wirksamkeit sowjetischer Propaganda," *Osteuropa*, no. 8 (August 1974), pp. 575–85.

ample, can find substantial room for their aspirations in the ideology. Although it sanctions the political supremacy of an institutionally Russian party and the hegemony of the Great Russians, it also permits the non-Russians to "blossom" and develop, not only to "draw together." More important, the ideology sanctions the "symbolic sovereignty" of the republics[32]—their possession of formal republican substate structures, parties, legal codes, flags, anthems, and constitutions, all of which act both to maintain national identity and to satisfy certain needs. As Soviet theorists like to emphasize, all republics enjoy "sovereignty." Clearly, though, the Ukraine and Belorussia, as members of the United Nations and of many other international organizations, are more symbolically sovereign than the rest.[33] And of the two, the Ukraine, whose representatives play a particularly active role in international bodies, is obviously first.[34]

In what ways does the Ukrainian SSR's symbolic sovereignty manifest itself? The republic is a charter member of the United Nations and belongs to fifty-five permanent and temporary bodies of fifteen intergovernmental organizations, among them the International Atomic Energy Agency, the International Labor Organization, and UNESCO.[35] The Ukraine was a member of the United Nations Security Council in 1948–49 and 1984–85. It is a signatory to more than

---

32. There is some similarity between symbolic sovereignty and the concept of "tactical nation-states," which denotes "units designed largely exogenously, that is at the initiative and under the control of outside powers, to serve as temporary and expedient means towards larger ends" (Gregory J. Massell, "Modernization and National Policy in Soviet Central Asia: Problems and Prospects," in *The Dynamics of Soviet Politics*, ed. Paul Cocks et al. [Cambridge: Harvard University Press, 1976], p. 268).

33. On republican sovereignty, see E. V. Tadevosian, *Sovetskaia natsional'naia gosudarstvennost'* (Moscow: Izdatel'stvo Moskovskogo Universiteta, 1972).

34. For a sampling of articles on the Ukrainian SSR's sovereignty, see *Radians'ke pravo*, no. 6 (September–October 1962), pp. 3–8; *Radians'ke pravo*, no. 1 (January 1966), pp. 3–7; *Radians'ke pravo*, no. 12 (December 1966), pp. 15–18; *Radians'ka Ukraina*, May 12, 1967, pp. 2–3; *Radians'ka Ukraina*, August 6, 1968, p. 2; *Ekonomika Radians'koi Ukrainy*, no. 4 (April 1970), pp. 3–12; *Radians'ke pravo*, no. 2 (February 1972), pp. 3–7. The following works in particular are suffused with the spirit of sovereignty: *Istoriia derzhavy i prava Ukrains'koi RSR* (Kiev: Naukova Dumka, 1967) and *Ukraina v period rozhornutoho budivnytstva komunizmu: Politychna orhanizatsiia suspil'stva* (Kiev: Naukova Dumka, 1967). See also Friedrich-Christian Schroeder and Boris Meissner, eds., *Bundesstaat und Nationalitätenrecht in der Sowjetunion* (Berlin: Duncker & Humblot, 1974).

35. Stanislav Lazebnyk and Pavlo Orlenko, *The Ukraine Today* (Kiev: Ukraina Society, 1980), p. 69. For a list of international organizations of which the Ukraine is a member, see *Soviet Ukraine* (Kiev: Academy of Sciences of the Ukrainian SSR, 1969), p. 552.

120 international agreements, treaties, and conventions; it has its own permanent representations in New York City, Paris, and Geneva; and it is host to the consulates general of Bulgaria, Cuba, Czechoslovakia, East Germany, Hungary, Poland, Rumania, the United States, and Yugoslavia in Kiev, and of Bulgaria, Cuba, India, and, until recently, Egypt in Odessa.[36] (Belorussia, its nearest republican competitor, has only two consulates, those of Poland and East Germany in Minsk.) Finally, as is the right of all diplomats, Soviet Ukrainian delegates deliver long-winded speeches at august world bodies, while their comrades at home greet foreign presidents, premiers, and ministers who make courtesy calls in Kiev.[37]

By the standards of real sovereignty, symbolic sovereignty is, of course, just that—symbolic, a facade for a lack of sovereignty. Yet there are probably many Ukrainians who do not judge their republic's status by such measuring sticks. I suspect that these unquantifiable multitudes accept the ideology's interpretation of the Ukrainian SSR's status and appreciate the opportunity it gives them to engage in the national rituals that symbolic sovereignty sanctions. In this manner, the Soviet state acquires substantial Ukrainian compliance with its institutionally Russian character by means of a purely formal acknowledgment of the republic's exceptional nature.

Most susceptible to the attractions of symbolic sovereignty are (I believe but cannot prove) the eastern Ukrainians. Western Ukrainians have a long tradition of intense nationalism.[38] Many of them either participated in, experienced, or still remember the "national liberation struggle" that was waged after World War II. Comparisons with

36. See Alexander J. Motyl, "The Foreign Relations of the Ukrainian SSR," *Harvard Ukrainian Studies*, no. 1 (March 1982), pp. 65–67. On the issue of the U.S. consulate in Kiev, see Alexander J. Motyl, "Kto Kavo? A Consulate in Kiev," *Commonweal*, March 9, 1984, pp. 134–35, and "A U.S. Consulate in Kiev?" *Freedom at Issue*, no. 69 (November–December 1982), pp. 22–23. The U.S. consulate, slated to open in mid-1986, still had not done so by the end of the year.

37. Helmut Kohl's stopover in the Ukrainian capital in July 1983, for example, although diplomatically of little or no significance, was a form of tacit recognition by the Federal Republic of Germany of the Ukraine's existence (which, incidentally, is to say a great deal) and importance within the Soviet context. Predictably, the Soviet Ukrainian press ran front-page stories about Kohl's meeting with CPU First Secretary Volodymyr Shcherbyts'kyi (*Radians'ka Ukraina*, July 7, 1983). The message, obviously, was that two statesmen representing two states were involved in discussions.

38. On the nationalist traditions of the western Ukrainians, see Alexander J. Motyl, *The Turn to the Right: The Ideological Origins and Development of Ukrainian Nationalism, 1919–1929* (Boulder, Colo.: East European Monographs, 1980), and "Ukrainian Nationalist Political Violence in Inter-war Poland," *East European Quarterly*, no. 1 (March 1985), pp. 45–55.

the past probably evoke negative emotions among the older members of this minority segment of the Ukrainian population. Among the far larger majority in the east (83% of the total population of the Ukrainian SSR), however, and especially among those who lived through the Stalinist terror, the Ukraine's present symbolic sovereignty may appear to be a step forward in comparison with the past they remember. After all, very few can recall that their republic enjoyed far broader diplomatic prerogatives in the 1920s.[39]

Most important perhaps, the Ukraine's symbolic sovereignty appears to be appealing to members of the Soviet Ukrainian substate— its prime beneficiaries.[40] The General Assembly speeches of Soviet Ukrainian representatives subtly reveal its attractiveness for these individuals. Of the ten presentations delivered between 1946 and 1955, for example, only one, in 1947, gives an openly, if superficially, Ukrainian perspective on an issue. In the rest, the term "Ukrainian SSR" appears only perfunctorily, first in the introduction and then in expressions of support for the USSR's position.[41] Starting with 1956 and continuing through 1979, all but three speeches provided the Soviet Ukrainian government's presumed view of things.[42] An additional nuance is also apparent. From 1946 to 1961 and from 1965 to 1970, the speakers almost invariably invoked the "Ukrainian SSR." Only very rarely did the phrase "delegation of the Ukraine" or "government of the Ukraine" arise. Between 1962 and 1964, on the other hand, the standard usage was not "Ukrainian SSR" but the more nationally minded "Ukraine."[43] The terminological changes are surely attributable at least in part to changes in the internal Soviet political climate—that is, to Khrushchev's de-Stalinization speech at the 20th Party Congress in 1956; to the 22d Party Congress in October 1961, which gave an additional impulse to de-Stalinization; and to Khrushchev's ouster and replacement by Brezhnev and Kosygin three years later, in October 1964.

If Arkady N. Shevchenko's revelations are accurate, the Ukraine's delegates to the United Nations can be under no illusions about the

39. Motyl, "Foreign Relations," pp. 67–70.

40. See Ukrainian SSR Minister of Foreign Affairs Hennadyi Udovenko's reaction to his republic's election to the United Nations Security Council in Visti z Ukrainy, no. 47 (November 1983).

41. Ukrains'ka RSR na mizhnarodnii areni: Zbirnyk dokumentiv i materialiv, 1944– 1961 rr. (Kiev: Politvydav Ukrainy, 1963), pp. 123–99.

42. Ibid., pp. 200–265; Ukrains'ka RSR na mizhnarodnii areni: Zbirnyk dokumentiv i materialiv, 1962–1970 rr. (Kiev: Politvydav Ukrainy, 1977), pp. 23–116.

43. Ukrains'ka RSR na mizhnarodnii areni (1977), pp. 23–46.

real scope of their republic's international importance.[44] They must realize that the Ukraine's international role is completely subordinated to the policy imperatives of the USSR; they must be aware of the exclusively symbolic nature of the Ukrainian SSR's "sovereignty." Nonetheless, their behavior at the United Nations strongly suggests that Ukrainian substate officials draw satisfaction bordering on pride from the Ukrainian SSR's international status, and therefore take advantage of expansions of political autonomy to express it. In this sense, symbolic sovereignty offers Ukrainians with middle- to low-level positions on their ethnic ladder the opportunity to pursue the material comfort associated with membership in an international delegation while experiencing the ersatz sensation of climbing the ladder.

Are such feelings a threat to the Soviet Russian state? I think not. The limited pride of Ukrainian functionaries is fully consistent with official pronouncements of republican sovereignty. Ersatz pride in the Ukrainian SSR is tolerated, sometimes even encouraged, as long as it is the pride of passport Ukrainians who have accepted and fully adjusted to the reality of their republic's subordination to the Soviet Russian state. In particular, symbolic sovereignty permits passport Ukrainian officials the luxury of indulging in certain national rituals and satisfying certain national needs while remaining wholeheartedly committed to their national benefactor and material provider, the Soviet Russian state. By accepting the logic of symbolic sovereignty, these Ukrainians also accept the logic of the state's ideological message. More than that, they are accepting the logic of the state's institutionally Russian structure.

44. Arkady N. Shevchenko, *Breaking with Moscow* (New York: Knopf, 1985).

CHAPTER 6

Politics and Language

Even if ideology fails to envelop perceptions in the manner desired by the state, antistate attitudes will remain socially meaningless so long as they are confined to particular individuals: only by entering the public sphere can such attitudes become converted into forms of behavior that convey messages and mobilize supporters. Antistate collective actions, therefore, will not—indeed, cannot—occur in the absence of deprivatized antistate attitudes. In attempting to forestall such deprivatization, states employ two techniques. The first, which is the subject of this chapter, blocks the entry of inimical attitudes into the public sphere. The second, to be discussed in Chapter 7, blocks access to those behavioral arenas within the public sphere where antistate activity can occur.

While the function of ideology is to obfuscate and to persuade, that of ideology-in-action is to affect behavior. A complex body of ideas imparts desired attitudinal norms; the ideological statements of state functionaries, better known as propaganda, convey their imperative behavioral forms. Even if Soviet citizens choose to disentangle themselves from the conceptual cobwebs described in Chapter 5, propaganda enjoins them to privatize their antistate attitudes and keep them to themselves. Since the state makes no secret of its intention to neutralize wreckers of the "common cause of communist construction," the risks of political deviance become abundantly apparent, and citizens who choose to violate the state's behavioral cues in public forums do so consciously, in the full awareness that they are court-ing official displeasure and reprisal.

One Soviet ideological expert, Evgenii Nozhin, has issued a typ-ically explicit and inelegant warning: "If, in laying the foundations of a new house, someone thinks differently from the united collective of builders, his dissidence is a personal affair, but if, figuratively speak-ing, he pours fuel oil into the good concrete prepared by the hands of others, in the expectation that the foundations of the new house will sink, this is no longer dissidence, but counteraction, and this cannot be permitted by our people."[1] Nozhin's analysis is fully consistent with my own. Political disagreement is fine as long as it remains private; open political disagreement, especially openly disagreeable political behavior, is a crime and must be prevented or contained.

The knowledge that antistate attitudes, if discovered, will be punished, whether by the censure of a labor collective, dismissal from work, or arrest, acts as an effective internal deterrent on the public ventilation of such attitudes. Simply put, no one wants to be accused of pouring oil into Professor Nozhin's concrete. In light of such conse-quences, openly deviant behavior is an act of enormous audacity. By the same token—and I do not doubt that the Soviet state is fully cognizant of this—the fact that such behavior is accessible only to those with large reserves of courage makes it inaccessible to the vast majority of Soviet citizens. The "masses" may no longer be so fearful as they were during Stalin's time, but they know full well—from their reading of the state's propaganda signals—what kind of political be-havior is and is not allowed. Consequently, publicly if not privately, the vast majority of Soviet citizens appear to conform to what Soviet propaganda expects of them politically—to be model "Soviet men and women."

The linguistic behavior of the Ukrainians provides a particularly revealing illustration of how this self-inhibiting dynamic works. As the following discussion demonstrates, the Soviet Russian state's lin-guistic preferences transform language use into a political act. In this manner, language use becomes a touchstone of political loyalty and

1. *Soviet Nationality Survey*, no. 4 (April 1984), p. 5. See also L. Kravchuk, "Pereko-nuvaty slovom i dilom, vesty za soboiu," *Pid praporom leninizmu*, no. 5 (March 1982), p. 16; M. Shul'ha, "Vykhovannia v trudovomu kolektyvi," *Pid praporom leninizmu*, no. 2 (January 1985), pp. 53–59; "Ot narusheniia distsipliny do prestupleniia—odin shag," *Kommunist Estonii*, no. 3 (March 1984), pp. 26–32; V. Tkachenko, "Grani obshchestvennoi distsipliny," *Kommunist Moldavii*, no. 2 (February 1984), pp. 51–57.

an officially preferred language becomes the medium through which such loyalty is expressed. Those who choose to use a different language are, as a result, making a conscious political statement and embarking on a high-risk confrontation with the state.

Contemporary Ukrainian linguistic behavior makes no sense outside this interpretive framework. After all, why is it that Ukrainians use Russian as a language of social intercourse? Why does a nation of close to forty million, with its own state structure, capital, and United Nations seat, in possession of a developed economy, and enjoying extensive historical, cultural, and linguistic traditions, use a foreign language in its everyday dealings? Why do people who have engaged in various forms of nationalist activity in the last sixty years not do what any minimally conscious nation would do—use their own language? Such behavior is strange and out of the ordinary in this ethnically conscious day and age, sufficiently so for scholars to devote special attention to this case of Ukrainian "exceptionalism." (As will shortly become clear, the Ukraine is not all that exceptional, since my arguments can be extended to another Slavic nation, the Belorussians.)

The question is not why Ukrainians *can* speak Russian, or why they use it in other regions of the USSR, or even why they lose their ethnic identity. As Soviet scholars like to argue, it is not unreasonable for knowledge of the Russian language to exist in an environment of almost universal Russian-language school instruction, for Russian to be used in certain mixed marriages, for ethnic identities to be fluid and therefore changeable, and for Russian to be a "language of internationality intercourse" within a multinational state such as the USSR. Rather, one is mystified by the fact that Ukrainians do as the Romans do and adapt to local conditions everywhere in the USSR—everywhere, that is, except in their own republic. The standard Soviet explanation is to point to the many nations inhabiting the Ukraine, and especially its cities, and to argue that they must communicate in the only language they have in common—Russian. While such reasoning may hold in principle for such exotic republics as Uzbekistan, Lithuania, and Armenia, where the native languages are totally unintelligible to Russian-language speakers, it does not apply to the Ukraine (and Belorussia). Since Ukrainian and Russian are mutually intelligible, if Ukrainians (or Belorussians) can comprehend Russian, then it should also be possible for Russians or Russian-language speakers to comprehend Ukrainian, especially if they were born in the Ukraine or have lived there most of their lives. And it is, after all, primarily Russians and Jews (many of whom are very proficient in Ukrainian), and not Yakuts, Chukchi, and Nentsy, who comprise the vast majority of the Ukraine's ethnically non-Ukrainian inhabitants.

Apparently the Russian language is most commonly used by Ukrainians in social situations, while the Ukrainian language is generally spoken only in the home and among close friends. I draw this conclusion partly from soft data, such as the well-nigh unanimous testimony of tourists, journalists, and émigrés, as well as from personal experience. Some hard data are also available in a study by V. I. Naulko, who conducted extensive language surveys in clusters of villages in the Ukrainian south. Although these rural settlements included large numbers of Bulgarians, Greeks, and Moldavians and are therefore not reflective of the Ukraine's ethnic structure, the language patterns of their inhabitants suggest that even in the countryside the use of Russian is extremely widespread. In several surveyed raions of Donets'k and Zaporizhzhia oblasts, for example, Naulko found that the "congruence of the native tongue with the basic conversational" one used in "social life and during production" was markedly different for Ukrainians and Russians engaged in the following four categories of work: skilled mental labor, 72.2 percent for Ukrainians and 91.6 percent for Russians; unskilled mental labor, 69.2 percent for Ukrainians and 94.4 percent for Russians; skilled physical labor, 91.1 percent for Ukrainians and 94.4 percent for Russians; unskilled physical labor, 89.7 percent for Ukrainians and 100.0 percent for Russians. At the workplace alone, 33.3 percent of Ukrainian skilled and unskilled mental laborers (99.9% and 75.0% for Russians, respectively), 69.2 percent of Ukrainian skilled physical laborers (77.8% for Russians), and 67.7 percent of Ukrainian unskilled physical laborers (99.9% for Russians) used their native language.[2] Despite internal, apparently socially determined differences within the cohorts, the Russians consistently used their language far more extensively than the Ukrainians.

Naulko's statistics are especially suggestive for our purposes. If Ukrainian-language use is so low in the traditionally conservative environment of the Ukrainian countryside, then surely it must be lower still in the socially mobilized setting of the republic's cities. And second, at least in the raions of Kirovohrad oblast for which Naulko provides data, a large percentage of the non-Ukrainian

2. V. I. Naulko, *Razvitie mezhetnicheskikh sviazei na Ukraine* (Kiev: Naukova Dumka, 1975), pp. 140–43.

groups—Russians, Moldavians, and Bulgarians—claim to have a mastery of Ukrainian, an aptitude that is probably less typical for the Ukraine's cities.[3] Knowledge of the Ukrainian language by ethnic non-Ukrainians obviously tends to support its social use, again suggesting that the corresponding figures would be much lower in an urban environment.

Naulko's data concur with the findings of the Harvard Refugee Project in revealing that many rural Ukrainians choose to speak Russian at home, with their parents and especially with their children—a fact that blurs the fine line I wish to draw.[4] Are these the same Ukrainians who speak Russian outside the home? One cannot tell from Naulko's findings. Although there is in principle no reason for the same set of motivational variables to be at work in both domestic and social environments, it is methodologically impossible to claim that there is no connection between these two spheres of life. More than that, it would be methodologically incorrect to do so. How, then, do we bridge the gap between public and private? Although many factors account for domestic and social language use, I suggest that causal primacy belongs to those that motivate the latter. People are social beings, not isolated atoms. Their actions and thoughts may or may not be determined by their environment, but they are obviously affected by it. Since personal behavior cannot be divorced from the social context, conceptually and methodologically it is reasonable to give priority to the public sphere and to focus on the forces that play a determining role in it.

From this perspective, it makes little sense to suggest, as Naulko and other Soviet scholars do, that ethnically mixed marriages in and of themselves account for the fact that Ukrainians and other non-Russians speak Russian with their children. Since there are two partners and two languages in a mixed marriage, why choose one language over another consistently? Clearly, for extralinguistic reasons involving the political and social status of the given languages. Naulko, to his credit, does state that "in the process of contact among peoples the choice of language is determined above all by social, cultural-ideological, and political factors."[5] I fully agree; unlike Naulko and most Soviet and Western scholars, however, I suggest that,

---

3. Ibid., pp. 146–47.
4. Ibid., pp. 142–43; Yaroslav Bilinsky, *The Second Soviet Republic: The Ukraine after World War II* (New Brunswick: Rutgers University Press, 1964), pp. 153–54.
5. Naulko, *Razvitie*, p. 147.

with respect to the use of the Ukrainian and Russian languages in the exceptional Ukraine, political factors play a very important, though by no means exclusive, and heretofore neglected role.

Why, then, *do* so many Ukrainians apparently use the Russian language in their everyday dealings, and especially at their places of work? Why does the speaking of Russian appear to be the norm in most public environments in the Ukraine?[6] Which conditions are *necessary* to account for such extensive Russian-language use by Ukrainians? Which are *sufficient*? Which are *facilitating*? I adopt a conditional analysis in order to cut through the conceptual confusion so common to exclusively behavioral studies that correlate linguistic behavior with independent "base-type" variables.[7]

Some Western scholars, including Brian D. Silver, Alfred Bohmann, and Peter Zwick, have suggested that "exposure to Russians," the "Russian element," and the "spread of Russian culture through migration" contribute to the acquisition of the Russian language by non-Russians and, eventually, to their assimilation.[8] Of this there can be no doubt. The presence of Russian-language speakers is also a necessary condition of Russian-language use by Ukrainians and other non-Russians. But that is all it is, because, logically, there is no reason for the mere presence of Russians in the Ukraine—where they are, after all, in the minority—to produce Russian-language use by Ukrainians and not, say, the reverse, Ukrainian-language use by Russians. Despite New York City's large Hispanic population, for instance, English, and

6. Soviet scholars have provided direct testimony on the importance of language use by suggesting that the census question regarding "native language" be replaced by one regarding language used in everyday life. These scholars, clearly, are aware that the use of a language, and not knowledge or adoption of it, is the key to linguistic processes in the USSR. See Yaroslav Bilinsky, "The Concept of the Soviet People and Its Implications for Soviet Nationality Policy," *Annals of the Ukrainian Academy of Arts and Sciences in the United States*, nos. 37–38 (1978–80), p. 126; P. G. Pod'iachikh, "Programma i osnovnye voprosy metodologii Vsesoiuznoi perepisi naseleniia 1970 g.," in *Vsesoiuznaia perepis' naseleniia 1970 goda: Sbornik statei*, ed. G. M. Maksimov (Moscow: Statistika, 1976), p. 32.

7. See Robert J. Brym's devastating critique of Wesley A. Fisher and Brian D. Silver's attempts to explain ethnic intermarriage in the USSR: "Cultural versus Structural Explanations of Ethnic Inter-Marriage in the USSR: A Statistical Re-Analysis," *Soviet Studies*, no. 4 (October 1984), pp. 594–601.

8. Brian D. Silver, "Social Mobilization and the Russification of Soviet Nationalities," *American Political Science Review*, no. 1 (March 1974), p. 64; Alfred Bohmann, "Russians and Russification in the Soviet Union," *Aussenpolitik*, no. 3 (1981), p. 253; Peter R. Zwick, "Soviet Nationality Policy: Social, Economic, and Political Aspects," in *Public Policy and Administration in the Soviet Union*, ed. Gordon B. Smith (New York: Praeger, 1980), p. 155.

not Spanish, is the language of social intercourse. So, too, in Austria, Switzerland, and West Germany, German, and not the languages of their *Gastarbeiter,* is dominant in the public sphere.

A sizable group of both Western and Soviet scholars believe that the use and adoption of the Russian language are the natural outcomes of the breakdown of "primordial" ethnic loyalties which inevitably takes place during economic development. The Soviet view, which is grounded in the traditional Marxist-Leninist belief that national differences will disappear in the course of the construction of communism, emphasizes the Russian language's vital role in the "drawing together" of the USSR's fraternal socialist nations.[9] Western scholars prefer the more prosaic language of modernization theory. Typical is Allen Kassof's statement that "as the processes of modernization [in the USSR] continue . . . the extreme differences between peasant and bureaucrat, between the educated and the uneducated, between European and non-European areas . . . will diminish in scope and importance."[10]

While Soviet scholars and modernization theorists properly note the importance of what Karl Deutsch has labeled "social mobilization," the problems associated with their overly narrow perspective are substantial and ultimately fatal.[11] First, empirically it has simply not proven true that economic development inevitably leads to assimilation. Quite the contrary, as Seweryn Bialer has pointed out, "to the extent that ethnically non-Russian regions were swept by the tide of modernization, they have developed a new type of intense, urban-centered ethnic identity."[12] Second, there is, logically, nothing "by

9. On the role of Russian in "developed socialism," see Iu. D. Desheriev, "Iazykovye problemy mnogonatsional'nogo sovetskogo obshchestva," *Voprosy iazykoznaniia,* no. 6 (June 1982), pp. 14–27; Iu. Desheriev, "Vazhneishii faktor v sblizhenii vsekh natsii i narodnostei strany," *Partiinaia zhizn',* no. 1 (January 1983), pp. 20–26; M. N. Guboglo, "Leninskaia natsional'no-iazykovaia politika KPSS—Internatsionalizm v deistvii," *Sovetskaia etnografiia,* no. 1 (January 1984), pp. 3–15; E. A. Bagramov, "Deistvitel'no proletarskoe otnoshenie k natsional'nomu voprosu i mify antikommunizma," *Voprosy istorii KPSS,* no. 6 (June 1984), pp. 87–100.

10. Allen Kassof, "The Future of Soviet Society," in *Prospects for Soviet Society,* ed. Kassof (New York: Praeger, 1968), p. 500.

11. According to Deutsch, "social mobilization can be defined . . . as the process in which major clusters of old social, economic and psychological commitments are eroded or broken and people become available for new patterns of socialization and behavior" ("Social Mobilization and Political Development," in *Comparative Politics: A Reader,* ed. Harry Eckstein and David E. Apter [New York: Free Press, 1963], p. 583).

12. Seweryn Bialer, *Stalin's Successors: Leadership, Stability, and Change in the Soviet Union* (Cambridge: Cambridge University Press, 1980), p. 208.

nature" linguistically Russian about industrialization, urbanization, or other aspects of economic development as such. There is no reason why, to use rather obvious illustrations, the mere act of riding a bus to work, working in a factory, operating a machine, or living in a city in and of themselves should either encourage or discourage the speaking of Russian. Simply put, there is no conceptual connection between economic development and Russian-language use. Conditionally, economic development is neither sufficient nor necessary; in the presence of factors that are, it may be at most facilitating. Roman Szporluk sums up my own feelings nicely: "we are sceptical of the thesis that the size of the Russian minority, or the degree of a region's urbanization, is invariably a predictor of the degree of assimilation of non-Russians in the USSR. Those disparities between ethno-demographic processes in west Ukraine and west Belorussia ought to be explained by a complex of factors, including Soviet language policies and the pre-Soviet experience in these regions."[13]

Finally, other scholars emphasize what Vernon V. Aspaturian calls "Russianization"—the "superimposition of Russian language and culture on the daily life of the non-Russian nationalities."[14] According to this view, penetration of linguistically non-Russian spheres by the Russian language causes that language to be used and adopted—an argument that is both sensible and straightforward. But is it correct? Admittedly, as Russian-language schools, books, journals, newspapers, street signs, posters, banners, films, and songs increasingly enter non-Russian environments, the pressures to *learn* Russian will grow correspondingly. Silver makes just this point: "The evidence strongly suggests that acquisition of Russian as a second language is essentially a pragmatic adjustment to incentives and opportunities to learn Russian. . . . [S]econd-language learning is a direct response to demands and opportunities to learn Russian created by both social circumstances and social policy."[15] But Russianization is neither necessary nor sufficient for Russian-language use. Without Russianization, Russian could still be spoken in the presence of Russian-language speakers. More important, with *some* Russianization, Russian

---

13. Roman Szporluk, "West Ukraine and West Belorussia," *Soviet Studies*, no. 1 (January 1979), p. 93.

14. Vernon V. Aspaturian, "The Non-Russian Nationalities," in *Prospects for Soviet Society*, ed. Kassof, pp. 159–61.

15. Brian D. Silver, "Language Policy and the Linguistic Russification of Soviet Nationalities," in *Soviet Nationality Policies and Practices*, ed. Jeremy R. Azrael (New York: Praeger, 1978), p. 300.

need not be spoken as there is no logical reason for responding to an objectively Russianized—though still not fully Russian—environment with Russian speech: after all, one speaks Russian not to films and books but to people. Complete Russianization, which would be tantamount to a totally Russian environment, might be a sufficient reason for speaking Russian. But Kiev is still not Moscow, and the Ukraine is still not Russia. The vast majority of individuals with Ukrainian passports consider Ukrainian to be their native language (94% in 1959, 91% in 1970, and 89% in 1979),[16] thus proving that, despite growing Russian-language inroads into the republic's schools, passport Ukrainians are continuing to learn their native tongue— something that would be manifestly impossible in a fully Russianized setting.[17] Like economic development, however, Russianization probably facilitates the use of the Russian language by encouraging knowledge of it. The greater the Russianization, the greater the chance—but only the chance—that Russian will be spoken.

But perhaps the Russianization of the Ukrainian SSR really is proceeding by leaps and bounds? If so, the Ukraine may indeed be in danger of becoming a little Russia. Affirmative answers to this question generally center on book publishing, and they note that the ratio of Ukrainian titles to total titles published in the Ukraine has steadily declined since the late 1950s.[18] Is this phenomenon incontrovertible evidence of massive Russianization? Alas, no. Unless they are correlated with population, book figures are meaningless. Correlation of the two sets of data requires one to determine the cumulative ratio— the percentage of Ukrainian titles with respect to total titles divided by the percentage of Ukrainians with respect to total UkSSR inhabitants. A cumulative ratio of 1 expresses an "ideal" condition, in which title ratios are equal to population ratios. (This calculation, obviously, says nothing about the total availability of titles, which may be appallingly low.)

16. *Chislennost' i sostav naseleniia SSSR* (Moscow: Finansy i Statistika, 1984), p. 71; *Itogi vsesoiuznoi perepisi naseleniia 1970 goda* (Moscow: Statistika, 1973), IV, 152; *Itogi vsesoiuznoi perepisi naseleniia 1959 goda: Ukrainskaia SSR* (Moscow: Gosstatizdat, 1963), p. 168.

17. See Barbara A. Anderson and Brian D. Silver, "Equality, Efficiency, and Politics in Soviet Bilingual Education Policy, 1934–1980," *American Political Science Review*, no. 4 (December 1984), pp. 1019–39.

18. Yaroslav Bilinsky, "Shcherbytskyi, Ukraine, and Kremlin Politics," *Problems of Communism*, no. 4 (July–August 1983), p. 7; Myroslav Shkandrij, "Literary Politics and Literary Debates in Ukraine, 1971–81," in *Ukraine after Shelest*, ed. Bohdan Krawchenko (Edmonton: Canadian Institute of Ukrainian Studies, 1983), pp. 64–66; Ivan Dzyuba, *Internationalism or Russification?* (New York: Monad, 1974), pp. 118–19.

TABLE 6

Cumulative ratios for titles and copies of books, journals,
and newspapers published, Ukraine, 1959–1979[a]

	Titles		Copies	
Medium and year	Passport Ukrainians	Political Ukrainians	Passport Ukrainians	Political Ukrainians
Books				
1959[b]	0.77	0.82	0.99	1.04
1970	0.51	0.55	1.01	1.10
1979	0.36	0.40	0.88	0.98
Journals				
1959	0.61	0.65	1.08	1.14
1970	0.48	0.52	1.19	1.29
1979	0.68	0.76	1.25	1.58
Newspapers				
1959	1.07	1.13	0.94	0.99
1970	1.08	1.17	0.89	0.97
1979	0.99	1.11	0.88	0.98

[a]Percentages of total titles and copies published represented by Ukrainian titles and copies divided by percentages of total population of the Ukrainian SSR represented by passport and political Ukrainians.

[b]Average of book data for 1958 and 1960.

Sources: Narodnoe khoziastvo SSSR, 1922–1982 (Moscow: Finansy i Statistika, 1982), pp. 534, 535, 537; Narodne hospodarstvo Ukrains'koi RSR v 1965 rotsi (Kiev: Tsentral'ne Statystychne Upravlinnia, 1966), pp. 646–47; Bohdan Krawchenko, ed., Ukraine after Shelest (Edmonton: Canadian Institute of Ukrainian Studies, 1983), p. 64.

If we apply this reasoning to the census years 1959, 1970, and 1979, we find that Ukrainian titles represented 59.4, 38.2, and 26.7 percent, respectively, of total book titles, and that passport Ukrainians comprised 76.8, 74.9, and 73.6 percent of their republic's total population.[19] Our cumulative ratios, however, are 0.77 (1959), 0.51 (1970), and 0.36 (1979) (see Table 6). There is a downward trend, but the situation, while far from ideal—in both senses of the word—is not quite so bad as the unadjusted statistics suggest. If we correlate title ratios with the percentage of political Ukrainians (all individuals, with or without Ukrainian passports, who acknowledge Ukrainian as their mother tongue—72.7% of the republic's total population in 1959, 69% in 1970, and 66% in 1979), the cumulative ratios markedly improve: 0.82 (1959), 0.55 (1970), and 0.40 (1979). If we repeat the same calculations for numbers of copies of books (not of titles), our

19. The figures throughout this paragraph are from Chislennost' i sostav naseleniia SSR (1984), p. 71; Itogi vsesoiuznoi perepisi naseleniia 1970 goda (1973), IV, 152; Itogi vsesoiuznoi perepisi naseleniia 1959 goda: Ukrainskaia SSR (1963), p. 168.

cumulative ratios are quite different: 0.99 (1959), 1.01 (1970), and 0.88 (1979) for passport Ukrainians, and 1.04 (1959), 1.10 (1970), and 0.98 (1979) for political Ukrainians. Indeed, they are close to ideal.

These figures may be misleading, since large-circulation editions of Marx, Engels, and Lenin, which few Ukrainians (or other Soviet citizens) appear to buy or read, are usually published in the Ukrainian language. But how important *are* books as an index of the Russianization of a non-Russian environment? Is it not reasonable to assume that newspapers and journals are the primary medium through which most Ukrainians come in contact most often with the printed word, be it Russian or Ukrainian? Is there evidence of Russianization here as well? Consider again the data in Table 6, which show cumulative ratios for journals and newspapers in 1959, 1970, and 1979. The statistics support our expectations.

If nothing else, these calculations demonstrate that there is no obvious evidence of steadily increasing Russian-language penetration of the Ukrainian-language print environment. A number of authors have argued that statistics alone do not tell the whole story. (Why, then, are statistics used to demonstrate Russianization?) Ukrainian literature, so this argument goes, is more provincial than Russian-language literature. Ukrainian newspapers draw much of their news from *Pravda*, *Izvestiia*, and other central Russian-language organs, and are therefore derivative and uninteresting to many readers. Finally, as Roman Solchanyk has shown, Ukrainian-language books tend to be confined to the humanities, while the sciences are the realm of the Russian language.[20] True or not, these objections are irrelevant. They may suggest that the Ukraine is a backwater and they may even suggest that the state has special reasons for wanting it that way, but they say nothing about language use—unless, of course, one is to make the fantastic assumption that all or most Ukrainian-language printed materials go unread.

What *is* the sufficient condition of Russian-language use by Ukrainians in the Ukraine? If Russian presence is a necessary condition, while economic development and Russianization are facilitating ones, which factors are left to consider? What is the missing link? The key to finding it is to appreciate that the above variables do not exist in a vacuum; unlike our conceptualizations of the state, they do not have an independent, rarefied existence of their own. Rather, they are

---

20. Roman Solchanyk, "The Non-Russian Languages in the USSR—Only for Poetry and Memoirs?" *Radio Liberty Research*, RL 376/84, October 3, 1984.

inseparable from and the products of a political milieu created by the Soviet Russian state. Politics, in a word, is the missing link, and political relationships are the sufficient condition of Russian-language use.

Vsevolod Holubnychy correctly considers Russification to be an "act of violence," a "political, and not spontaneous and natural, process," and the "consequence of the conquest of the Ukraine."[21] Roman Szporluk argues in a similar vein, noting that the "role of force, including terror and deportation, was no less instrumental in producing Russification" than "sociological pressures" and the "advantage enjoyed by the Russian language."[22] Their comments are also relevant to our concerns. Russian-language use is a response to the threat of coercion implicit in what I call "Russification policy."[23] What precisely is Russification policy and how does it threaten non-Russians? The Soviet Russian state and its leading spokesmen—such as the good Professor Nozhin—continually and ubiquitously underline the primacy of the Russian language as the "language of internationality intercourse," of the "friendship of peoples," and, most of all, of "the Soviet people." Iurii Andropov's statement of this theme is as succinct as any by other Soviet leaders:

> The peoples of our country address special words of gratitude to the Russian people. In none of the Republics would the present achievements have been conceivable without their disinterested fraternal assistance. The Russian language, which has naturally entered the life of millions of people of every nationality, is a factor of exceptional importance in the country's economic, political, and cultural life, in the drawing together of all its nations and nationalities, in making the riches of world civilization accessible to them.[24]

The same sentiments are contained in the 1986 Party program: "the mastering, together with the language of one's own nationality, of the Russian language, voluntarily accepted by Soviet people in the capacity of a means of internationality intercourse, expands access to the

---

21. Vsevolod Holubnychyi, "Tezy pro rusyfikatsiiu," *Journal of Ukrainian Graduate Studies*, no. 2 (Fall 1977), p. 74.

22. Roman Szporluk, "Russians in Ukraine and Problems of Ukrainian Identity in the USSR," in *Ukraine in the Seventies*, ed. Peter J. Potichnyj (Oakville, Ont.: Mosaic, 1975), p. 199.

23. See Yaroslav Bilinsky, "Expanding the Use of Russian or Russification?" *Russian Review*, no. 3 (1981), pp. 317–32.

24. Iu. V. Andropov, *Izbrannye rechi i stat'i* (Moscow: Politizdat, 1983), p. 8.

achievements of science, technology, of our own and world culture."[25] Russian, clearly, is the Soviet Russian state's preferred language.

Language use has a potent symbolic quality in a politicized linguistic environment: it immediately assigns the user to one of two sides of the ideological barricade described in Chapter 5.[26] Oleksa Tykhyi and Vasyl' Romaniuk, both former Ukrainian dissidents (Tykhyi died in a camp, Romaniuk recanted), were fully aware of this symbolism when they quixotically exhorted their countrymen to protest against the state's preference for Russian by speaking Ukrainian "not only in the family, but also at work, in public activity, and on the street."[27] The use of Ukrainian, they realized, is tantamount to opposition to the Soviet state, which, as Andropov's comments indicate, demands that non-Russians show their loyalty by speaking Russian. Although no laws forbid deviations from this behavioral norm (as one Soviet Ukrainian representative once told me, no is "is holding a gun to their heads"), non-Russians in general and Ukrainians in particular appear to understand that insistence on speaking one's native language—especially among Russians—will be perceived as rejection of the "friendship of peoples" and as hostility to "the Soviet people." Precisely because Ukrainian and Russian are mutually intelligible, using Ukrainian in relations with Russian-language speakers is so obviously an affront against the spirit, if not quite the letter, of Russification policy as to qualify the obstinate user as a "Banderite," "Petliurite," "bourgeois nationalist," or, minimally, an ungrateful sibling of the "elder brother." A Soviet survey conducted in several plants in Dnipropetrovs'k and Nykopil' supports this conclusion. According to its findings, 90 percent of the surveyed "young workers" stated that they would "adopt an internationalist position if, in their presence, actions occur or conversations are held that contradict the spirit of the friendship of peoples."[28] Such near-unanimity, reminiscent of elections to the Supreme Soviet, is unconvincing, but it is

25. *Prohrama Komunistychnoi Partii Radians'koho Soiuzu* (Kiev: Politvydav Ukrainy, 1986), p. 43.

26. See Kenneth C. Farmer's illuminating discussion of this issue in *Ukrainian Nationalism in the Post-Stalin Era* (The Hague: Martinus Nijhoff, 1980), pp. 28–33.

27. Oleksa Tykhyi and Vasyl' Romaniuk, "Istorychna dolia ukraintsiv," *Ukrains'kyi pravozakhysnyi rukh* (Toronto: Smoloskyp, 1978), p. 55.

28. A. I. Kholmogorov, "Deiatel'nost' partii v oblasti natsional'nykh otnoshenii," *Voprosy istorii KPSS*, no. 12 (December 1984), p. 32.

testimony to the degree to which Ukrainians have internalized proper ethnic behavior.[29]

In light of the above, anecdotal evidence assumes special significance, particularly because it indicates that the state's linguistic preferences reinforce popular chauvinism and thereby create local guardians of the ethnic status quo. Leonid Pliushch, for example, a Ukrainian dissident now living in the West, was told to speak "human" upon using Ukrainian in a store in, of all places, the republic's capital, Kiev.[30] Even more telling is the case of a certain Nina Lashchenko, a Komsomol member "accused . . . of speaking Ukrainian in a Ukrainian school." According to the samizdat journal *Ukrains'kyi visnyk* (Ukrainian Herald), her conversation with the Party organizer in the school went as follows:

> "You insist on speaking Ukrainian everywhere. Why is this necessary?"
> "But this is a Ukrainian school!"
> "You enter the Russian tenth grade and speak Ukrainian there as well."
> "To me, language is not attire. I cannot change it like a dress—one for the theatre, another for work."
> "Take me, for example. I teach English but I do not speak it outside class."
> "That is merely your job, but to me my native language is an indispensable part of my life."

In the course of her talk with the Party organizer, Lashchenko was "advised to resign."[31]

Few Ukrainians are audacious enough to risk such unpleasantness as public censure, loss of employment, or even jail for the sake of linguistic purity. As a result, they signal their loyalty to the state and

---

29. Victor Zaslavsky and Robert J. Brym argue in similar fashion about the ritual importance of Soviet elections: "elections encourage citizens to demonstrate that they have adjusted to the fiction of democracy in the Soviet Union. Elections buttress the regime—not by legitimizing it, but by prompting the population to show that the illegitimacy of its 'democratic' practice has been accepted and that no action to undermine it will be forthcoming" ("The Functions of Elections in the USSR," *Soviet Studies*, no. 3 [July 1978], p. 371).

30. Leonid Plyushch, *History's Carnival* (New York: Harcourt Brace Jovanovich, 1977), p. 114; Dzyuba, *Internationalism or Russification?*, pp. 100–101.

31. *The Ukrainian Herald, Issue 6: Dissent in Ukraine* (Baltimore: Smoloskyp, 1977), pp. 129–30.

sidestep chauvinist reactions by speaking Russian. John Kolasky, a Ukrainian-Canadian Communist who became disillusioned with the USSR after living for several years in the Ukraine, describes this process well:

> So the pressure to Russify goes on continually and relentlessly. Anyone with the courage to offer opposition invariably suffers the consequences of being publicly ostracised, of being mocked and laughed at, of losing favors such as a trip to the much-talked-about workers' sanitariums or a chance of promotion. He may even be dismissed, suffer unemployment . . . and later be given work on a lower level at less pay. Worse still, he may be forced to leave Ukraine to find employment. In extreme cases he may even be arrested and sentenced to prison or banishment.[32]

Ivan Dziuba sums up this linguistic dynamic: "the actual secondary position of the Ukrainian language (and culture)—with implacable force, past comparing with that of any whip, any rod, any command or legal enactment—with all-crushing might *compels* and *forces* the individual Ukrainian and the Ukrainian masses in general to speak Russian and to renounce their mother tongue."[33]

It is thus in the context of Russification policy that Russian demographic presence, economic development, and Russianization both allow and facilitate the speaking of Russian. Proving one's loyalty to the state by speaking Russian is made either easier, when one's interlocutors do not understand one's native language (as when Russians are present among non-Slavs), or imperative, when they do (as when Russians are with Belorussians and Ukrainians). To speak a non-Russian language in the former context is downright silly; to speak it in the latter context is downright dangerous. Dziuba argues in similar fashion: "Where 'the authorities' speak Russian, soon everybody will also be forced to start speaking Russian. The language of the 'commanding elements' gradually triumphs over the whole environment."[34] The *political supremacy* of the Russian language, as manifested in the state's Russification policy, best accounts for and is the sufficient condition of Russian-language use by Ukrainians.

Although Russian-language use need not imply any psychological transformation, it is equivalent to descent down the ethnic ladder. It represents behavioral adjustment to the ethnic status quo and a concomitant rejection of non-Russian claims to republican hegemony. As

32. John Kolasky, *Two Years in Soviet Ukraine* (Toronto: Peter Martin, 1970), p. 42.
33. Dzyuba, *Internationalism or Russification?* p. 156.
34. Ibid., p. 135.

a form of self-accommodation, Russian-language use may be called "Little Russianization," a term derived from an earlier nomenclature for Ukrainians and one we may now employ to denote an acceptance, however unwilling, of non-Russian subordination to Russian ethnic hegemony. Little Russians, generically understood, are unlikely to challenge Russian societal hegemony or Russian dominance of the Soviet state, since their use of Russian as a language of ritualized social intercourse has provided them with secure niches in the structure of Russian ethnic power.

Although all non-Russians are potential candidates for Little Russianization, elites and workers, among whom Russian is generally acknowledged to be most widely spoken, appear to be the state's primary targets. Why are these two republican strata singled out? The answer, apparently, is that both groups occupy strategic positions within the Soviet system. The elites are indispensable politically, the workers are indispensable economically, and both figure prominently in Soviet ideology. National elites are supposed to testify to the success of "Leninist nationality policy," while workers are claimed to be living proof of the proletarian nature of the Soviet state. Control over both groups' behavior—especially at the critically important workplace—is imperative. Little Russianization thereby acts as a behavioral filter: officials or workers willing to use Russian at the workplace are declaring their loyalty to the state. With respect to elites in particular, I hypothesize that only those non-Russians who act as Little Russians will advance up the *nomenklatura* ladder. Those who do not behave properly will be weeded out at each progressively higher level of the state. John Armstrong hints at just such a process when he writes that "Ukrainians (and to a lesser extent Belorussians) have been employed in key control and managerial positions throughout the U.S.S.R. and abroad. This is concrete evidence that members of these groups are not discriminated against if they acquire the proper education and submit to Russification."[35] As Little Russians par excellence, Ukrainian representatives to the United Nations are permitted to indulge in Little Russian pride, because they fully realize that symbolic sovereignty is Little Russian sovereignty. Of course, none of this is to say that Little Russianization invariably produces ethnically

35. John A. Armstrong, "The Ethnic Scene in the Soviet Union: The View of the Dictatorship," in *Ethnic Minorities in the Soviet Union*, ed. Erich Goldhagen (New York: Praeger, 1968), p. 20. See also A. Nove, "History, Hierarchy, and Nationalities: Some Observations on the Soviet Social Structure," *Soviet Studies*, no. 1 (July 1969), p. 88.

submissive elites—P. Iu. Shelest is proof that it does not. But it does introduce a certain predictability to recruitment of native elites by institutionalizing a process of loyalty formation.

Another consequence of Russification policy (as well as, proximately, of Little Russianization) is attitudinal and involves Aspaturian's concept of Russification—the transformation of non-Russians into Russians "objectively and psychologically."[36] Operationalizing such categories is all but impossible, and census statistics on native language may or may not be adequate indicators of so total a transformation. Nevertheless, it must be assumed that some Russification has occurred and still occurs. This much seems obvious. Scholars often focus on the apparently small degree of actual Russification as proof of the tenacity with which non-Russians hold on to their languages and cultures.[37] As correct as this view is, it is also incomplete. It overlooks the fact that even marginal Russification is an enormous boon to the maintenance of Russian hegemony. Were it not for the addition to the Russian cohort of small percentages of Russified non-Russians, Russian demographic dominance would be in a far more precarious position than it currently is. Nevertheless, since Russification is at most a long-term goal, it is far less important than Little Russianization, whose benefits in behavioral conformity are immediate and enormous.

One final question, concerning history, remains to be addressed. Why, in the 1920s, did the Soviet state, already then a Russian state, discourage Little Russianization by pursuing *korenizatsiia*? Why did the state exercise its autonomy with respect to Russian societal hegemony? Concerned with its ethnic stability, which appeared to be precarious in the early 1920s, the state hoped to improve its survival capacity by making concessions to non-Russian ethnic power in general and to Ukrainian ethnic power in particular.[38] Clearly, the state succeeded. Like NEP, in Szporluk's words, *korenizatsiia* facilitated the "acceptance of communism and the Soviet form of government in the non-Russian areas, making it possible to reach the peasantry and

---

36. Aspaturian, "Non-Russian Nationalities," pp. 159–61.

37. Farmer, *Ukrainian Nationalism*, pp. 127–31; Jonathan Pool, "Soviet Language Planning: Goals, Results, Options," in *Soviet Nationality Policies*, ed. Azrael, p. 244.

38. On non-Russian opposition, see Arthur E. Adams, *Bolsheviks in the Ukraine* (New Haven: Yale University Press, 1963); Michael Rywkin, *Moscow's Muslim Challenge* (Armonk, N.Y.: M. E. Sharpe, 1982), pp. 34–44; Edward Allworth, ed., *Central Asia: A Century of Russian Rule* (New York: Columbia University Press, 1967), pp. 207–65.

win the collaboration of the national intelligentsias with the Soviets."[39] As *korenizatsiia* progressed, however, it increasingly became counterproductive. Although it manifestly enhanced the Soviet Russian state's ethnic stability in the 1920s, it also undermined the major source of stability—Russian societal hegemony. The danger for the Soviet Russian state lay in the fact that, as Bohdan Krawchenko points out, "its principal source of strength in Ukraine—the urban population and the proletariat—was rapidly becoming predominantly Ukrainian rather than Russian, and could move toward a more distinctly 'national' political posture." As a result, Ukrainization was abandoned in 1933, perhaps "because . . . the party realized that it could succeed."[40] Ukrainian-language use enjoyed a slight revival in the 1960s, for reasons that will be touched on in Chapter 8, but Shelest's fall marked its demise and a full-scale return to Russification policy.

This cursory sketch suggests a conclusion that is both discouraging and encouraging for opponents of Russification policy. Although the exigencies of survival and autonomy maximization may result in the temporary setting aside of Russification policy (as in the 1920s and 1960s), that policy and its goal, Little Russianization, are unlikely to be abandoned as long as Russian societal hegemony is the mainstay of the Soviet Russian state's ethnic stability. Paradoxically, though, by being based on a contradiction, Russification policy can also be a liability. Russification policy has greatest value with respect to individuals and nations positioned too highly on the ethnic ladder. Forcing them to descend the ladder is necessary for stability, but doing so may provoke resistance and produce tensions. In particular, the behavioral adjustments Russification policy demands represent a tendency contrary to the one that ethnic hegemony facilitates—ascent up the ethnic ladder. In this manner, Russification policy may have the contradictory effect of underpinning the Soviet Russian state's ethnic stability while simultaneously intensifying antistate attitudes and complicating the state's effective pursuit of survival. As non-Russian nations grow increasingly hegemonic in their own regions, the double-edged effect of Russification policy will correspondingly increase. Indeed, it may one day prove to be the Achilles' heel of Soviet nationality policy.

39. Roman Szporluk, "Nationalities and the Russian Problem in the U.S.S.R.: An Historical Outline," *Journal of International Affairs*, no. 1 (1973), p. 28.

40. Bohdan Krawchenko, "The Impact of Industrialisation on the Social Structure of Ukraine," *Canadian Slavonic Papers*, no. 3 (September 1980), p. 357.

A second problem with Russification policy is its tendency to encourage (if only by appearing to encourage) Russian nationalism.[41] While Russian nationalists generally support the state's Russian pattern of domination, their insistence on an openly Russian national state is a threat to the Soviet Russian state's high level of autonomy and therefore to the state itself. Ironically, Russian nationalism may actually be a greater threat to the Soviet Russian state's ethnic stability than non-Russian nationalism. The complete suppression of Russian nationalism may be impossible, since it would be tantamount to the abandonment of Russification policy—which the state's ethnic authority pattern, as a confining condition, cannot permit. Should this conclusion be valid, its implications for non-Russian nationalists are sobering. Successful opposition to the Soviet Russian state may require an alliance with their greatest enemies—the Russian nationalists. To the degree that such an alliance is unlikely, the Soviet Russian state appears to have little to fear from its non-Russian subjects in the near future.

41. On Russian nationalism, see John B. Dunlop, *The Faces of Contemporary Russian Nationalism* (Princeton: Princeton University Press, 1983); Alexander Yanov, *The Russian New Right* (Berkeley: University of California Press, 1978).

CHAPTER 7

Coercion and Control

Just as Soviet officials are no longer so visionary as to believe that attitudinal transformations come easily on a mass scale, they are not fanatical enough to pursue the complete elimination of all forms of deviance. Their current goal is to confine deviant thoughts to the individual mind and deviant behavior to the home. The effects of this approach are threefold. First, as we have seen, antistate attitudes are effectively neutralized by being privatized and thus eliminated from the public sphere; second, a safety valve is retained in that individuals with subversive sentiments are allowed to indulge in their fantasies in the proper setting, the home; and third, by confining such individuals and their attitudes to the home, the state prevents their engagement in public collective activity in general and antistate collective activity in particular.

The consequences of such distinctions have been earth-shattering. By drawing a fairly exact line between the public and private spheres, the post-Stalinist state automatically increased the scope of each individual's political autonomy. In the home, with friends and family, Soviet citizens can now engage fearlessly in a far greater variety of actions and sentiments than they could under Stalin. Certain topics still remain taboo, even in family circles, but the things that may be and are said at home would often qualify as subversive if they were expressed publicly. Apparently even dedicated Communists believe that their homes are their castles. According to an Estonian defector,

Valdo Randpere, "these very same Communists also laugh at the end of the day. They take off their Party membership along with their jackets and become almost normal people. They talk about whatever they want to and they say things that could easily be called anti-Soviet propaganda."[1]

Such a lifestyle would have been unimaginable under Stalin, when the state actively interfered in its subjects' personal lives. In contrast, the post-Stalinist strategic elite understands that massive intrusions into the private lives of individuals inevitably enhance the power of the secret police and thus threaten its own supremacy. Moreover, it realizes that withdrawal to and consolidation within the public sphere—defined earlier as that area of human activity located between the private lives of members of society and the political authority of the state—is just as effective as continued occupation of the private sphere, and certainly less costly. It is in the public sphere that individuals come together, engage in joint activity, and—if granted sufficient political autonomy—undertake autonomous and possibly antistate collective actions. Consequently, close supervision of the public sphere and the points of entrance to it should suffice to prevent and contain antistate collective activity.

To explain how the Soviet state goes about this task I borrow two concepts from the natural sciences—time and space. All Soviet (and, for that matter, all non-Soviet) citizens have limited amounts of free time.[2] This is obviously and almost trivially true. Work, sleep, the procurement, preparation, and consumption of food, and involvement with family and/or friends are the mundane facts of life that structure and take up most of one's day. In this respect, the time remaining for any kind of collective activity (political, cultural, sport, religious, or other) is small even under the best of circumstances. And when much of that time is occupied with officially sanctioned, nonautonomous forms of collective activity, regardless of the enthusiasm or listlessness with which these activities may be greeted, it follows that both time and opportunity for unofficial, autonomous forms of collective activity are proportionally reduced.[3]

---

1. "Interview: Valdo Randpere," *Soviet Nationality Survey*, no. 1 (January 1985), p. 2.

2. See I. P. Mokerov, "Ispol'zovanie svobodnogo vremeni trudiashchimsia promyshlennykh predpriiatii," in *Trud, byt, otdykh* (Moscow: Finansy i Statistika, 1983), pp. 59–69.

3. Of course, the Soviet state was not the first to discover the prophylactic value of state-sponsored participation. Aristotle recognized this simple truth when he wrote of

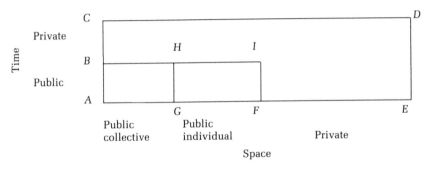

Figure 3. Time-space matrix

State-sponsored collective activity in the USSR also occupies much of the space available at any given time for public activity. The focus here is on the totality of public activity and the degree to which it has been expropriated by the state. In principle, this totality would appear to have no bounds; within the context of any given society, however, we can more or less imagine all of the activities that will be pursued in such an environment, and then group them in political, social, economic, cultural-intellectual, and sports- and military-related "boxes." The size of the boxes these activities represent will vary from society to society, but a box of some kind will almost certainly be there. Were the state to expropriate all the boxes to itself, residual space would be reduced to zero. The lesser the state expropriation, the greater the space available for autonomous activity; the greater the expropriation, the lesser the space.

Figure 3 illustrates how time and space may be combined into a single theoretical construct. The y axis represents all available time, the x axis all available space. Rectangle *ACDE* thus stands for all available time-space in, say, one day. Segment *AB* represents time spent in public; segment *BC* represents private time. Segment *FE* stands for private activity; *GF* for the public activity of individuals, or public individual activity; *AG* for the public activity of groups, or public collective activity. Exclusively private time-space (*BCDEFI*), or the private sphere, is, as I noted above, for the most part free of state control. Public collective time-space (*ABHG*), which is equivalent to

---

the means by which tyrannies could be preserved. One such policy, he noted, was "to require every resident in the city to be constantly appearing in public, and always hanging about the palace gates" (Ernest Barker, ed., *The Politics of Aristotle* [London: Oxford University Press, 1958], p. 244).

the public sphere, is occupied by the leading institution of the post-Stalinist state—the Party. Finally, public individual time-space (*FGHI*), which is a bridge between the private and public spheres and thus contains the points of entrance into the latter, is supervised by the KGB. This division of labor and the relegation of the KGB to only one part of the time-space matrix stand in sharp contrast to the Stalinist state's expropriation, by means of the secret police, of most available time-space in the private, public, and intervening public individual spheres.

Although the Committee for State Security (KGB) has fallen out of vogue among scholars since the totalitarian model's demise and the rise of détente, it continues to be a formidable machine.[4] Its cadres consist of an estimated 250,000 uniformed armed forces, about 15,000 signal troops, some 150,000 technical and clerical workers, and 1.5 million officers, plain-clothes agents, and informers.[5] A Ukrainian samizdat journal claims that in 1970 the KGB had a staff of 2,000 in L'viv (1970 population: 553,000) and that in 1969 there were 400 KGB employees in Ternopil' (1970 population: 85,000).[6] The KGB's annual budget may be in the area of $5 billion.[7]

The KGB's task in controlling public individual time-space is to supervise the public behavior of private individuals, spot and remove

4. Those who do write about the political police—Soviet defectors and émigrés, such scholars as Amy Knight and Jonathan R. Adelman, and qualified observers such as John Barron—are a small lot compared to the legions of Western specialists who prefer to focus on the more savory aspects of the Soviet system. The illogic of this approach is obvious. Ignoring so important a state agency as the KGB will not make the Soviet system more humane or more amenable to reasoned discourse. See Amy W. Knight, "The Powers of the Soviet KGB," *Survey*, no. 3 (Summer 1980), pp. 138–55, and "The KGB's Special Departments in the Soviet Armed Forces," *Orbis* (Summer 1984), pp. 257–80; Jonathan R. Adelman, "Soviet Secret Police," in *Terror and Communist Politics: The Role of the Secret Police in Communist States*, ed. Adelman (Boulder, Colo.: Westview, 1984), pp. 79–134; John E. Carlson, "The KGB," in *The Soviet Union Today*, ed. James Cracraft (Chicago: Bulletin of the Atomic Scientists, 1983), pp. 81–94; Frederick C. Barghoorn, "The Security Police," in *Interest Groups in Soviet Politics*, ed. H. Gordon Skilling and Franklyn Griffiths (Princeton: Princeton University Press, 1971), pp. 93–130; John Barron, *The KGB* (New York: Reader's Digest Press, 1974); Peter Deriabin and Frank Gibney, *The Secret World* (Garden City, N.Y.: Doubleday, 1959); Aleksei Myagkov, *Inside the KGB* (New Rochelle, N.Y.: Arlington House, 1978).

5. Carlson, "KGB," pp. 82–83.

6. *The Ukrainian Herald, Issue 7–8: Ethnocide of Ukrainians in the U.S.S.R.* (Baltimore: Smoloskyp, 1976), p. 151; *Narodnoe khoziastvo Ukrainskoi SSR v 1983 godu* (Kiev: Tekhnika, 1984), pp. 7–8.

7. John L. Scherer, ed., *USSR Facts and Figures Annual* (Gulf Breeze, Fla.: Academic International Press, 1983), VII, 358.

political deviants, and thereby filter potential entrants into the public sphere. Although not so bloodthirsty as in Stalin's time, the KGB has remained no less thorough in its handling of suspected opponents. Violence is no longer a trademark of its *modus operandi*, but intimidation, threats, and coercion still are. At present the KGB's first line of attack usually consists of informers who ferret out and report untoward signs of public individual behavior. Potential troublemakers are singled out and placed under surveillance. If "wrong" kinds of behavior continue, KGB agents first attempt to reason with the problem citizen. Veiled threats may be made—regarding employment, housing, career opportunities, educational chances for one's children, and so on. If the deviant persists, certain threats will be carried out. Especially stubborn asocial types may get mugged by Voluntary People's Squads (*druzhinniki*) masquerading as "hooligans." Finally, if none of these prophylactic measures works, the dissident will invariably be arrested—either on political grounds (anti-Soviet activity or defamation of the state) or for rape, drug abuse, or parasitism. Several suspicious deaths of dissidents, especially in the Ukraine and Lithuania, suggest that the KGB does have occasional recourse to its tried and true methods.

The most daunting of the KGB's features is not its ruthlessness—after all, Soviet citizens know what to expect from their secret police—but the apparent ubiquity of its presence. All public locales—hotels, restaurants, cafés, and bars—are popularly assumed to be bugged, and probably are. Informers are also assumed to be lodged at all levels of public life. Whether listening devices and *seksoti* truly are all that pervasive is immaterial, since Soviet citizens not unreasonably act on the assumption that "even the walls have ears." Consequently, most forms of politically uncertain behavior are squeezed out of public individual time-space and driven into the home, where they are immediately disqualified for potential social significance.

While the KGB screens potential entrants into the public sphere, the Party occupies it, thus setting the terms for those individuals who desire to enter. Entrance is permitted, indeed it is encouraged, but only on condition that the applicants surrender their political autonomy and join the state-sponsored and Party-penetrated organizational forms packed into the public sphere. Significantly, the mechanism for expropriating public time-space is enshrined in laws that evince a great deal of continuity with Stalin's times. Now, as then, the state's internal affairs organs have an enormous amount of leeway in deciding whether or not to license a public meeting or register an association.[8] With regard to the latter, according to Andrii Bilyns'kyi, they consider such factors as "whether the founding of such a society or union is expedient," "whether the statute and goals of the society correspond with the general task of the given branch of socialist construction," "whether the personal composition of the founders of the society is 'trustworthy,'" and "whether the goals and statute of the society harmonize with the goals of the appropriate state organs and public organizations." The result is that today, as in the 1930s, "associations are not founded, but simply created by the appropriate state-Party organs."[9] More than that, as befits a party constitutionally decreed to be their "core," the leading cadres of associations are expected to be and are CPSU members.[10] Having penetrated the non-autonomous associations, the Party proceeds to supervise them from within as well as from without.

Before we see how the public sphere is occupied, it will be useful to place Soviet behavior vis-à-vis this sphere into a broader conceptual framework. The corporatist approach currently sweeping the political science profession is ideal for our purposes, since its specific focus is on the relationship of state, society, and the intermediate public organizations. Philippe Schmitter, for example, speaks of "monism," "state" and "societal" corporatism, and "pluralism" as four possible categories of the ways in which states occupy the public sphere in general and the collective activities that comprise it in particular. A monist state, such as the USSR, creates and attempts to control all public collective formations.[11] State corporatism, as represented by

8. John Hazard, *The Soviet System of Government*, 4th ed. (Chicago: University of Chicago Press, 1968), pp. 57–59.

9. Andrii Bilyns'kyi, *Hromads'ki orhanizatsii v SRSR* (Chicago: Ukrainian Research and Information Institute, 1969), p. 42.

10. *Konstitutsiia (Osnovnoi Zakon) Soiuza Sovetskikh Sotsialisticheskikh Respublik* (Moscow, 1977), p. 8.

11. A monist state is one "in which the constituent units are organized into a fixed number of singular, ideologically selective, noncompetitive, functionally differentiated and hierarchically ordered categories, created, subsidized, and licensed by a single party and granted a representation role within that party and vis-à-vis the state in exchange for observing certain controls on their selection of leaders, articulation of demands and mobilization of support" (Philippe Schmitter, "Still the Century of Corporatism?" *Review of Politics*, no. 36 [January 1974], p. 97). For a critique of attempts to apply the corporatist approach to Soviet politics, see Susan Gross Solomon, "'Pluralism' in Political Science: The Odyssey of a Concept," in *Pluralism in the Soviet Union*, ed. Susan Gross Solomon (New York: St. Martin's Press, 1982), pp. 4–36. Valerie Bunce and John M. Echols III characterize the USSR as a "mixture of corporatist types" ("Soviet Politics in the Brezhnev Era: 'Pluralism' or 'Corporatism'?" in *Soviet Politics in the Brezhnev Era*, ed. Donald R. Kelley [New York: Praeger, 1980], p. 19). But

the countries of Eastern Europe, is best described for our purposes as a watered-down version of monism, while societal corporatism presupposes that the public collective institutions co-opted by the state were initially generated by society and therefore retain substantial autonomy (West European social democracies presumably fit into this category). Pluralism, such as is supposed to be found in the United States, consists of a multiplicity of autonomous public groups not co-opted by the state and independent of its control.

Although the monist Soviet state proscribes autonomous public collectivities, this does not mean, as supporters of the totalitarian model at one time insisted, that it is characterized by a "circular flow of power," that all initiative comes from the top, that public organizations have no input to make, and that quasi-interest groups—or, as Franklyn Griffiths calls them, "tendencies of association"—do not exist.[12] Nor does it mean that there is no politics in the USSR. Quite the contrary, it is obviously true that the Soviet political process is complex, involving variously weighted inputs from a variety of sources. My view, that public collectivities in the USSR are incapable of engaging in autonomous activity, accommodates both this complexity and the possibility that these groups do in fact contribute to policy formation. But that, of course, is precisely their purpose. By creating nonautonomous forms of public collective activity, the Soviet state ensures that diverse popular and elite energies will be tapped and—ideally—channeled only in directions desired by the state. Although critical of the corporatist approach, Jerry Hough is therefore quite correct to insist that the "absolutely crucial point to understand is that in any meaningful sense there *is* some societal autonomy in the Soviet Union," since the nonautonomous public collective activity located in the public sphere is only a small part of a time-space matrix that also includes the private and the public individual spheres.[13]

Since Hough's rejection of corporatism appears to be based on a misunderstanding, it will be worth the trouble to embark on a small digression and determine why. According to Hough,

> state corporatism does at least admit of the input side of politics, which
> is an advance on the old totalitarian and directed society models, but

---

this label only deepens the confusion they attempt to resolve and subverts the very purpose of classifications—to arrive at precise distinctions.

12. Franklyn Griffiths, "A Tendency Analysis of Soviet Policy-Making," in *Interest Groups in Soviet Politics,* ed. Skilling and Griffiths, p. 77.

13. Jerry F. Hough, "Pluralism, Corporatism and the Soviet Union," in *Pluralism in the Soviet Union,* ed. Solomon, p. 57.

my suspicion is that this will fade from view in our descriptions of the "corporatist" Soviet Union. The comparative textbooks will compare Soviet corporatism with Western pluralism, Soviet "groups" nearly to-tally manipulated by the all-powerful state with "autonomous" groups in the West. We will be able to retain all the old black-and-white ster-eotypes, with all the desired ideological overtones.[14]

Clearly, Hough's dissatisfaction is based on worst-case reasoning. If instead we follow Douglas A. Chalmers's nonalarmist advice and treat corporatism only as a conceptual guide, a heuristic—and that is all that it has ever pretended to be—we can easily avoid stereotypes and discover its not insubstantial utility for studying the Soviet public sphere.[15] Moreover, Hough forgets that not concepts but scholars pro-duce stereotypes. If someone is intent on blackening the USSR, "in-stitutional pluralism"—as opposed to good ol' American pluralism—will do just fine to point out the difference between us and them. (Ironically, Archie Brown's criticism of Schmitter's definition of monism undermines Hough's critique of corporatism. For Brown, who is no adherent of black-and-white stereotypes, monism is a "mis-leading understatement" in the Soviet context, because it implies that the intermediate categories actually select their own leaders.)[16]

The most important public collective activity in the Soviet public sphere and hence the one that draws most of the state's attention is the workplace. It is here that workers daily come into contact with one another, exchange stories, listen to grievances. As the site of the most intensive and extensive social contacts, the workplace offers the most opportunities for disseminating antistate sentiments and mobilizing antistate activity—something prerevolutionary Russian Marxists un-derstood very well. Furthermore, the production process takes place at the workplace and endows workers with enormous potential eco-nomic power.[17] Georges Sorel's vision of a cataclysmic general strike may never materialize in the USSR, but the innate disruptive capacity of Soviet workers is sufficiently worrisome to the state to have condi-tioned it to respond to factory strikes or riots in one of only two

14. Ibid., p. 56.

15. Douglas A. Chalmers, "Corporatism and Comparative Politics," in *New Direc-tions in Comparative Politics,* ed. Howard J. Wiarda (Boulder, Colo.: Westview, 1985), pp. 56–79.

16. Archie Brown, "Pluralism, Power, and the Soviet Union: A Comparative Perspec-tive," in *Pluralism in the Soviet Union,* ed. Solomon, pp. 77–78.

17. Harry Braverman, *Labor and Monopoly Capital* (New York: Monthly Review Press, 1974), pp. 59–152.

fashions—either by giving in to the demands (after which concessions are eventually rescinded and repressive measures employed) or by sending in the troops.[18] In both cases the state avoids prolonged or tardy responses, since they contribute to the formidability and complexity of worker demands.

The state's occupation of the blue-collar workplace involves two complementarily related collectivities—trade unions and labor collectives. Trade unions exclude worker elites from the real decision-making process (or what there is of it that involves unions), while labor collectives include the mass of workers in a bogus decision-making institution. This is not the place to discuss the merits and demerits of Soviet trade unions or to resolve the question of whether or not they are mere cogs within the state machine. Recent studies of Soviet *profsoiuzy* suggest that, although unions are not a vehicle for worker self-expression, they are also far from being mere transmission belts of state-to-worker directives: they do influence the distribution of wages and benefits, the setting of plan targets, and the rationalization of production. In addition, some conflict, generally involving trade union representatives and factory managers only, has been discerned.[19] True enough, but from the perspective of autonomous—and especially antistate—activity in the public sphere, such considerations are more or less irrelevant. The fact that unions are salutary, useful, and lively organizations may strike a death blow against the totalitarian model, but, as Blair Ruble demonstrates, it only strengthens the appeal of the corporatist approach.[20] As nonautonomous organizations supervised by members of the Party *nomenklatura* and subordinate to the state, Soviet unions are monist creatures par excellence.

Incidentally, though not insignificantly, some Soviet workers have recognized that official unions are not fully representative of their interests. Indeed, they have committed the darkest of monist sins: they have founded independent trade union organizations. The Donbass coal miner Vladimir Klebanov, the first to succumb to temptation

18. See Donna Bahry, "Politics, Generations, and Change in the USSR," Soviet Interview Project, Working Paper no. 20 (Urbana: University of Illinois, April 1986).

19. See Blair A. Ruble, *Soviet Trade Unions: Their Development in the 1970s* (Cambridge: Cambridge University Press, 1981); Mary McAuley, *Labour Disputes in Soviet Russia, 1957–1965* (Oxford: Clarendon, 1969).

20. Blair Ruble, "The Applicability of Corporatist Models to the Study of Soviet Politics: The Case of the Trade Unions," Carl Beck Papers in Russian and East European Studies, no. 303 (University of Pittsburgh, 1983).

in early 1978, was immediately repressed and incarcerated in a psychiatric prison-hospital for his strange ideas. A group of Moscow dissidents followed his example later in the year and founded the Free Interprofessional Association of Workers (SMOT). By the early 1980s, SMOT apparently had several hundred members in at least twenty-one groups.[21] Its vitality notwithstanding, SMOT, too, was forced to do penance for violating the corporatist code.

Whereas unions have at least some positive role to play, labor collectives appear to be almost exclusively intended to occupy space and control workers. The ideal labor collective consists of the entire work force of an enterprise and is the purported sovereign over all enterprise activity. A collective's sovereignty, however, like that of a republic, is mostly symbolic, since its decision-making authority is lodged in the hands of Party and trade union activists and management. Seen in this light, a vague 1983 law that enshrined the labor collectives' importance by purporting to expand their power over the enterprise in general and the production process in particular appears ominous. Evidently its real purpose is just what one would expect from a monist organization—to impose stricter discipline on and ideological control over the workers, in effect to reduce further still whatever personal autonomy workers possessed. Soviet authors betray this motive by specifically calling for the "center of ideological efforts to [be transferred to] the labor collective and the primary Party organization" and for labor collectives to become "schools" of labor discipline, socialist morality, and proletarian internationalism.[22] A labor collective in Zhytomyr oblast provides us with an interesting illustration of how this process of worker control may work:

> A workers' meeting of the Berdychiv Bread Products Combine discussed the behavior of the cabinetmaker M. N. A supporter of the "council of churches of Evangelical Christians-Baptists" and an extremist, he did not recognize the laws on cults and stubbornly refused to abide by their requirements. He organized slanderous group letters and mailed them all around. He forbade his children to join the Pioneers and Komsomol, and he attempted to raise them as believers-fanatics. Explanatory talks with M. N. were held more than once; he was called upon to abide by the laws on religious cults, but he continued with his

21. Betsy Gidwitz, "Labor Unrest in the Soviet Union," *Problems of Communism*, no. 6 (November–December 1982), pp. 35–37.
22. G. Maksimenko, "Tsentr ideologicheskikh usilii—trudovoi kollektiv," *Partiinaia zhizn'*, no. 18 (September 1984), p. 56.

activity: he disseminated all sorts of fables and inventions about the Soviet state's attitude toward religion, the church, and believers, about the "violation of freedom of conscience," etc.

And then at their meeting the workers openly stated that they are not about to endure the tricks of a hypocrite, who takes advantage of all the blessings given him by society while simultaneously disregarding the norms of socialist communal life and Soviet laws and who spreads lies and calumnies. They unanimously declared public censure of the violator and warned him that, if he does not change his behavior, the collective will petition to bring him to criminal responsibility. This influenced M. N., and he ceased his calumnious activity.[23]

Did all of M. N.'s colleagues truly believe that he was an antisocialist malcontent in need of "influence"? According to dissident and émigré accounts, worker attitudes are hardly so unanimous as this case would have us believe. Why, then, did the Berdychiv toilers condemn M. N.—and in language so reminiscent of Soviet behavioral expectations? The answer, as I have suggested, lies in the nonautonomous character of labor collectives. Supervised by Party and trade union activists, who undoubtedly help set the tone of the debate, labor collectives deprive workers of autonomy, keep them well informed of the consequences of putting heady ideas into practice, and thereby control their workplace behavior. Which of M. N.'s comrades wanted to be reprimanded for defending so mendacious and rapacious an obscurantist? The question, of course, is rhetorical.

State occupation of public time-space extends far beyond the workplace to all the boxes involving collectively based activities. Nonautonomous unions of writers, artists, architects, composers, journalists, and cinematographers, as well as republican academies of sciences, cover the public space available for most professional activities. Creative unions do not extend their tentacles into the homes of intellectuals and artists, where their freedom and autonomy are unlimited. But intellectuals who step outside and try to pursue professional careers in public find that they can do so only within the confines of the particular union to which people of their calling have been assigned. (Even amateur talents are relegated to "amateur creative groups" under the supervision of the primary Party organization of the enterprise under whose auspices they were created.) Similar options are available to a variety of other professionals and nonprofes-

23. V. Ie. Ostrozhyns'kyi, "Zhyttiestverdzhuiucha aktyvnist' materialistychnoho svitohliadu," *Komunist Ukrainy*, no. 3 (March 1985), p. 36.

sionals. Atheists and scientifically inclined individuals have a choice of the Knowledge Society, known as the Union of Militant Atheists until 1947, or the All-Union Society of Inventors and Rationalizers. Believers can join a plethora of church bodies—the Russian or Georgian Orthodox church, the All-Union Council of Evangelical Christians and Baptists, the Evangelical Lutheran church, the Armenian Apostolic church, the Catholic church, official Judaism, and the Islam of the spiritual directorates. Humanitarians may opt for the Red Cross or Red Crescent Society. Sports enthusiasts are grouped in a variety of all-Union and republican associations. Patriots and military buffs have the Voluntary People's Squads and the All-Union Voluntary Association for the Support of the Army, Air Force, and Navy (DOS-AAF). Civic-minded individuals may choose from among comrades' courts, people's control committees, volunteer fire brigades, street and house committees, peace groups, women's councils, and many others. Children have their own groups—the Octobrists and Pioneers—while youths can join the Komsomol. Evidently, as soon as it espies a potentially emergent collective activity, the state creates an organization into which it can be molded. The growing popularity of insufficiently supervised dance locales, for example, has led some Ukrainian Party functionaries to seek to transform them into "political discotheques."[24]

A striking example of the extreme character that the corporatist logic of the Soviet state occasionally assumes is its policy toward religiously inclined citizens. Believers, like others who venture into the public sphere, may practice their faiths only within the confines of official church institutions. Those who refuse to recognize the authority of established religious boxes, such as certain Baptists, Fifth-Day Adventists, and Uniate Catholics, immediately qualify as dissidents and, as a result, tend to represent a substantial proportion of the concentration camp population. But Soviet monism goes beyond confining believers to institutions: it also confines them and their activities physically—to designated religious buildings. "In the Ukrainian SSR, the main forms of religious and atheist convictions are constitutionally protected and justifiably placed on an equal [sic] footing. . . . Along with atheist propaganda, religious propaganda is conducted in the Ukrainian SSR," states a frankly cynical Ukrainian diplomatic report at the United Nations. "Nevertheless, there are some appropriate limitations both for religious and atheist propagan-

24. *Radians'ka Ukraina*, May 12, 1984.

da. . . . Religious propaganda is allowed only in specially appointed places—churches, mosques, synagogues, houses of prayer, monasteries, religious seminaries and academies, etc. . . . *Nor do atheists conduct atheist propaganda in places intended for religious worship.*"[25] Priests, ministers, rabbis, or mullahs who proselytize outside their officially designated structures are trespassing on the state's turf and are therefore treated as criminals.

The state's occupation of public collective time-space has two principal effects. First, since no collective activity may be legally undertaken without state sponsorship and Party supervision, all attempts at autonomous collective action in a box already expropriated by the Soviet Russian state are, by definition, antistate. It is, as a result, very easy to become a dissident in the Soviet Union, because the boundaries of antistate activity are never far away. On the other hand, the visibility of these boundaries and popular awareness of the penalties that befall those who overstep them also act as effective deterrents on autonomous ventures into the public sphere. The motivation for such self-restraint is, I venture to guess, quite simple: such activity is just not worth the consequences to most people.

Second, all organizations that decline to apply for registration, however innocent their goals by world standards, immediately fall outside the pale of Soviet law and, in a very real sense, become anti-Soviet. At the same time, those less than orthodox, legalistically inclined groups that try unsuccessfully to register are placed in a legal and moral bind. Having expressed a willingness to go through accepted Soviet legal procedures, they can all the more easily be accused of intentional antistate activity if they refuse to accept the verdict of the state. The Ukrainian Helsinki Group, for example, applied to be registered in 1976 and, naturally enough, was turned down.[26] Having embarked on the path of legalism, the group willfully and consciously broke Soviet laws by remaining in existence without the state's formal approval.

Besides preventing the formation of antistate collectivities, state occupation of the public sphere forestalls the emergence of antistate leaders. Managing the elites of regional hegemons is, as we know, critical to the effective pursuit of survival, since it is these very groups that are best situated to exploit conflict tendencies and propel their hegemonic constituencies up the ethnic ladder. Ambitious, talented,

---

25. *Soviet Nationality Survey*, nos. 7–8 (July–August 1985), pp. 6–7; italics added.
26. Victor Haynes, "The Ukrainian Helsinki Group: A Postmortem," *Journal of Ukrainian Studies*, no. 2 (Winter 1983), pp. 102–13.

and educated individuals with aspirations to careers in the public sphere or the republican substate—which, in relation to the central state, may be considered an extension of the public sphere—are given two options: they may pursue their elite ambitions nonautonomously or autonomously. They may conform to the state's organizational designs or not conform and then accept the consequences.

Most non-Russians (and Russians) prefer the first option, and, especially since Stalin's death, many of them have been given ample opportunities to join the substate. In 1983, 80 percent of oblast, city, and raion first secretaries of the Communist Party of the Ukraine were passport Ukrainians.[27] Since the mid-1950s, most top positions within the Ukrainian SSR Politburo, Council of Ministers, and KGB also belong to Ukrainians.[28] Although such individuals formally renounce antistate behavior by entering the public sphere or substate, their potential for developing autonomous tendencies is still strictly, if imperfectly, regulated by means of the system of personnel supervision and assignment known as *nomenklatura*. By maintaining vertical control over cadres, the strategic elite effectively prevents the formation and protracted existence of antistate local elites within these sectors. Naturally, this mechanism does not always work. Substate or public-sphere officials, and particularly first secretaries of important republics, may attempt to build indigenous power bases. Given sufficient resources, favorable political circumstances, and a modicum of political autonomy, they may even succeed in engaging in untoward activity for extended periods of time. The examples of P. Iu. Shelest of the Ukraine, V. N. Mzhavanadze of Georgia, and Sh. R. Rashidov of Uzbekistan stand out. Sooner or later, however, local officials who step out of line appear invariably to get caught and punished. The 1984–85 purge in Uzbekistan, which involved substate officials at all levels of the republic, is an especially noteworthy example of the *nomenklatura*'s self-purgative efforts.[29]

Not only are substate officials subjected to Party supervision from above, but their prerogatives are purposely circumscribed, very much in the manner of public associations located in the public sphere.

27. V. V. Shcherbyts'kyi, "Pro zavdannia partiinykh orhanizatsii respubliky, iaki vyplyvaiut' z dopovidi Heneral'noho sekretaria TsK KPRS tovarysha Iu. V. Andropova 'Shistdesiat rokiv SRSR,'" *Komunist Ukrainy*, no. 4 (April 1983), p. 31.

28. Hélène Carrère d'Encausse, *Decline of an Empire* (New York: Newsweek Books, 1979), p. 144.

29. See I. S., "Purge in Uzbekistan," *Soviet Nationality Survey*, no. 12 (December 1984), pp. 1–2.

(Indeed, conceptually it might be fruitful to think of republican sub-states as glorified public associations.) With respect to agenda setting, it is Moscow that determines all the policy issues and most of the policy answers for the republics. Republican substate elites can and do affect the central decision-making process, but it is unrealistic to exaggerate their impact.[30] The planning process, for example, testifies to Moscow's centrality. Republican Gosplan organs do make inputs and can suggest adjustments, but it is the USSR State Planning Commission that finally and fundamentally determines republican economic goals. Another area of limited competence involves the division of ministries into Union, Union-republican, and republican types and the delegation of strategically important economic sectors to the first. Not only is republican decision making thereby confined to regional economic spheres, but a large number of republican enterprises—those subservient to Union ministries—are completely beyond republican control. In effect, republican organs are reduced to provincial administrators with limited powers and jurisdiction.[31] Finally, the budgetary process, like the planning process, is still Moscow's prerogative—a fact that perturbed such economists as M. Volobuiev even in the 1920s.[32] Whether or not Western scholars are correct in estimating the degree to which the Ukraine is a net exporter of capital, their arguments do convincingly show that the republic itself, as an administrative entity, has at most indirect control over its own financial resources.[33] Soviet spokesmen admit as much when they speak of the primacy of all-Union interests, of the fact that the USSR is a "single economic mechanism," and of the identity of all-Union and republican interests.

If talented, educated, and ambitious non-Russians reject the non-autonomous option offered them by the state, the only way they can pursue their elite aspirations without joining the substate or the organizations it sponsors is to try to enter the public sphere on their own, autonomously. In the 1960s and 1970s, such individuals became dis-

30. Jerry F. Hough and Merle Fainsod, How the Soviet Union Is Governed (Cambridge: Harvard University Press, 1979), pp. 547–48.

31. Fyodor Kushnirsky, Soviet Economic Planning, 1965–1980 (Boulder, Colo.: Westview, 1982), pp. 73–78.

32. See James E. Mace, Communism and the Dilemmas of National Liberation: National Communism in Soviet Ukraine, 1918–1933 (Cambridge, Mass.: Ukrainian Research Institute, 1983), pp. 161–90.

33. See Zinowij Lew Melnyk, Soviet Capital Formation: Ukraine, 1928/29–1932 (Munich: Ukrainian Free University Press, 1965).

sidents; in the 1940s and 1950s, they usually had ties to nationalist or national Communist traditions. Regardless of their ideological preferences, the Soviet state has never hesitated to respond to their activities within the public individual sphere with coercion. Public individual dissident activity, therefore, while not a form of antistate collective activity, does represent the activity of relatively autonomous elite individuals and is repressed, lest it lead to the penetration of the public sphere and the mobilization of antistate activity. The dissidents were a threat to the state not because of the popular support they commanded but because of the support that they *could* in principle have eventually come to command.

The career options facing potentially elite Ukrainians are supplemented by a third that appears to be unique to them—to leave their republican public sphere and substate altogether. While the number of Ukrainians who acquire secondary education in their republic is quite high, the percentage of Ukrainians in the Ukraine with a completed higher education is very low.[34] Since Ukrainians living outside of the Ukrainian SSR tend to be unusually well educated,[35] educated Ukrainians evidently leave their republic in large numbers. Although employment opportunities may be better in other parts of the USSR, when the outflow of educated Ukrainians is viewed in conjunction with the inflow of educated and skilled Russian cadres, we have to doubt that lucrative jobs and sunny steppes alone are at the root of such wanderlust.[36] When, in addition, we consider that official permission is necessary to acquire certain jobs and to settle in certain closed cities, the conclusion is all but inescapable that the Soviet state's heavy hand is at work in what may best be described as a brain drain.[37] The Ukraine's educated cadres, the national elite that would be most likely to seize upon latent conflict tendencies and to express or support demands for autonomy, are simply removed.[38] The remaining members of the Ukrainian elite are so reduced in numbers that they are relatively easy to control. The technique, not inciden-

34. Bohdan Krawchenko, *Social Change and National Consciousness in Twentieth-Century Ukraine* (New York: St. Martin's Press, 1985), p. 220.

35. Ibid., p. 218.

36. F. Douglas Whitehouse and David W. Bronson, "Manpower," in *The Ukraine within the USSR*, ed. I. S. Koropeckyj (New York: Praeger, 1977), p. 143.

37. For an excellent discussion of closed cities, see Victor Zaslavsky, *The Neo-Stalinist State* (Armonk, N.Y.: M. E. Sharpe, 1982), pp. 130–64.

38. For a similar interpretation, see Roman Szporluk, "Russians in Ukraine and Problems of Ukrainian Identity in the USSR," in *Ukraine in the Seventies*, ed. Peter J. Potichnyj (Oakville, Ont.: Mosaic, 1975), pp. 196–97.

tally, bears some resemblance to that practiced by the USSR, Poland, East Germany, and other East European countries in allowing or forcing prominent dissidents—Aleksandr Solzhenitsyn, Petro Grigorenko, Wolf Biermann, Rudolph Bahro, and numerous members of Solidarity come to mind—to emigrate to the West.

Finally, the brain drain is most evident in the elevation of Ukrainian officials to nonrepublican rungs of the *nomenklatura* ladder. Removing a non-Russian official from his substate matrix completely precludes his development into a potential republican leader.[39] The official loses his base both in the substate and among the republican population and is ipso facto transformed into a Little Russian member of the central state apparatus. The official may still cause trouble with respect to the state's political or class authority patterns, but, as a potential non-Russian antistate leader, he has ceased to exist. From this perspective, the induction of large numbers of Ukrainians into the central state apparatus represents much more than an attempt to satisfy their career ambitions or to create a Slavic bloc.[40] It is, as well, a time-honored mechanism that harks back to tsarist days, a means of preventing the formation of a native—that is, autonomous—Ukrainian elite.

39. Bohdan Harasymiw, "Political Mobility in Soviet Ukraine," *Canadian Slavonic Papers*, nos. 2–3 (June–September 1984), pp. 160–81.

40. Roman Solchanyk, "Molding 'The Soviet People': The Role of Ukraine and Belorussia," *Journal of Ukrainian Studies*, no. 1 (Summer 1983), pp. 3–18.

CHAPTER 8

Why Non-Russians
Have Not Rebelled

If history really is a guide to the future, past disturbances among non-Russians may hold clues to the possibility of their recurrence or development into rebellions. A variety of sources indicate that the Soviet Union has led and continues to lead a turbulent existence: strikes, riots, demonstrations, and even some antistate collective actions have always been and still are regular, if not quite common, occurrences.[1] Large and chronologically concentrated sets of sizable, intense, and protracted antistate collective actions, however, have been far less frequent.

Such collective-action sets describe two related, though quite different, forms of opposition—rebellion and resistance. Rebellion is large-scale opposition to established authority; resistance is large-scale opposition to the establishment of authority. Rebellions are premised on the firm existence of Soviet rule; resistance assumes that Soviet power is only in the process of being consolidated. In contrast to rebellions, examples of anti-Soviet resistance by non-Russians abound, especially in the years during and after the world wars, when Soviet power was weak. Ukrainians, Balts, Armenians, Georgians, and Central Asian Turks opposed the imposition of Soviet rule from 1917 to 1921, as did the Basmachi and the guerrillas of the North Caucasus

---

1. Charles Lewis Taylor and Michael C. Hudson, *World Handbook of Political and Social Indicators* (New Haven: Yale University Press, 1975), p. 191.

in the 1920s and 1930s.[2] (The term *civil war* is actually a misnomer when applied to the non-Russian regions, because it glosses over the fact that the invading Red Army consisted overwhelmingly of Russians, while its opponents consisted almost entirely of non-Russians.)[3] Following near-defeat in World War II, the advance and gradual reimposition of Soviet power in the course of 1943–44 again provoked substantial resistance by non-Russians. Some made the political mistake of joining German-sponsored military or Waffen-SS units, while others signed up with General Andrei Vlasov's Russian Liberation Army.[4] Still others—Ukrainians, Lithuanians, Estonians, and Latvians—established independent guerrilla movements, the strongest and most prominent of which survived into the 1950s.[5]

Numerous disturbances among non-Russians have occurred since World War II. Uzbeks rioted in 1966 and 1969, Georgians protested the status of their language in 1978, and a relatively large number of protest demonstrations have been documented in the Ukraine and the Baltic republics.[6] Although many more such disturbances have taken place, all of them lack the defining characteristics of rebellions—or, for that matter, of resistance—and therefore remain isolated manifestations of discontent. Although it may be somewhat heterodox to view them in such terms, the dissidents were the only oppositionists whose activity came even close to qualifying as a rebellion. The so-called dissident movement involved a certain degree of anti-Soviet

2. On non-Russian resistance to Soviet power, see Richard Pipes, *The Formation of the Soviet Union* (New York: Atheneum, 1974); Martha B. Olcott, "The Basmachi or Freemen's Revolt in Turkestan, 1918–24," *Soviet Studies*, no. 3 (July 1981), pp. 352–69; Alexandre Bennigsen, "Muslim Guerrilla Warfare in the Caucasus (1918–1928)," and Marie Broxup, "The Basmachi," *Central Asian Survey*, no. 1 (July 1983), pp. 45–81.

3. Indeed, in 1921 Russians represented 62.4% of soldiers on the Turkestan front, 74.0% of the 9th Kuban Army on the Caucasian front, and 74.7% of the 6th Army on the southern front. In the Ukraine alone they accounted for 57.1% and 62.3% of the Kiev and Kharkiv Military Districts, respectively (V. Iu. Mel'nychenko, "Istorychne znachennia voienno-politychnoho soiuzu radians'kykh respublik," *Ukrains'kyi istorychnyi zhurnal*, no. 1 [January 1986], p. 39).

4. See Alexander Dallin, *German Rule in Russia, 1941–1945* (New York: St. Martin's Press, 1957).

5. See V. Stanley Vardys, "The Partisan Movement in Postwar Lithuania," *Slavic Review*, no. 3 (September 1963), pp. 500–522; John A. Armstrong, *Ukrainian Nationalism* (Littleton, Colo.: Ukrainian Academic Press, 1980); Romuald J. Misiunas and Rein Taagepera, *The Baltic States: Years of Dependence, 1940–1980* (Berkeley: University of California Press, 1983), pp. 81–104.

6. David Kowalewski, "Ukrainian Opposition in the Light of Demonstrations," *Ukrainian Quarterly*, no. 2 (Summer 1980), pp. 171–82, and "Dissent in the Baltic Republics: Characteristics and Consequences," *Journal of Baltic Studies*, no. 4 (1979), pp. 309–19.

sentiment; it was widespread, deeply rooted, and remarkably persistent; and it presented the Soviet state with one of its most serious postwar challenges. Just as obviously, however, the dissident movement never did develop into a rebellion. Why not?

A partial answer to this question is that it is inaccurate to speak of the dissident "movement" as if it were one entity. In fact, it was a fairly loose conglomeration of individuals, organizations, movements, and groups whose only common features were dissatisfaction with official Soviet practices and a healthy respect for Western journalists. Not only were there numerous political, ideological, and regional cleavages within the movement, but they were compounded by national divisions. Democrats opposed fascists; liberals opposed conservatives; Baptists and Fifth-Day Adventists ignored the lot; nationalists worked for the dismemberment of the system; nonnationalists strove for its transformation. If samizdat publications—whose variety and number are astounding—are an accurate measure of the various kinds of currents within the dissident movement, then it becomes manifestly clear that there was no one movement to instigate rebellion and no one movement to succeed or fail.[7]

But not only is it an exaggeration to speak of a Union-wide dissident movement, it is also inaccurate to refer to single dissident movements in the various republics. Some appear to have experienced little or no dissent. Belorussia, the Central Asian republics, and Moldavia stand out in this regard. Others, such as the Baltic republics, the Ukraine, Georgia, and Armenia, produced a plethora of indigenous dissenters.[8] Like participants in the all-Union movement, however, republican dissidents differed in their goals, their tactics, and their degrees of commitment. It was only in the mid-1970s, during the demise of the dissident phenomenon, that some measure of intrarepublican consolidation took place with the formation of Helsinki groups in the Ukraine, Lithuania, Armenia, Georgia, and Moscow. But this was clearly a case of too little too late, since most dissidents had already been exiled or arrested by that time.

In addition to their lack of unity, intrarepublican dissidents almost universally rejected rebellion as a serious option. Most non-Russian (and Russian) dissenters emphasized that theirs was a legal struggle concerned only with the fulfillment of rights already enshrined in the

7. Alexander Motyl, "USSR's Alternative Press," Index on Censorship, no. 2 (March–April 1978), pp. 22–28.

8. Hélène Carrère d'Encausse, Decline of an Empire (New York: Newsweek Books, 1980), pp. 209–27.

Soviet Constitution. Not the Party's overthrow but its return to "true" Leninism was the oft-stated goal[9]—and for good reason. In the aftermath of Stalinism and in light of the post-Stalinist state's unconcealed opposition to openly antistate activity, most dissidents not unreasonably concluded that the pursuit of minimal goals had an immeasurably greater chance of success than an insistence on all or nothing. Moreover, "human rights" was the ideal dissident motto: human rights were sanctified by international covenants signed by the USSR and one could claim that they were totally devoid of political content (which, of course, was not at all the case). Nevertheless, it is obvious that rebellions will not be started by humanists opposed to the very idea of rebellion.

Further complicating the matter for most non-Russian dissident movements was the fact that they, unlike their Russian counterparts, lacked leadership. They lacked men of stature, charisma, and influence—such as Aleksandr Solzhenitsyn, Andrei Sakharov, Iurii Orlov—who, whether imprisoned, exiled, or free, could speak as the conscience of the nation and be regarded as the moral leaders of the opposition. The absence of leaders is due not to some innate deficiency of talent but to the non-Russians' far greater lack of political autonomy. Thanks to the Western journalists and diplomats stationed in Moscow, the USSR's capital city enjoys two enormous advantages over other urban areas. First, its residents are always in the limelight: the arrest of a Moscow-based dissident will almost invariably receive coverage in, say, *The New York Times*.[10] Second, Moscow's international and somewhat open stature forces the KGB to deal more circumspectly with the capital's troublemakers than with those of the periphery. The cumulative effect of both factors is that Moscow's Russian and Jewish dissidents enjoy substantial political autonomy, while their colleagues in the non-Russian republics do not and thus are far easier to repress. Had Anatoly Shcharansky been an Uzbek from Tashkent, for example, he would never have attained celebrity status and his arrest almost certainly would not have provoked public protests throughout the world. The major impact of the agreement to establish an American consulate in Kiev may thus be to expand, however slightly, the political autonomy of Ukrainian oppositionists by exposing the Ukraine's capital to the diplomats, journalists, tourists, and business representatives sure to use the consulate's resources.

9. Petro Grigorenko, *Memoirs* (New York: Norton, 1982), pp. 262–76.
10. Alexander Motyl, "The Soviet Union through the Eyes of *The New York Times*," *Journal of Ukrainian Graduate Studies*, no. 2 (Fall 1979), pp. 69–82.

Finally, most non-Russian dissidents remained isolated from their local populations. Indeed, they are often faulted for having expressly neglected their republics' working people by focusing only on human and national rights. The implication is that their message was too abstruse, too abstract to appeal to broad sections of the population. Human, civil, or national rights are presumably beyond the understanding and interest of ordinary Soviet men and women; a stronger emphasis on immediate and tangible social problems and on the rights and grievances of workers and peasants was, it is argued, the missing ingredient. The objection may or may not be valid; as I have already argued, there is no a priori reason to think that workers will innately respond more to a worker-oriented message than to a nation-oriented one. Moreover, there are too many concrete historical examples to the contrary—the circumstances of the Second International's demise and the high proportion of workers in the NSDAP being just two.[11] Most important, the criticism is irrelevant, since no ideology can be appealing to the masses in the absence of some vehicle to bring the message to them.

That vehicle is an autonomous organization free of police interference. Lenin recognized the importance of this obvious truth in *What Is to Be Done?* Without such an organization, no amount of goodwill and rhetorical persuasiveness will suffice to mobilize a public in support of some cause. Moreover, without such an autonomous organization, rebellions and revolutions are impossible. The recent experience of Poland confirms this view. Although many other factors make comparing Poland with the USSR a risky business, it is surely true that the prior existence of the Catholic church, the Workers' Defense Committee, KOR-KSS, free trade union committees in Katowice, Szczecin, and Gdansk, and the underground newspaper *Rabotnik* provided the leadership, organization, and autonomous base for the workers who took part in the unrest that led to the formation of Solidarity in August 1980.[12] Polish dissidents already were organized and their autonomous organizations could easily accommodate the new forms of protest that were emerging in those hot summer months. Polish dissent, to use Samuel P. Huntington's terminology, was sufficiently institutionalized to absorb the growing participatory

11. Barrington Moore, *Injustice: The Social Bases of Obedience and Revolt* (White Plains, N.Y.: M. E. Sharpe, 1978), pp. 398–433.

12. Roman Laba, "Worker Roots of solidarity," *Problems of Communism*, no. 4 (July–August 1986), pp. 47–67.

tendencies of Polish society.[13] But autonomous organization is pre-cisely what most non-Russians lacked. Individual grouplets existed in all the republics, but never long enough to serve as the foundation for a network. The inability of most non-Russian dissidents to establish relatively autonomous organizational networks in the public sphere is thus the main reason for their failure to develop ties with the masses.

Consider a notable exception—the Lithuanian dissident movement, perhaps the most resilient, mass-based, and persistent of all the USSR's dissident strands. Although repression of Lithuanians has been particularly severe (they constitute proportionately the largest national contingent in the concentration camps),[14] new cohorts of dissidents continually appear, petitions frequently bear the names of thousands of ordinary Lithuanians (one petition, in 1979, was signed by some 150,000 faithful, approximately 4% of the republic's popula-tion),[15] and the major samizdat work, "The Chronicle of the Catholic Church in Lithuania," has been coming out regularly since 1972. What accounts for the obvious strength of Lithuanian dissent? The answer is evident in the name of the above-mentioned samizdat jour-nal. Lithuanian dissent is based on the political autonomy provided by the institutional strength of the Lithuanian Catholic church; in this respect it is very similar to the dissident movement in Poland and the peace movement in East Germany. Although officially neglected and frequently persecuted, the Lithuanian church is legal, independent of church bodies in Moscow, and rooted in the religiosity—whether real or feigned is immaterial—of well-nigh the entire Lithuanian popula-tion. As a result, nationalist and human rights activists who ply their trade within the autonomous presence of the Catholic church have automatic access to the public sphere, even if only to a tiny corner of it. Since the nationalist movement centers on Roman Catholicism, Lithuanian dissidents are spared the necessity of penetrating the pub-lic sphere on their own, building organizations from scratch (which is not to say, of course, that no such organizations have been estab-lished), and forging completely new links with potential constitu-encies.

In contrast to Lithuania and Poland, the Ukraine lacks an already

13. Samuel P. Huntington, *Political Order in Changing Societies* (New Haven: Yale University Press, 1968), pp. 55–79.

14. Cronid Lubarsky, "Soziale Basis und Umfang des sowjetischen Dissidenten-tums," *Osteuropa*, no. 11 (November 1979), p. 927.

15. Misiunas and Taagepera, *Baltic States*, p. 244.

existing semi-autonomous institutional focus for dissent. The Ukrainian Catholic, or Uniate, church, which had served as a conduit for Ukrainian nationalist sentiments in the interwar period, was officially dissolved in 1946; the Ukrainian Autocephalous Orthodox church had been disbanded in 1930, and its successor, the Russian Orthodox church, is subordinate to the patriarch of Moscow. The nonofficial Council of Churches of Evangelical Christians and Baptists, which broke away from the official Baptist body in the early 1960s, remains remarkably active, but it represents too small a part of the overall population to serve as an autonomous base for a republic-wide dissident movement.[16] Consequently, it has always been incumbent on Ukrainian oppositionists to seek a niche within the public sphere via their own organizational creations—the Ukrainian Workers' and Peasants' Movement in 1960, the Ukrainian National Front in 1964–67, the Union of Ukrainian Youth of Galicia in the late 1960s, the Ukrainian Helsinki Group in 1976, the Ukrainian Patriotic Movement in 1980, and others of lesser importance.[17] All of these organizations were short-lived, and all but the Helsinki Group had very limited memberships. Why? Lacking legally based autonomy while aspiring to boxes within the public sphere already occupied by the state, they were exceedingly vulnerable to assaults by the political authorities, who correctly perceived them as trespassers.

The Lithuanian and Ukrainian cases prove that the major reason for dissidents' inability to institutionalize truly was their lack of appeal—to the state, not necessarily to their potential popular constituencies. The seeming marginality of the dissident movement—whether Ukrainian or not—is a direct result of the KGB's determination quite literally to push all dissident activity to the geographical margins of Soviet society—Siberia. Autonomously organized, large-scale dissident activity will therefore be impossible in the Soviet Union in general and the Ukraine in particular as long as the state's coercive agency, the KGB, remains so effective in preventing and containing it.[18] A certain weakening of the KGB or its partial withdrawal from the public indi-

---

16. See Bohdan R. Bociurkiw, "Religious Situation in Soviet Ukraine," in *Ukraine in a Changing World,* ed. Walter Dushnyck (New York: Ukrainian Congress Committee of America, 1977), pp. 173–94.

17. Kenneth C. Farmer, *Ukrainian Nationalism in the Post-Stalin Era* (The Hague: Martinus Nijhoff, 1980), pp. 154–60.

18. On the importance of coercion, see Harry Eckstein, "On the Etiology of Internal Wars," in *Why Revolution?* ed. Clifford T. Paynton and Robert Blackey (Cambridge, Mass.: Schenkman, 1971), pp. 124–50; Chalmers Johnson, "Revolution and the Social

vidual sphere, followed by an expansion of political autonomy, is the minimal necessary condition for the emergence of non-Russian dissident leaders and of successful institutionalization of dissent.

These conclusions have important implications. If the KGB was so large an obstacle to the development of dissent, it may have been equally central to its origins and demise. As I shall presently argue, Ukrainian dissent was primarily the product of political circumstances, foremost of them being Khrushchev's de-Stalinization and Brezhnev's partial re-Stalinization of Soviet state and society. Before we explore this argument, however, it will first be necessary to dispose of its opposite, which minimizes political factors and exaggerates socioeconomic ones. An extended analysis of this nonpolitical thesis not only will demonstrate the fallacy of assigning primacy to the base and neglecting the political superstructure but also will corroborate the view expressed in Chapter 4, that the Soviet state's recent socioeconomic record has, if anything, mollified rather than aggravated Ukrainian opposition.

The central position of the nonpolitical approach, as vigorously argued by Wsevolod Isajiw and Bohdan Krawchenko, may be summarized as follows. The social mobilization of the Ukrainian population, which took place in the 1950s and 1960s largely as a consequence of postwar reconstruction and a booming economy, collided with the sizable Russian presence in the Ukraine's cities. The result was competition and the subsequent growth of ethnic tensions, one of whose manifestations was the dissident movement. According to Krawchenko, actual blockage has occurred. Russian occupation of top positions in the Ukraine, coupled with the extensive use of Russian in the republic's educational system, has blunted the expectations of upwardly mobile Ukrainians, sensitized them to a "Russian problem," and driven them to oppose the Russian presence and to defend the Ukrainian language as a symbol of their rising but frustrated aspirations. A final consequence is a cultural division of labor, with Ukrainians tending to occupy lower-level economic positions and Russians tending to occupy higher-level ones.[19]

————

System," in ibid., pp. 199–213; Theda Skocpol, *States and Social Revolutions* (Cambridge: Harvard University Press, 1979), pp. 289–90.

19. Wsevolod Isajiw, "Urban Migration and Social Change in Contemporary Soviet Ukraine," *Canadian Slavonic Papers*, no. 1 (March 1980), pp. 56–66; Bohdan Krawchenko, *Social Change and National Consciousness in Twentieth-Century Ukraine* (New York: St. Martin's Press, 1985).

Besides being an uncritical application of the by no means flawless theories of Karl Deutsch, Ted Robert Gurr, and Michael Hechter,[20] the views of Isajiw and Krawchenko suffer from a variety of methodological, theoretical, and empirical flaws. First, both scholars employ a concept of competition that is far too loose to be of much analytical value. At times they imply that "lost competition" is the decisive factor, a view in line with Gurr's. Thus the person who competes and loses becomes frustrated, conscious of the winner's ethnicity, and thus likely to seek an ethnic solution to the apparently ethnic problem of his inability to advance socially. As Krawchenko puts it, "the urbanisation of Ukraine, as a process of geographical and hence social mobility, was accompanied by competition between Ukrainians and Russians. At stake in this rivalry were higher status and better paying jobs, political and economic power and influence. In this competitive process, Russians enjoyed considerable advantages." Isajiw echoes these sentiments: "In this competition Ukrainians have been at a disadvantage as compared with the Russians, and the indications are that this disadvantage will probably increase." At other times, they imply that competition alone, in and of itself, is the crucial independent variable. According to Isajiw, "the movement for national rights in Ukraine today, rather than being a continuation of old nationalist movements, is evoked in sociological terms by the specific nature of social mobility and urbanisation processes." Or, as Krawchenko writes, "the question of competition is crucial in explaining the rise of national consciousness. With mobilised individuals, expectations race ahead of the real possibilities. These were the same people who had to compete with Russians for employment, and the rivalry led to an exacerbation of ethnic tensions."[21] Although both scholars do emphasize the primacy of the "lost competition" factor, they cannot have it both ways. Krawchenko and Isajiw are forced to resort to such fuzziness, I suspect, by the fact that "lost competition" is far more difficult to demonstrate than mere competition.

A more serious problem is the concept of competition itself. One can easily imagine a one-on-one contest between a particular Russian and a particular Ukrainian, in which both know exactly who the opponent is. But how do Ukrainians in general compete against Russians

20. Karl Deutsch, *Nationalism and Social Communication* (Cambridge: M.I.T. Press, 1953); Ted Robert Gurr, *Why Men Rebel* (Princeton: Princeton University Press, 1971); Michael Hechter, *Internal Colonialism* (Berkeley: University of California Press, 1975).

21. Krawchenko, *Social Change*, pp. 184–85, 198, 251; Isajiw, "Urban Migration," pp. 61, 65.

in general? Or, for that matter, how does an individual Ukrainian compete against Russians in general? How do we know that some particular Ukrainian is even aware of a competition with Russians? Is it not just as likely, perhaps more so, that such Ukrainians will also be competing with other Ukrainians? It takes quite a leap of imagination to comprehend that one's vague sense of social frustration, which may not have arisen from a direct conflict with a Ukrainophobe Russian, is due to the possibility that Russians occupy a somewhat more privileged position in Ukrainian society. Moreover, if we grant some validity to the concept of an ethnic ladder, then there is no a priori reason to think that a person with a Ukrainian passport will even be sensitive to such ethnic issues. The claim that competition will sensitize him to them runs the risk of circularity: is not some degree of ethnic sensitivity a prerequisite to understanding that actual competition, and not just the search for jobs, is going on? To argue in this manner is also to overlook the Soviet state's ideological adeptness at concealing undesirable facts. At the very least, if the Soviet media continually inform Ukrainians that success in competition by Ukrainians is the norm, how are individual Ukrainians supposed to generalize from their own particular negative experience?

Most important are the empirical objections to the Isajiw/Krawchenko thesis. As I demonstrated in Chapter 4, it is simply not true that Ukrainians in general have been losing the competition. So devastating an inconsistency notwithstanding, the Isajiw/Krawchenko thesis would find some support if Ukrainian dissidents—presumably those individuals who were so frustrated by the competition as to parlay their aggressiveness into dissent—were generally people who had competed and lost. But this is not at all the case. Ukrainian (as well as most Russian and non-Russian) dissidents are not losers. As even Krawchenko points out, "the opposition in Ukraine came from the socially mobilised sectors of society."[22] Viacheslav Chornovil's "typical biography of the average person convicted in 1966 for 'anti-Soviet nationalistic propaganda and agitation'" also typifies most dissidents of the 1970s and 1980s:

> The convicted N. was twenty-eight to thirty years old at the time of his arrest. He came from a peasant's or worker's family, graduated with honors from secondary school, entered university (perhaps after serving in the army), where he actively participated in scientific discussion

22. Krawchenko, *Social Change*, p. 251.

groups. Being an excellent student he obtained a good position, wrote a postgraduate dissertation (or succeeded in defending one) and his articles were published in periodicals (or he even published a book). Even if his profession was a technical one, he took an interest in literature and art and grieved for the state of his native language and culture. He is still unmarried or was married shortly after his arrest and has a small child.[23]

Chornovil, himself a dissident, convincingly demonstrates that the average Ukrainian dissident had competed and won. David Kowalewski and Cheryl Johnson's statistical analysis of Ukrainian dissidents supports Chornovil's journalistic account.[24] Indeed, even a quick survey of the most prominent dissidents confirms this view: Ivan Svitlychnyi, Ivan Dziuba, and Ievhen Sverstiuk were all up-and-coming young literary critics; Vasyl' Stus and Ihor Kalynets' were rising young poets; Mykola Rudenko and Oles' Berdnyk were established writers; Chornovil was a journalist, Valentyn Moroz was a teacher, Leonid Pliushch was a cyberneticist, Petro Grigorenko was a general and lecturer at the Frunze Military Academy. These were all individuals who in varying degrees had made it. Their commitment to the Ukrainian cause must surely be sought elsewhere than in some imagined anger at having lost to the Russians. Isajiw seems to be aware of this dilemma, for he argues that "the dissenter is still, to a large extent, a first-generation peasant. That is, most dissenters appear to be socially mobile people who have migrated from rural to urban areas. They represent those who are most aware of the threat to Ukrainian institutions."[25] Ironically, Isajiw has just undermined the very basis of the thesis he shares with Krawchenko. Now, apparently, not competition, not even lost competition, appears to be the critical factor. Rather, it is the peasant roots of successful competitors. This new hypothesis may be persuasive, but one thing it certainly is not: a confirmation of the nonpolitical Isajiw/Krawchenko thesis.

If we reject these arguments, how are we to explain the emergence of national opposition and dissent in the 1960s? Our perspective suggests that we look to the state and its policies for the answer. This more superstructural approach may be summarized as follows. As we

23. Vyacheslav Chornovil, *The Chornovil Papers* (New York: McGraw-Hill, 1968), pp. 80–81.

24. David Kowalewski and Cheryl Johnson, "The Ukrainian Dissident: A Statistical Profile," *Ukrainian Quarterly*, no. 1 (Spring 1984), pp. 52–53.

25. Isajiw, "Urban Migration," p. 65.

know, Stalin's death in 1953 produced a crisis within the leadership that succeeded him. With the terroristic secret police at the pinnacle of its power, physical survival became the immediate priority of his lieutenants. Curbing the police and neutralizing Beria—the first steps in de-Stalinization—were thus a political decision made by the strategic elite, not a functional necessity of modernization, urbanization, and the like. After Khrushchev emerged as *primus inter pares*, it was unquestionably he who made the decision to denounce Stalin. Why? Partly to dissociate himself from the Stalinist past and thereby to enhance his own legitimacy as a ruler; partly to outmaneuver his political opponents by winning the ideological high ground and putting them on the defensive; partly for international reasons, in order to refurbish the USSR's badly tarnished image and thus send positive signals to the newly liberated countries of the Third World and to the nations of the West; partly because Khrushchev may have actually believed that a loosening of controls was best for Soviet society; and finally, partly because Khrushchev's planned economic reforms necessitated certain political reforms. (Charles Lindblom and Wlodzimierz Brus have studied the theoretical relation between economic and political liberalization, while, most recently, Deng Xiao-ping has demonstrated it in practice.)[26] Whatever the reason, and for our purposes it is unnecessary to isolate the decisive one, de-Stalinization was a political decision of the Soviet state's strategic elite. Like Stalin's "revolution from above" and Mao Zedong's Cultural Revolution, Khrushchev's measures represented an attempt to change intrastate as well as state–society authority relations. Indeed, Khrushchev may be said to have created a new state characterized by new, non-Stalinist political authority patterns.

For reasons already discussed in Chapter 3, de-Stalinization was accompanied by Khrushchev's Sovnarkhoz reform. Both moves had several effects. In respect to intrastate relations, the non-Russian republics were granted more extensive powers as their economies were more or less subordinated to republican control. Authority, in a word, was deconcentrated. In addition, non-Russian cadres were co-opted in increasing numbers into the party—again, for a variety of possible reasons: to swamp the former Stalinists, to acquire needed legitimacy

26. Charles E. Lindblom, *Politics and Markets* (New York: Basic Books, 1977); Wlodzimierz Brus, "Political Pluralism and Markets in Communist Systems," in *Pluralism in the Soviet Union*, ed. Susan Gross Solomon (New York: St. Martin's Press, 1983), pp. 108–30.

among the long-neglected republics, to fill the increasing number of responsible posts being devolved to the republican level, to dampen potential national dissatisfaction. The sudden jump in Ukrainian Party membership in the 1950s was due, therefore, to a political decision and not to the increasing urbanization and social mobilization of the Ukrainian population.[27]

With regard to society, the state, in what came to be known as the "Thaw," expanded political autonomy by reining in the terror and loosening certain political and especially cultural controls. And a thaw it was indeed, producing an outpouring of adventuresome cultural works in the late 1950s and early 1960s by such authors as Ilia Ehrenburg, Evgenii Evtushenko, Andrei Voznesenskii, and the Sixties Generation in the Ukraine. Their creativity, too, was the product of political liberalization and not of economic development. As Soviet citizens were allowed to think more openly (even under Stalin they were allowed to think), as their sources of information and their ability to communicate with others increased—that is, as political autonomy expanded—they logically concluded that de-Stalinization should be only the start of a long-term and thoroughgoing process. The publication of Solzhenitsyn's *One Day in the Life of Ivan Denisovich* indicates that the post-Stalin state encouraged such beliefs. Very few of the original cultural activists can therefore be called dissidents, since their activity was almost exclusively cultural and wholly consistent with the premises of de-Stalinization.

But de-Stalinization soon fell short of its promise. Khrushchev began to backtrack, and for good reason. Carried to its logical conclusion, de-Stalinization would have swept him and the strategic elite out of power. By the mid-1960s, moreover, with the trial of Iurii Daniel and Andrei Siniavskii and the concomitant crackdown in the Ukraine, the post-Khrushchev leadership signaled that de-Stalinization was over. The repressive actions of Brezhnev and Kosygin had the effect of contracting political autonomy and delineating clearly what was and what was not culturally and politically tolerated—a line that Khrushchev had left somewhat blurred. As a result, large numbers of legalistically inclined activists suddenly found themselves on the wrong side of the law. In this sense, it was the Soviet state that created the dissidents. By contracting the field of permissi-

27. Bohdan Krawchenko, "Changes in the National and Social Composition of the Communist Party of Ukraine from the Revolution to 1976," *Journal of Ukrainian Studies*, no. 16 (Summer 1984), pp. 33–54.

ble activity, the state was declaring all those who found themselves beyond the new boundaries to be subversives. By not contracting it in a Stalinist fashion, however, the state was also guaranteeing that dissidents would always enjoy some political autonomy and become endemic to the system. My argument is thus rather different from that of Walter D. Connor, who believes that the collision between social differentiation and a "constricted" political system produced dissent.[28]

Partial re-Stalinization had an additional side effect. Not only did it create the dissidents, it also politicized them. Constitutional activists were in fact told that their legalistic efforts were incompatible with the Soviet political system. Not surprisingly, calls for legalism gradually, though not universally, changed into calls for a complete revamping of state and society. Many activists came to realize that their modest cultural demands, which were tolerated in the early 1960s, would not be met by a state that had become avowedly hostile to them. Many Ukrainians and other non-Russians not unreasonably concluded that republican rights were inauthentic, that the Soviet state was in fact a Russian state, and that political independence was the only guarantee of their nations' cultural and political development. Such reasoning is most evident in, for example, the politically sophisticated writings of the Ukrainian Helsinki Group and the Ukrainian Patriotic Movement.[29]

The vagaries of state policy constitute the analytical framework within which the emergence of national and nationalist currents in the non-Russian republics must be seen. In view of the political and cultural opportunities created by Khrushchev and rescinded by his successors, first legal and then illegal national activism was a perfectly natural response of the non-Russian elites to the initial expansion and later contraction of political autonomy. True, not all non-Russians behaved according to this pattern, and the reasons for the divergences must be sought in a variety of places: culture, history, political traditions, the vitality of local elites, and, of equal importance, socioeconomic conditions. It would be naive to claim that postwar developments in the society and economy of the republics had no role to play in the emergence of dissent. Certainly, as Charles Tilly

28. Walter D. Connor, "Dissent in a Complex Society: The Soviet Case," *Problems of Communism*, no. 2 (March–April 1973), pp. 46–47.

29. Osyp Zinkevych, ed., *Ukrains'ka Hel'sinks'ka Hrupa, 1978–1982: Dokumenty i materiialy* (Baltimore: Smoloskyp, 1983); *Dokumenty Ukrains'koho Patriotychnoho Rukhu, 1980 r.* (New York: Zakordonne Predstavnytstvo Ukrains'koi Hel'sinks'koi Hrupy, 1980).

might suggest, these changes affected the form that opposition assumed;[30] minimally, they more or less ensured that the cities would become the centers of opposition, for it was to the cities that the most active elements of the non-Russian populations had moved and it was in the cities that new elites arose. In this sense, modernization and social mobilization affected the range of political options that were open to the non-Russian elites and populations. But none of these base-type factors would have been operative had the state not made a number of political decisions—de-Stalinization and partial re-Stalinization—that first tolerated and then condemned incipient nonconformist activity.

Khrushchev's curbing of the powers of the secret police created the political autonomy that permitted dissidents-to-be to venture into the public sphere. Brezhnev returned to a watered-down version of Stalinism and correspondingly reduced autonomy (but not completely) by granting more prerogatives to the coercive apparatus. We return once again to the KGB and its powers. Although the Soviet Union is by no means totalitarian, there is no escaping the simple fact of the KGB's overpowering presence in Soviet society. It may be subordinate to the wishes of the Party elite, and coercion may not be the major source of state stability; but the KGB represents a nearly impregnable line of defense against assaults on the Soviet state's political, class, and ethnic patterns of authority. As long as the secret police remains intact, the state is likely to enjoy satisfactory levels of survival capacity and high levels of management effectiveness. The state, in a word, will continue to be quite stable.

30. Charles Tilly, "Does Modernization Breed Revolution?" *Comparative Politics*, no. 3 (April 1973), pp. 425–47.

CHAPTER 9

Rebellions from Outside?

The large number of externally supported rebel movements throughout the world shows plainly that, as the complaint goes, outside interference in the internal affairs of sovereign states is a common enough occurrence. Pious promises and indignant protests to the contrary, few states appear willing to translate alleged principles into actual behavior and desist completely from all forms of interference. More to the point, they could not do so even if they wanted to. Given the economic, political, and military interconnectedness of international state relations, complete noninterference would be tantamount to a policy of political isolationism and economic autarky on the order of that pursued by Enver Hoxha's Albania—hardly a realistic option for most state actors.

Strictly speaking, since foreign aid, trade, and tourism also are forms of interference, the true analytical distinction is not between interference and noninterference but between desired and undesired interference. The Soviet Union, for one, has experienced its share of both. The former does not concern us; the latter includes, among other things, military intervention in 1918–21, Western aid to post–World War II resistance movements, American and Israeli moral support of Jewish "refuseniks" and other dissidents, continuous Western radio sabotage, and ideological spill-over from such neighboring countries as Poland and Afghanistan. That undesired nonmilitary interference is a nuisance for the Soviet authorities goes without saying. But is it more than that as well? In particular, can outside forces generate a Ukrainian or, more broadly, a non-Russian rebellion in the USSR?

The experience of currently existing rebel movements suggests a negative answer. Few would dispute that external assistance can be a great boon to the fighting capacity of rebels. Nor would many deny that rebels with nothing but external support are unlikely to survive long in a hostile or indifferent social environment. Clearly, then, the precondition of successful, even if limited, outside interference is that internally generated recipients be there to receive it. South Africa's support of UNITA, Cuban support of the Salvadoran guerrillas, and American aid to the Afghan mujahidin and the Nicaraguan contras can produce results because interference only complements already existing rebel forces. But, as Chapter 8 argued, non-Russian rebels-in-waiting in the Soviet Union appear to be few and far between.

These remarks assume that the state within which an actually functioning or potential rebel group is active simply sits back and watches its opponents go about their subversive work. But this, of course, is never the case. States, as dedicated self-maintainers, adopt extensive measures to prevent unwanted interference: they attempt to interdict the flow of aid, be it men, matériel, or money; they actively combat actual and incipient insurgent forces; they wage a war of ideas. Indeed, as Theda Skocpol has made clear, even if relatively fertile social grounds for rebellion are assumed to exist, outside assistance will be ineffective in any but the short run as long as the coercive capacity of the threatened state is sufficient to prevent internal opponents from translating it into active opposition.[1] Poland in 1981, Czechoslovakia in 1968, Hungary in 1956, and East Berlin in 1953 testify to the validity of Skocpol's insight. Despite the intensity of their "popular liberation struggles," Soviet power was the ultimate guarantor of the continued existence of "real socialism" in all four countries.

Short of war, the armed forces and police of states generally do not just fall apart—a perhaps insurmountable problem for potential non-Russian rebels. Since the Soviet Union is a superpower, only an enormously destructive conflict—a nuclear war—could so debilitate its coercive agencies as to permit Soviet class- and nation-based insurrectionary forces to arise en masse. Of necessity, such a conflagration would involve the targeting of population and industrial centers of the non-Russian republics. Indeed, the republics of the Soviet west

---

1. Theda Skocpol, "What Makes Peasants Revolutionary?" *Comparative Politics*, no. 3 (April 1982), pp. 351–75.

would probably suffer most, since they are home not only to vital countervalue targets (Baltic and Black Sea ports, the Donbass, the Kryvyi Rih [Krivoi Rog] Basin) but also to counterforce ones, among them a plethora of theater nuclear weapons such as the SS-20s. The resultant devastation could make the issue of separation more or less moot, since there would, quite possibly, be no one left to break away.

But how likely is a war between the Soviet Union and the United States? Despite the recurrent American propensity for inflammatory rhetoric (about whose usual lack of substance the Hungarians learned the hard way), it is reasonable to suggest that no American president is going to bomb Russia, at least not without truly enormous provocation: the Americans know this, the Soviets know this, and both know that the other side knows it. (Bombing smaller countries such as Libya, of course, is another matter—and one that proves my point.) Neither, I suggest, is the United States or NATO about to launch a preventive first strike against the Soviets (especially in view of Western Europe's current disinclination to annoy the USSR), nor, for that matter, are the Soviets about to embark on suicide and attack Western Europe or the United States. Both sides stand to lose too much to upset the balance of terror intentionally and risk a nuclear exchange, at least under normal circumstances. Naturally, a major crisis in, say, the Middle East or a trigger-happy president or general secretary might create abnormal circumstances, but such contingencies necessarily fall outside our analysis. In a word, although Western relations with the USSR will probably continue to alternate between détente and quasi cold war, a hot war initiated by either of the two superpowers seems to be out of the question.

Economic warfare, on the other hand, is quite possible and may flare up from time to time. Its effects, however, are not about to undermine the Soviet state. Embargoes have proven notoriously ineffective in the past. U.S. efforts to halt the transfer of sensitive technology to the USSR have also been largely unsuccessful and are unlikely ever to close the large number of uncontrollable channels for smuggling such hard- and software. No less important, since the United States has too much to lose by cutting off all trade with the Soviets, its past economic boycotts have usually proven to be either halfhearted or provisional or both. If implemented, conservative calls for strangling the Soviets—by depriving them of needed commodities while embarking on a costly arms race—would certainly make life difficult for the Soviet Union, but they would be unlikely to lead to the collapse of a state of the USSR's power, magnitude, and resources. Moreover, such a course would probably elicit so much protest in the United States and impose such high costs on its populace as to be politically unimaginable in normal circumstances.

To argue that the West is not a source of system-threatening activity for the Soviet state is not necessarily to say that none exists. A variety of scholars have suggested that one such source may be the USSR's large Islamic population.[2] Specifically, they focus on the possibility that the Islamic revival in the Middle East may spread to the Muslims of Soviet Central Asia and thereby undermine the claims of communist ideology. There is some evidence to support this scenario. The Central Asian press regularly denounces a variety of stubborn Islamic religious and cultural practices, devotes extensive space to the valor of KGB border troops stationed on the USSR's southern borders (thus suggesting that Afghan guerrilla claims of having made forays into the USSR may not be unfounded), and frequently attacks "foreign intelligence services" for their attempts to subvert the Central Asians ideologically.[3] Obviously, if an Iranian-style fanaticism were to grip Central Asia, the Soviet state would be faced with a major crisis. But how likely is this darkest of scenarios? At worst, in the absence of extensive cross-border ties between Central Asia and Afghanistan and Iran, I doubt that militant Islam could spread as rapidly and as easily as this scenario implies. At best, I suspect that there is no way of really knowing. I concur with Daniel C. Matuszewski's reasoned judgment:

> The powerful cultural renaissance among the Turkic peoples can cut both ways. If manipulated properly by Soviet authorities and imbued with a substantial Soviet element, it can play a strong role in Soviet expansionary patterns in the East. If mishandled and alienated, it would become a tremendous subversive force tending to undermine the legitimacy of the Soviet regime. At present, the Soviet content of this phenomenon remains high. This is not to say that the Soviet Turkic peoples are immune to Islamic spiritual contagion.[4]

As the Soviet authorities no doubt realize, further sensitivity to Central Asian cultural and religious concerns and continued commitment

---

2. Alexandre Bennigsen and Marie Broxup, *The Islamic Threat to the Soviet State* (London: Croom Helm, 1983); Hélène Carrère d'Encausse, *Decline of an Empire* (New York: Newsweek Books, 1979); Michael Rywkin, *Moscow's Muslim Challenge* (Armonk, N.Y.: M. E. Sharpe, 1982).

3. Alexandre Bennigsen, "Mullahs, Mujahidin, and Soviet Muslims," *Problems of Communism*, no. 6 (November–December 1984), pp. 28–44.

4. Daniel C. Matuszewski, "Empire, Nationalities, Border: Soviet Assets and Liabilities," in *Soviet Nationalities in Strategic Perspective*, ed. S. Enders Wimbush (Lon-

to the region's development will prove as crucial to defusing any potential Islamic threat as they have been to consolidating Soviet rule in the past. Mikhail Gorbachev's apparent intention to increase economic efficiency may reduce Moscow's subsidies to Central Asia's growth rates, but its impact on political behavior is, as I shall argue in Chapter 10, quite indeterminate.

Far more important to Soviet ethnic stability is the USSR's East European empire. Almost all East European countries are undergoing varying degrees of economic decline and social unrest. Poland needs no comment, Hungary's demoralized population is experiencing an economic downturn, Rumania is extolling the virtues of sacrifice, while normally imperturbable East Germany has to contend with a rejuvenated Protestant church, a strong peace movement, and hordes of would-be emigrants. Czechoslovakia, although economically most fit, continues to have difficulties with Charter 77 activists and Czech and especially Slovak religious dissidents. Even staid Bulgaria has problems with bomb-throwers and Turks. East Germans, Hungarians, Czechs and Slovaks, and Poles have rebelled in the past, and there is no reason to think that they are incapable of such actions in the future. Indeed, it is probably a safe bet that another Polish outburst, although not necessarily on the scale of Solidarity, is inevitable.

In a very real sense, Eastern Europe is a no-win proposition for the Soviet state. To keep the Eastern Europeans materially satisfied the Soviet Union must either subsidize their economies, which it can ill afford to do for long (especially in light of the steep fall in the price of oil in 1985–86); let them intensify their contacts with the West, which only increase their exposure to nefarious influences; or more fully incorporate them into the Soviet economic and political sphere, thus risking even greater popular resentment (the 1986 Chernobyl catastrophe can but have increased East European suspicions of all winds from the East). The last option appears to be the Soviet leadership's current preference, despite the high ideological risks involved in associating with populations that have so obviously rejected Soviet domination. Soviet leaders are justifiably concerned, because Eastern Europe has exerted some ideological influence on parts of the Soviet Union in the past, especially during the Prague Spring and Solidarity's near-revolution.[5] Their worries are unlikely to diminish,

---

don: Croom Helm, 1985), pp. 92–93. See also Martha Olcott, "Soviet Islam and World Revolution," *World Politics*, no. 4 (July 1982), pp. 487–504.

5. Roman Szporluk, ed., *The Influence of East Europe and the Soviet West on the USSR* (New York: Praeger, 1975); Grey Hodnett and Peter J. Potichnyj, *The Ukraine and*

since Eastern Europe's extensive higher- and lower-level political, economic, cultural, and social contacts with border regions of the USSR—and the associated likelihood of spill-over—are bound to increase in tandem with CMEA integration.[6]

Eastern Europe, Poland in particular, is especially relevant to Soviet ethnic stability because of its proximity to and extensive ties with the Ukraine.[7] Solidarity's threat to Soviet power in the Ukrainian SSR is incomparably more significant than the Islamic threat to Soviet Central Asia—not only because of the many channels for transmitting its ideas into the Ukraine (say, the 150,000 Ukrainians in Poland and the 258,000 Poles in the Ukrainian SSR)[8] but also because the Ukraine is still the key to the Soviet Russian state's ethnic stability. Equally important, the conduit for ideas between Eastern Europe and most of the Ukraine is its western border oblasts, where nationalist sentiments, dissident activity, and receptivity to unorthodox views are still very much alive. It would, of course, be alarmist to suggest that the Soviet Ukraine will follow ineluctably in Poland's footsteps. But the possibility exists, and, as their decision to reduce sharply Polish-Ukrainian tourism in 1982–83 indicates, Soviet policy makers are quite sensitive to such a scenario.[9]

For all their corrosive ideological potential, neither militant Islamic countries nor the socialist states of Eastern Europe are willing or able to interfere directly and massively in Soviet affairs. Such interference in the concerns of a superpower is the prerogative only of another superpower. Although the United States does not appear to be hell-bent on the Soviet Union's destruction, some of its policies do pose a

the *Czechoslovak Crisis* (Canberra: Australian National University, 1970); V. Stanley Vardys, "Polish Echoes in the Baltic," *Problems of Communism*, no. 4 (July–August 1983), pp. 21–34; Roman Solchanyk, "Poland and the Soviet West," in *Soviet Nationalities*, ed. Wimbush, pp. 158–80; "Attitudes of Some Soviet Citizens to the Solidarity Trade Union Movement," RFE-RL Soviet Area Audience and Opinion Research, AR no. 5-82 (May 1982).

6. V. P. Kolesnik, *Internatsional'nye sviazi trudiashchikhsia prigranichnykh oblastei SSSR i evropeiskikh sotsialisticheskikh stran* (Lvov: Vyshcha Shkola, 1984).

7. See Peter J. Potichnyj, ed., *Ukraine and Poland: Past and Present* (Edmonton: Canadian Institute of Ukrainian Studies, 1980).

8. Borys Lewytzkyj, "Political and Cultural Cooperation between the People's Republic of Poland and the Ukrainian Soviet Socialist Republic," in *Ukraine and Poland*, ed. Potichnyj, pp. 209–10.

9. M. V. Znamens'ka, "Uchast' Ukrains'koi RSR u spivrobitnytstvi SRSR z ievropeis'kymy krainamy sotsializmu v haluzi turyzmu (70-i–pochatok 80-kh rr.)," *Ukrains'kyi istorychnyi zhurnal*, no. 1 (January 1986), p. 122.

direct challenge to the Soviet Russian state. How large a challenge and with respect to whom? It will be worth analyzing how the United States has gone about interfering in the Soviet Ukraine and why the results of its efforts have been relatively meager.

The simultaneously anti-Soviet and pro-Ukrainian activity of the United States is more or less synonymous with the policies of containment and roll-back pursued in the late 1940s and early 1950s. The Cold War was in its early stages, and the American commitment to stopping the Red menace and saving the world was still unshaken; the Truman Doctrine, the Marshall Plan, and the creation of NATO and other alliances represent significant milestones in this strategy. With respect to the non-Russians, however, the United States record is far more bleak. If we discount statements of solidarity with the captive nations, saber-rattling, and name-calling by presidents and other government officials and concentrate only on concrete attempts at interference, there is, frankly, not much left to consider. In effect, America's efforts are confined to the activity of the Central Intelligence Agency (and of CIA-sponsored or -affiliated organizations): direct clandestine support of resistance movements in the Ukraine as well as indirect attempts to influence the Ukrainian population by means of the airwaves.

It is best to begin with American radio infiltration of the Soviet Ukraine. Our focus, naturally, is on Radio Liberty. Founded in the early 1950s as Radio Liberation from Bolshevism, it was removed from the CIA payroll in 1973, when it began to receive its funding directly from the United States Congress. At the same time, Radio Liberty and its counterpart for Eastern Europe, Radio Free Europe, were rechristened an "independent radio service," RFE-RL, Inc.[10] Irrespective of these changes, it is an open secret—to which the USSR is privy—that Radio Liberty continues to spearhead American anti-Soviet activity.

Official Soviet denunciations, the testimony of Soviet émigrés, and RFE-RL audience surveys convincingly demonstrate that parts of the target audiences actually do listen to the broadcasts. According to Radio Liberty estimates, "RFE-RL is reaching between 6.8 and 9.5 million listeners on an average day; between 15.9 and 23.5 million in an average week; and between 17.7 and 25.6 million in an average

10. Donald R. Browne, *International Radio Broadcasting* (New York: Praeger, 1982), pp. 135–48; Board for International Broadcasting, *Sixth Annual Report, 1980* (Washington, D.C., 1980), p. 43.

month."[11] More important than mere numbers are the social groups that apparently tune in the broadcasts. "University students, the 'scientific intelligentsia,' the 'literary-artistic intelligentsia,' and the 'politically-oriented younger generation' all listen [to Radio Liberty] at higher rates, show a more marked preference for the station's informational and political programming, tune in more frequently, and say they like the station more than members of other audience categories." While 42 to 54 percent of these groups are supposed to be Radio Liberty listeners, 18 percent of agricultural workers and 28 percent of blue-collar workers also listen to it.[12] Not only are the latter two percentages not insignificant, if accurate, but they obviously represent a far larger audience in absolute terms. With respect to Radio Liberty's listeners in the Ukrainian SSR, another audience survey estimates that "12% of the population of the Ukraine aged 16 years and over are reached by Radio Liberty in the course of an average week." Not unexpectedly, the social profile of the Ukraine's Radio aficionados is similar to that of the larger Soviet audience.[13]

Just as impressive as these figures are the ideological, financial, technical, and manpower resources that the Soviet authorities devote to combating hostile radio voices. Jamming alone involves an estimated 2,500 transmitters priced at $250 million, and annual operating costs are supposed to exceed $100 million.[14] It is instructive to take note of the pattern of jamming employed by the Soviets. Almost without exception, it seems, jamming stations are situated in and around cities, while there is reason to believe that broadcasts can be heard loud and clear in the countryside.[15] Why this discrepancy? City dwellers are probably considered more susceptible to outside influence than villagers and more dangerous if they should be infected by the germs of imperialist propaganda. This pattern, I suggest, testifies to the Soviet state's confidence in its ability to keep the countryside pacified and its lack of confidence in its ability to keep the cities— that is, intellectuals and workers—under control.

11. "Trend Report: RFE-RL's Audience in the USSR, Jan.–Dec. 1984," AR no. 2-85 (April 1985), p. 4.

12. "Radio Liberty's Audiences in the USSR: A Behavioral Study," Audience Research and Program Evaluation Division, RFE-RL, AR no. 7-73 (1973), pp. 6, 10.

13. K. Mihalisko, "Nationality Listener Report: Belorussian and Ukrainian Services (1983 Data)," RFE-RL Soviet Area Audience and Opinion Research, NLR 1-84 (July 1984), pp. 12, 9.

14. John L. Scherer, ed., *USSR Facts and Figures Annual* (Gulf Breeze, Fla.: Academic International Press, 1983), VII, 288.

15. Information based on interviews with Soviet émigrés.

Do these considerations mean that the Soviet state has been able to counter the pernicious influence of RFE-RL? The recent development of counterpropaganda as a form of ideological activity specifically designed to neutralize Western propaganda *after* it has been imbibed suggests that Soviet fears about the attractiveness of bourgeois ideas are not insubstantial and perhaps not unsubstantiated.[16] But if my arguments regarding the behavioral functions of ideology and Russification policy are correct, then the private attitudes of radio listeners are not really at issue. Far more important is that very few listeners appear willing to translate their opinions into concrete actions (after all, if all listeners were dissidents, the dissident movement would be enormous). Thus Radio Liberty's programs appear to have become a permanent, though controllable, source of irritation for the Soviet Russian state. The same conclusion probably holds for Radio Liberty's less maligned cousins—Vatican Radio, Deutsche Welle, the BBC, the Voice of America, and other foreign "airwave saboteurs."

Direct American intervention in Soviet Ukrainian affairs is inversely proportional to indirect RFE-RL involvement. The 1940s and early 1950s, when a Ukrainian nationalist underground still existed, were the period of most intense CIA encouragement of anti-Soviet activity. Training Ukrainian émigré personnel, air-dropping them into the Ukraine, and providing financial and logistical support to the underground appear to represent the full scope of CIA operations.[17] Their significance, though slight, was not nil. By encouraging the underground without supplying it with the requisite military equipment, however, United States policy makers merely prolonged its inevitable demise. To be sure, there was little that the United States could do, since anything short of an all-out attack—which the Ukrainians, like their counterparts in Lithuania, unrealistically expected[18]—would have been insufficient to meet the needs of the resistance.

For obvious reasons, the United States has generally used Ukrainian

16. L. M. Kravchuk, "Kontrpropahanda v systemi ideolohichnoi roboty partiinykh komitetiv: Dosvid, problemy," *Ukrains'kyi istorychnyi zhurnal*, no. 6 (June 1984), pp. 5–17.

17. A scholarly study of American relations with the Ukrainian nationalists has still to be written. For references to the issue, see Bruce Page, David Leitch, and Phillip Knightley, *The Philby Conspiracy* (New York: Ballantine, 1981), pp. 185–89; William Colby and Peter Forbath, *Honorable Men: My Life in the CIA* (New York: Simon & Schuster, 1978), p. 104; Thomas Powers, *The Man Who Kept the Secrets* (New York: Knopf, 1979), pp. 39–43.

18. Osyp Diakiv-Hornovyi, *Ideia i chyn* (New York: Association of Former UPA Fighters, 1968), p. 98.

émigrés in its subversive efforts: they speak the language, know (or knew) local conditions, and have strong political commitments. (The Soviet caricature of émigrés as venal mercenaries relegated to the garbage heap of history is just that, a caricature.) No less important than their involvement with "imperialist circles," however, Ukrainian émigrés engage on their own in a variety of anti-Soviet activities deserving of our attention. Notorious for their optimism, all émigrés— even such luminaries as Lenin and Trotsky in the years before 1917— tend to exaggerate the importance of what they do. Since Ukrainian émigrés are no exception to this rule, we may ignore bombastic pronouncements of imminent revolution, protest marches, hunger strikes, and demonstrations, and proceed to evaluate only their attempts at direct and indirect involvement in the homeland. Since the end of World War II they have consistently if variably provided support for oppositionist elements, engaged in subversive tourist activities, and mailed nationalist propaganda.[19]

As long as the nationalist underground existed, Ukrainian émigrés of most political persuasions in West Germany and in several other European countries were involved in both open and clandestine operations in support of their colleagues in the homeland (with the assistance of, apparently, the American, British, and West German secret services).[20] Émigré couriers were smuggled into the Ukraine; money, propaganda, and presumably some firearms were siphoned to the underground; an exchange of information and directives was continually in progress. How effective these measures were is hard to say if only because both the underground and the émigrés were thoroughly riddled with Soviet agents. Indeed, there is reason to believe that the Soviets refrained from crushing what remained of the underground in the late 1940s in order to have more time to capture its leaders and penetrate the emigration. In any case, 1954 marked a symbolic turning point. That year, Vasyl' Okhrymovych, a leading nationalist, was air-dropped into the Ukraine. Caught and subsequently tried and shot, he appears to have been the last important émigré to return to the Ukraine on a subversive mission.[21]

With the elimination of the underground and the sealing off of the

19. Such antistate actions par excellence as attacks on Soviet officials or buildings in the Ukraine may be immediately dismissed from consideration, since they have never, to my knowledge, occurred. There were, however, several fire bombings of Soviet property in Paris, Luxembourg, and Munich in 1978–80.

20. E. H. Cookridge, *Gehlen* (New York: Random House, 1971), pp. 237–348.

21. "U viis'kovomu Trybunali Kyivs'koho viis'kovoho okruhu," *Radians'ka Ukraina*, May 19, 1954.

Soviet border, the émigrés were effectively severed from the Ukraine. Propaganda mailings, clandestine broadcasting independent of Radio Liberty, and attempts to penetrate the Iron Curtain by such means as hot-air balloons appear to have become the norm of émigré anti-Soviet activity in the mid- to late 1950s.[22] While the latter two forms fell victim to the demise of the Cold War, propaganda mailings have been encouraged by "peaceful coexistence" and détente and continue to preoccupy many Ukrainian émigré groups.

The 1960s witnessed two significant developments: the rise of the Ukrainian dissident movement and official Soviet encouragement of tourism. Émigré circles were quick to use the latter development in their attempts to aid or influence the former. Inevitably, as tourists arrived in the USSR its border would become "one of the channels through which our enemies strive to acquire espionage information, carry out hostile acts, engage in ideological diversions and other subversive acts."[23] The Soviet Ukrainian press is replete with references to the vigilance of the border guards, who annually interdict the flow of thousands of purportedly anti-Soviet publications. According to the chief of the Political Sector of the Army's Red Flag Western Border Command, "each year, especially during the last few years, the border guards in our command on the control entry points confiscate many tens of thousands of copies of ideologically harmful publications. There were cases in which these publications were disguised as books of innocent content; they were bound in covers with titles of well-known classical and Soviet works, or published in the form of microbooks and microbrochures."[24] In 1981 alone, about 60,000 "ideologically harmful materials"—the bulk of which presumably consisted of Western newspapers and magazines—were confiscated at Soviet Ukrainian frontier checkpoints.[25]

22. *Ukraina: Suchasne i maibutnie: Zbirnyk stattei* (New York: Proloh, 1959), p. 75, discusses clandestine broadcasting. According to *Vitchyzna*, no. 9 (September 1957), "during the 1955–56 period, about two thousand balloons with all kinds of apparatus and with containers of hostile literature were captured over the territory of the Ukrainian SSR" (*Digest of the Soviet Ukrainian Press*, no. 2 [December 1957], p. 3). Despite the doubtful effectiveness of such measures, even as late as 1957 and 1959 the Ukrainian émigré nationalist leaders Lev Rebet and Stepan Bandera were considered to be sufficiently threatening to warrant elimination by KGB agent Bohdan Stashyns'kyi. For additional information on the Stashyns'kyi case, see *Moskovs'ki vbyvtsi Bandery pered sudom* (Munich: Ukrains'ke vydavnytstvo, 1965).

23. I. Kalynychenko, "V boiovomu dozori," *Radians'ka Ukraina*, February 25, 1984.

24. *Radians'ka Ukraina*, May 28, 1970, as translated in *Digest of the Soviet Ukrainian Press*, no. 7 (July 1970), p. 27.

25. *Soviet Nationality Survey*, no. 2 (February 1984), p. 5.

Although émigré anti-Soviet activity has been consistently high throughout the years, it remains no more than a very minor threat to Soviet ethnic stability. First, it is exclusively supportive and therefore ultimately dependent on developments in the Ukraine. Second, émigré resources—mailings, propaganda, and so on—are so limited as to be of scarcely any danger to a superpower such as the Soviet Union. Third, the Soviet Union can neutralize émigré activity by maintaining tight control of tourists and of incoming mail at the borders. Relatedly, the KGB's penetration of émigré groups has made it relatively easy to entrap émigré emissaries, much to the embarrassment of their sponsors. The cases of Yaroslav Dobosh of Belgium, in 1972, and of Andrew Klymchuk of Great Britain, in 1977, have been the most sensational recent examples of the KGB's prowess.[26] Fourth, denunciations of émigrés continue to be regular features of the Soviet Ukrainian press, reminding the citizenry that émigrés and nationalism are taboo in any and all guises.[27] Last and most important, even when control fails and a subversive letter or tourist manages to get through, there is no guarantee that the target wants to be or can get involved in émigré schemes. A recent example is illustrative. One M. Kukhtiak, an instructor in Ivano-Frankivs'k, appears to have been the focus of émigré attempts at recruitment in 1982–83. But Kukhtiak, whether out of fear or conviction, resisted these blandishments and immediately reported them to the KGB. The result was a press conference at which this loyal, self-styled "ordinary village boy" exposed the nefarious exiles.[28]

Attempts at external intervention in the Ukrainian SSR are likely to be even less successful in the future than they have been in the past. Both the postwar nationalist resistance and, to a far lesser extent, the dissident movement were well-organized forces, with networks of activists and the means for establishing contacts with external allies. If even they failed, we should expect far less from the nonorganized, relatively isolated groups, grouplets, and individuals active today. Considering the enormous controls imposed by the Soviet state on

26. Kenneth C. Farmer, Ukrainian Nationalism in the Post-Stalin Era (The Hague: Martinus Nijhoff, 1980), pp. 197–99. See also Ia. Radchenko and B. Chaban, "Turyst na zamovlennia," Radians'ka Ukraina, March 13, 1973, p. 3.

27. For typical examples of this genre, see V. Iu. Ievdokymenko and V. O. Ihnatov, Natsionalizm i natsii (Kiev: Naukova Dumka, 1981); Iu. I. Rymarenko, Burzhuaznyi natsionalizm ta ioho 'teoriia' natsii (Kiev: Naukova Dumka, 1974). For a critique of Rymarenko, see Omelian Pavliv, "Fal'shyvyi idealizm Iu. I. Rymarenka i do choho vin vede," Suchasnist', no. 10 (October 1975), pp. 100–106.

28. Soviet Nationality Survey, no. 3 (March 1984), p. 7.

borders, tourism, the mail, and radio, it is all but impossible for "imperialist secret services" or "Ukrainian bourgeois nationalists" to penetrate the thick wall of security. The term *Iron Curtain* may have a variety of unsavory connotations, but it accurately reflects the conditions confronting external "enemies" of the Soviet state, be they Ukrainians, Russians, Jews, Lithuanians, Latvians, Estonians, or other belligerent émigrés.

Evidently a non-Russian or, more specifically, a Ukrainian rebellion will have to be generated within the Soviet Union itself. If such a rebellion is to occur, it will have to be the doing largely, if not quite exclusively, of the inhabitants of the USSR. Western interference may help create hostile attitudes, it may inspire some individuals to engage in samizdat, it may even impel them to communicate their convictions to close friends or family members. But translating such feelings into public sentiments and public activities—that is, deprivatizing them—is something Western actors cannot do for the simple reason that they are physically separated from their target constituencies in the USSR.

Thus Russian and non-Russian oppositionists are left with one option only, and that is to follow the advice of interwar Ukrainian nationalists and view their "own forces" (*vlasni syly*) as the key to victory.[29] Such self-reliance is laudable, but are their own forces enough to start a rebellion against the Soviet state? Irrespective of state controls, are the forces of any one non-Russian nation sufficient to engage in successful rebellion? As I suggested in Chapter 3, the only non-Russian nation with a fighting chance against the state is the Ukrainians. Still, as *postwar* Ukrainian nationalists realized, even the Ukrainians cannot topple the Soviet state on their own. If armed intervention is excluded and if outside economic pressure is dismissed as ineffective and probably unrealizable, the only possibility of a successful Ukrainian rebellion against the state must involve Ukrainian alliances with other nations. How good are the chances of such coalitions' coming about?

The task is formidable. The Belorussians, for example, are natural allies of the Ukrainians. Similar languages and cultures, internationally experienced elites, and no record of enmity make these two Slavic nations the ideal partners for a coalition against the state. Nev-

29. Alexander J. Motyl, *The Turn to the Right: The Ideological Origins and Development of Ukrainian Nationalism, 1919–1929* (Boulder, Colo.: East European Monographs, 1980), pp. 29, 69.

ertheless, a Ukrainian-Belorussian alliance is probably next to impossible. At present, the Belorussian elite appears largely to have been co-opted by the state, the masses seem to be positioned quite low on their ethnic ladder, and both groups are the targets of a wide-ranging and apparently effective Russification policy.[30] Moreover, the Belorussian contribution to dissent has been virtually nonexistent. If not the Belorussians, then who? The Balts and Caucasians, though more or less active nationally, are both too far and too few to be effective partners. The Moldavians are insignificant. Central Asia's Muslims may become a threat someday, but they are simply too distant from the Ukraine for representatives of both constituencies to forge workable coalitions under Soviet conditions. Geopolitics, in a word, makes a successful Ukrainian alliance with other nations highly unlikely.

Subjective factors may be more important than objective ones in preventing such a coalition from forming. According to Zvi Gitelman, persistent Soviet complaints, and the accounts of émigrés, journalists, and tourists, substantial barriers still divide the USSR's nations.[31] Survivals of the past or not, national arrogance, racism, chauvinism, intolerance, mistrust, and just plain dislike appear to be widespread among all of the USSR's ethnic groups. If, as Gitelman argues, the hostility between Ukrainians and other nations really is exceptionally high, then Ukrainian unwillingness to associate with "foreigners"—and vice versa—may torpedo any chance for the emergence of coalitions with other non-Russians.

Do potential Ukrainian rebels have to go it alone? Not necessarily. As a number of Ukrainian dissident and émigré writers have suggested, there is still the USSR's largest nation—the Russians. The rationale for such an alliance is obvious. Since Russian ethnic power is so enormous, unless many Russians actually turn against their own state, it will probably remain more or less immune to assaults by non-Russians. The problem with this scenario, however, is that it demands that the Russians act with the selflessness that Soviet ideology attributes to them and spurn the privileges of ethnic hegemony. No wonder, then, that very few Russian dissidents, such as Valery Chalidze, Pavel Litvinov, Iurii Orlov, and Ludmilla Alexeyeva, appear to be willing to embark on such a course. Most Russians appear to take

---

30. The samizdat *Letter to a Russian Friend* (London: Association of Byelorussians in Great Britain, 1979) offers a gloomy yet hopeful assessment of Belorussian political potential.

31. Zvi Gitelman, "Are Nations Merging in the USSR?" *Problems of Communism*, no. 5 (September–October 1983), pp. 35–47.

satisfaction from the state's endorsement of the Russian language and culture and view the USSR as theirs. They may prefer democracy, they may even desire workers' control, but they do not seem to be terribly enthusiastic about or, for that matter, even interested in self-determination for non-Russians.

There are even more grounds for pessimism if Ukrainian feelings toward Russians are taken into account. Many eastern Ukrainians appear to be favorably disposed toward the elder brother and are least inclined to question Russian authority and engage in nationalist activity. Those who are most inclined toward nationalism, the western Ukrainians, bear an enormous antipathy to Russians. Indeed, whether or not Ukrainians will ever find partners among other Soviet nations, how likely is it that western and eastern Ukrainians will be able to forge an alliance? Radically different historical experiences have produced profoundly different and mutually mistrustful types.[32] The westerners developed under relatively tolerant Habsburg Austria and interwar Poland, while the easterners are products of tsarist Russia and the worst excesses of Stalin. Different religions—Uniate Catholicism in the west, Orthodoxy in the east—and different linguistic patterns compound the cleavages. Tourist and émigré accounts indicate that western Ukrainians almost unanimously mistrust the easterners, generally consider them Russophile and slavish, and sometimes suspect them of being agents of the state. Apparently it is not too uncommon for nationally committed western Ukrainians not to reveal their true feelings about a variety of political issues to their east Ukrainian spouses.[33] Easterners, for their part, often cast westerners as Banderites, Hitlerites, collaborationists, and cutthroats. Although the level of mistrust and stereotyping appears to have subsided since the immediate postwar years, impressionistic evidence suggests that the cleft is still substantial.

Although Soviet propaganda continually stresses the desirability of the "friendship of peoples" and "proletarian internationalism," I suspect that Soviet authorities are not overly concerned with eliminating all forms of national enmity and overcoming east–west mistrust in the Ukrainian SSR. The state's practice of associating most forms of concern for national traditions and culture with "bourgeois nationalism" tends to reinforce prejudicial attitudes among individuals and groups

---

32. For a classic treatment of these differences, see Osyp Nazaruk, *Rik na Velykii Ukraini* (Vienna: Ukrains'kyi Prapor, 1921).

33. Information based on interviews with tourists from the Ukrainian SSR.

already inclined to believe that certain nations are innately untrust-
worthy. Ukrainian–Jewish relations are an excellent example of how
this unfortunate dynamic works.[34] Official anti-Zionism legitimizes
Ukrainian anti-Semitism; official condemnation of "Ukrainian bourgeois nationalism" reinforces Jewish Ukrainophobia. In addition, the
co-optation of Belorussians and Ukrainians into authoritative positions in other republics, the stationing of nonnative troops in the non-
Russian republics, and the pattern of nationality representation in the
army's officer corps also serve to reinforce ethnic boundaries.[35] Finally, the centralized economic system fosters nationality tensions, as
republican elites fight one another for a greater piece of the budget.

The outlook for Ukrainian and other non-Russian rebels, if any ever
arise, is therefore anything but rosy. Outside help is unlikely to come
and unlikely to be effective if it does. On their own, they are too weak;
unity, however, appears to be a pipe dream. Most important, as I have
continually emphasized, the Soviet state possesses a formidable array
of techniques to prevent and contain antistate collective activity. Is
there any chance of the state's becoming less formidable? Chapter 10
considers various problem areas that may weaken the state and thus
facilitate non-Russian assaults on its heretofore very effective pursuit
of survival.

34. See the scurrilous brochure by Olexiy Kartunov, Yellow-Blue Anti-Semitism
(Odessa: Mayak, 1981).
35. S. Enders Wimbush and Alex Alexiev, The Ethnic Factor in the Soviet Armed
Forces, Rand Corporation Report R 2787/1 (March 1982).

Systemic Crisis and the Soviet Russian State

That the Soviet Union is beset by severe difficulties is a truism voiced by Western and Soviet scholars. Naturally, the terms they use to describe the reality differ. Western analysts like to speak of a "crisis"; in their parlance, the term refers to a complex set of structural problems whose effective solution demands profound systemic change. Their Soviet counterparts prefer to talk of "difficulties," "problems," and the concomitant need for their "accelerated resolution." The term *crisis*, according to Soviet thinking, is inapplicable to so developed a socialist society as the USSR, because crises stem from antagonistic socioeconomic contradictions, which can occur only in capitalist states.[1] Semantic and ideological differences notwithstanding, both sides are speaking of a system that is muddling through. Mikhail Gorbachev's urgent tone at the ground-breaking Party plenum of April 23, 1985, was very much reflective of this scholarly consensus. "Comrades," intoned the new general secretary, "we must become thoroughly aware of the present situation and draw the most serious conclusions. The country's historical destiny and the positions of socialism in the world today depend to a large degree on how we conduct matters from now on."[2]

---

1. See Ernst Kux, "Contradictions in Soviet Socialism," *Problems of Communism*, no. 6 (November–December 1984), pp. 1–27.

2. *Pravda*, April 24, 1985.

Scholarly agreement also extends to the diagnosis: that a troubled economy is at the root of the USSR's ailments. Deteriorating health care, ideological stagnation, youth rebelliousness, rampant theft and corruption, and many other "negative phenomena" contribute to the crisis, but economic decline is the single most important variable within the complex configuration of the country's malaise. Most worrisome is the nature of the decline, which appears to involve a long-term trend, not just a temporary slump. Although the economic trends of the 1950s and 1960s were for the most part positive, they already evinced a tendency toward secular decline. The seriousness of the downturn became especially visible by the mid to late 1970s, when even optimists acknowledged that the economy was rapidly sliding into what could only be called dire straits. Indeed, all the indexes of economic health—gross national product, consumption, energy availability, labor and capital productivity, capital investments, and labor supply—reached low points by the time the 1980s came around. Minor improvements in some sectors were registered by the middle of the decade, but most economists seemed to agree that they were mere blips in the downward curve and, as such, were analytically irrelevant to the long-term prospects for the Soviet economy. To be sure, if, as Soviet policy makers hope, these expectations prove to be unfounded, my own analysis may become irrelevant.

The average annual percentage growth of GNP, for example, has fallen steadily from a high of 5.9 percent in the late 1950s to a low of 1.2 percent in 1980.[3] Industrial production, a key sector of the Soviet economy, grew annually by an average of 10.9 percent in 1951–55, 6.8 percent in 1961–65, 5.9 percent in 1971–75, and only 2.3 percent in 1981–82.[4] Consumption levels have dropped from an average annual rate of growth per capita of 4.3 percent in the 1950s to 2.5 percent in the 1970s.[5] Nor is all quiet on the energy front. Oil production has peaked (while the price of petroleum has plunged), the pell-mell expansion of natural gas extraction is gobbling up investments in an increasingly inefficient manner, the costs of mining Donbass coal and

---

3. USSR: Measures of Economic Growth and Development, 1950–80 (Washington, D.C.: Government Printing Office, 1982), p. 15; John L. Scherer, ed., USSR Facts & Figures Annual (Gulf Breeze, Fla.: Academic International Press, 1983), VII, 105.

4. Gertrude E. Schroeder, "The Slowdown in Soviet Industry, 1976–1982," Soviet Economy, no. 1 (January–March 1986), p. 42.

5. Gertrude E. Schroeder, "Consumption," in The Soviet Economy: Toward the Year 2000, ed. Abram Bergson and Herbert S. Levine (London: Allen & Unwin, 1983), p. 312.

of transporting its Siberian competitor are high, while the effects of Chernobyl on the nuclear power industry are still indeterminate.[6]

Labor productivity has declined to alarmingly low levels, and its radical and immediate improvement has become a centerpiece of Gorbachev's speeches. Its average annual growth rate was 2.0 percent in the early 1970s, 1.3 percent in the late 1970s, and only 0.9 percent in 1981.[7] Capital productivity is no less problematic. Gross fixed capital investment, which grew by 6 to 8 percent in 1961–75, has fallen to just over 3 percent in 1976–80. More fundamentally, Soviet investments are notoriously unproductive. Capital–output ratios for the entire economy increased from 1.6 in 1960 to 2.2 in 1970 to 3.3 in 1980, while capital productivity growth has been negative throughout the entire 1959–79 period.[8] Agricultural investment is in even worse condition than its industrial counterpart. Although the state has made massive capital infusions into the countryside since Stalin's death, so that agriculture proper currently accounts for about 20 percent of total Soviet investment,[9] that sector continues to perform under par. Capital–output ratios have increased from 0.6 in 1960 to 2.9 in 1980, while negative growth of capital productivity has been even higher in

6. See Leslie Dienes, "The Energy System and Economic Imbalances in the USSR," *Soviet Economy*, no. 4 (October–December 1985), pp. 340–72.

7. Herbert S. Levine, "Possible Causes of the Deterioration of Soviet Productivity Growth in the Period 1976–80," in *Soviet Economy in the 1980's: Problems and Prospects* (Washington, D.C.: Government Printing Office, 1983), p. 154; Scherer, *USSR Facts & Figures*, p. 104. Levine has identified a large number of possible causes of this downturn, ranging from such "exogenous factors" as weather and external economic conditions to "consequences of a maturing economy," such as the "depletion of the resource base" and the "aging of the capital stock," to "strategic planning decisions" regarding defense expenditures, investment, and technology transfer, to such "systemic elements" as inadequate planning and labor discipline and the "second economy" (pp. 153–68). Whatever the decisive cause, and for our purposes it is unnecessary to isolate it, the decline in labor productivity is clearly no simple phenomenon that will lend itself to an easy remedy. The increased production discipline imposed by Andropov and Gorbachev has had beneficial results, but, as even Soviet leaders realize, it only scratches the surface of the problem.

8. Robert Leggett, "Soviet Investment Policy in the 11th Five-Year Plan," in *Soviet Economy in the 1980's*, pp. 132, 134; Boris Rumer, "Soviet Investment Policy: Unresolved Problems," *Problems of Communism*, no. 5 (September–October 1982), pp. 53–68; Stanley H. Cohn, "Sources of Low Productivity in Soviet Capital Investment," in *Soviet Economy in the 1980's*, p. 172.

9. Robert W. Campbell, "The Economy," in *After Brezhnev: Sources of Soviet Conduct in the 1980s*, ed. Robert F. Byrnes (Bloomington: Indiana University Press, 1983), p. 96.

agriculture than in industry.[10] The visible manifestation of these statistics is erratic and occasionally catastrophic grain yields.[11]

A declining and regionally skewed labor supply is another serious
and seemingly unsolvable problem. In general, the average annual
growth rate of the Soviet population has fallen from 1.34 percent
between the 1959 and 1970 censuses to 0.92 percent between the 1970
and 1979 censuses. These figures conceal important regional disparities, however. In the Slavic republics, the growth rate fell from
0.93 percent in the RSFSR, 1.08 percent in the Ukraine, and 1.01
percent in Belorussia in the 1960s to 0.62, 0.61, and 0.67 percent,
respectively, in the 1970s. Population growth in the Turkic-language
republics, on the other hand, has generally been three times as high as
that in the Slavic republics in the 1959–70 period and from three to
five times as large in 1970–79. Uzbekistan, for instance, with a total
population of 15.4 million in 1979, experienced a 3.46 percent annual
growth rate in the earlier period and a 3.00 percent rate in the later
one.[12]

These seemingly inexorable trends have several implications, none
of them heartening. Owing to the reduction in overall population
growth, the net increase in the Soviet work force is projected to decline from some 24 million in the 1970s to about 6 million in the
1980s.[13] According to Robert W. Campbell, "the startling feature of
this projection is that the entire increment between 1980 and 1985
will occur in the Moslem areas and that between 1985 and 1990 the

10. Leggett, "Soviet Investment Policy," p. 133; Cohn, "Sources of Low Productivity," p. 172.

11. Several consecutive years of miserable weather have greatly contributed to such
poor results, but even Soviet scholars and policy makers generally acknowledge that
such contingencies are not the primary culprit. The formation of progressively smaller
work units, the introduction of technology and elimination of wasteful procedures, the
development of agro-industrial complexes, a rejuvenation of the village work force,
and, most important perhaps, the use of rational pricing may eventually serve to reform
agriculture effectively and provide Soviet citizens with a steady output of high-quality
agricultural products and a good diet. None of these eventualities is going to happen
overnight, however, and if Brezhnev's food program—whose recipe for increased agricultural growth is increased use of factors of production—represents the extent of
Soviet ingenuity, agriculture will continue to be a problem area for some time to come.
Gorbachev made some nods in the direction of an agricultural "tax in kind" and other
reform measures at the 27th Congress, but at present it is impossible to judge whether
these ideas will be put into practice and prove actually to be effective.

12. Murray Feshbach, "Population and Labor Force," in *Soviet Economy*, ed. Bergson
and Levine, p. 82.

13. Ibid., p. 96.

working-age population in the non-Moslem areas will actually decline."[14] Consequently, the Soviet economy is facing and will continue to face a severe labor shortage compounded by the fact that additions to the work force will have to come from those southern nationalities that have a weak knowledge of Russian and appear to be least willing to migrate to the country's labor-poor areas.

To state the problem somewhat baldly: Siberia has the resources, the European USSR has the industry and infrastructure, while Central Asia has reserves of underemployed labor. Resource extraction and industrial development will be difficult as long as Central Asian workers are reluctant to leave their ancestral homelands for the inhospitable north or the Slavic west. Soviet efforts to lure Central Asians to these regions have thus far been only minimally successful, and most Western experts agree with Campbell that "there is little reason to expect migration on any significant scale, since the ethnic groups of Central Asia are reluctant even to leave the countryside."[15] Naturally, this unbalanced distribution of factors of production should have a negative impact on regional equalization. Without labor, western industry, unless rapidly modernized, is likely to stagnate; without industry, the southern tier may become overpopulated and suffer a decline in living standards; without labor and capital investments, Siberia will be unable to provide the minerals and energy resources deemed crucial to economic development in the rest of the USSR. Neglect of Siberia and its enormous appetite for capital and workers could be economically suicidal; neglect of the Soviet west and south, however, could be no less detrimental, above all politically. The choice facing Soviet planners is, to put it mildly, unenviable.

The secular trends outlined above are generally reproduced at the level of republican economies. As Ellen Jones and Fred W. Grupp have demonstrated, declining rates of growth and consumption are having a negative impact on regional equalization by restraining Soviet leaders from investing in regions that offer lower than maximal returns.[16] Recent talk of the harmony between national and republican economic interests is in fact a smoke screen for Moscow's commitment to give priority to the national economy—a perhaps understandable view at a time of stringency. The priority of central interests is

14. Campbell, "Economy," pp. 81–82.
15. Ibid., p. 82.
16. Ellen Jones and Fred W. Grupp, "Modernisation and Ethnic Equalisation in the USSR," Soviet Studies, no. 2 (April 1984), pp. 159–84.

especially evident in the new edition of the Party program. Whereas the 1961 version said it was the Party's task "to continue to pursue . . . the line of the all-round development of the economy of the Soviet republics," Gorbachev has shifted the emphasis "to the building up of the material and spiritual potential of each republic within the framework of the single economic complex."[17]

Growth in net material product has fallen even more rapidly in the Ukraine than in the USSR as a whole.[18] With respect to consumption, argues Gertrude Schroeder, the Ukraine's "position may have deteriorated slightly" vis-à-vis the other republics.[19] And "starting with the second half of the 1960s," according to Murray Feshbach, "the Ukraine's position deteriorated relative to the USSR as a whole in regard to productivity growth." Population growth has been on a par with that of the RSFSR and Belorussia, so that the Ukraine's labor force is expected to experience a net decline in the 1980s and 1990s, falling from 29.3 million in 1980 to 29 million in 1995.[20] All these factors will have a negative impact on the Ukraine's continued ability to maintain its developed status. Vastly complicating the problem is the disaster at the Chernobyl atomic energy station. The exact human and economic costs of the accident may be indeterminate, but it is certain that they will be enormous.

Broadly speaking, three related factors account for the Ukraine's relative economic decline. First, since the mid-1960s Soviet planners have preferred to focus their investments on Siberia and, to a less significant degree, on Central Asia. Second, a large part of Soviet investment revenues have been and still are extracted from the Ukrainian SSR, which functions as an exporter of capital. And third, the Ukraine's industrial plant is relatively old and its energy resources are neither as accessible nor as abundant as they were in the relatively recent past.[21] Naturally, all three factors are connected, the result being a vicious circle of sorts. To break it the Soviet Union must invest massively in the Ukraine's industrial and extractive base; such large-scale investments, however, would undermine a long-standing economic priority, the development of Siberia. As long as primacy is

17. *Soviet Nationality Survey*, no. 1 (January 1986), pp. 5–8.

18. Stanley H. Cohn, "Economic Growth," in *The Ukraine within the USSR*, ed. I. S. Koropeckyj (New York: Praeger, 1977), p. 70.

19. Gertrude E. Schroeder, "Consumption and Personal Income," in *Ukraine*, ed. Koropeckyj, p. 106.

20. Feshbach, "Population and Labor Force," pp. 82, 94.

21. Cohn, "Economic Growth," pp. 78–80.

accorded the Soviet east, the Soviet west in general and the Ukraine in particular may be expected to be neglected comparatively.

What is the solution to this apparently intractable complex of seemingly worsening economic ailments? In the final analysis, Western scholars see the root problem in the Soviet system's overly centralized character. A greater degree of enterprise autonomy, less authority for Union ministries in general and Gosplan in particular, alignment of prices with supply and demand, small-scale entrepreneurship, increased private ownership—these and similar market-type measures are generally viewed as indispensable to Soviet economic health.[22] The Soviet diagnosis is not uniform. Some analysts think that the "economic mechanism," being basically sound, requires only some tinkering; others view the economic situation as more serious. Of the latter, some are attracted by the Hungarian experiment, others opt for a balanced combination of continued central supervision coupled with increased enterprise autonomy, more along the lines of the East German model—a position apparently advanced by Gorbachev himself.[23] Indeed, Gorbachev has proposed that the State Planning Committee be transformed into a "scientific and economic body that gathers together major scientists and leading specialists," that republican-level ministries be pared, and that the "center of gravity of all day-to-day economic work" be shifted to basic production units "directly subordinate" to the central ministries.[24] Whether such plans will be put into practice—and, if so, whether they will have the desired effect—only time will tell.

These at least in part ideologically based differences aside, all Soviet and non-Soviet analysts agree that the proximate cause of economic decline is the Stalinist growth model. An "extensive" model premised on massive injections of capital, labor, and land is bound to lead to a dead end in an age of economic complexity and capital and labor scarcity. Consequently, so goes the argument, the answer to the economy's secular decline is to transform it along "intensive" lines. As Soviet sources recognize, intensivity means efficiency, and efficiency requires elimination of waste, improved product quality, enhanced work and plan discipline, establishment of labor incentives, reduced drunkenness, expanded enterprise initiative, a search for hidden re-

22. Joseph S. Berliner, "Managing the USSR Economy: Alternative Models," *Problems of Communism*, no. 1 (January–February 1983), pp. 40–56.

23. *Izvestiia*, June 1, 1985; *Pravda*, June 12, 1985.

24. *Pravda*, June 12, 1985.

serves, and, most important of all, harnessing of the "scientific-technical revolution"—all goals of the "large-scale economic experiment" introduced in the mid-1980s. Technology is the key, since only it can "accelerate" the economy's transformation into a modern mechanism. In Gorbachev's own words, "the Party views the acceleration of scientific-technical progress as the main direction of its economic strategy, as the main lever for the intensification of the national economy and the raising of its efficiency, and hence for the resolution of all other economic and social issues."[25]

How likely is it that scientific-technical progress will have the impact Gorbachev desires? While Soviet scientists do not appear to lack inventiveness (many of the innovations for modernizing industry that Japan adopted in the early 1970s were of Soviet origin),[26] various impediments stand in the way of the practical application of their innovations to the production process. Abram Bergson mentions "bureaucratic obstacles attendant on multiple clearances and organization of interdepartmental cooperation for a new technology; the weakness of domestic and foreign competition, that might spur innovation; impediments to labor transfers from lagging to more technologically advanced enterprises, and inadequate incentives." This last point is critical. Soviet managers inured to plan fulfillment and to playing by certain rules dislike taking chances with newfangled experiments that may result in economic failure. Workers with similar "obsolete habits" may be no more inclined to work harder under a system of full employment. Things may change, of course, but, in light of these obstacles, Bergson's conclusion appears eminently sensible: "A distinct acceleration [in technological progress] is not precluded, but more likely advance will continue at a slow pace more or less comparable to that which has prevailed lately."[27] All in all, the prospects for the Soviet economy's rapid and trouble-free transition to "intensive tracks" appears bleak.

What, if anything, does this prognosis mean for Gorbachev? Despite his lackluster performance at the 27th CPSU Congress and during the first two weeks of the Chernobyl crisis (is it possible that Western analysts have overestimated the man?), Gorbachev still appears committed to reinvigorating the Soviet economy. But if the array of diffi-

25. Moscow Television Service, June 11, 1985, as translated in FBIS, June 12, 1985, R3.

26. Lecture by Leslie Dienes at Columbia University, March 27, 1986.

27. Abram Bergson, "Technological Progress," in Soviet Economy, ed. Bergson and Levine, pp. 65–66.

culties is truly as imposing as Western scholars believe it to be, his voluntarist predilections are unlikely to overcome ingrained economic inertia and produce a Great Leap Forward—unless, of course, he decides to resort to coercion on a massive scale. Moreover, Gorbachev has political problems to contend with. To the extent that he may eventually run into difficulties of a purely bureaucratic nature—snags in his consolidation of power, which has so far proceeded quite smoothly and quite rapidly, or the obstructionism of the middle-level bureaucrats excoriated by Academician T. Zaslavskaia[28]—his ability to effect a rapid turn-around in the economy will deteriorate. Indeed, says Bialer, since "the conditions for a relatively rapid change to intensive growth would require fundamental changes in the economic-political system," they "are unlikely to be accomplished in the foreseeable future."[29] But even if Gorbachev overcomes all political obstacles and manages to push through truly radical economic reforms—a very big if—chances are that the immediate aftermath, the period of transition, will be marked by a temporary decline in efficiency, productivity, living standards, and economic growth. As Gorbachev seems fated to be damned if he does and damned if he doesn't, it appears certain that the Soviet economy will face at least stagnation, if not continued decline, for the foreseeable future. Irrespective of the small upturn in economic indexes in 1984–86 (due, apparently, to improved labor discipline), consumption will probably either stagnate or decline and living standards may fall. What will happen farther down the road is, at this point, anybody's guess.

Western analysts conclude on the basis of this not unreasonable prognosis that the Soviet state will increasingly have to contend with citizen dissatisfaction as well as with labor and consumer unrest, strikes, riots, and dissident activity. The Western view is grounded partly on official Soviet perceptions of the state's social contract with the citizenry. "The store, the cafeteria, the laundry, the dry cleaners are places people visit every day," Brezhnev noted in his speech to the 26th Party Congress. "What can they buy? How are they treated? How are they spoken to? How much time do they spend on all kinds of daily cares? The people will judge our work in large measure by how these questions are solved. They will judge strictly, exactingly."[30] More important—and inspiring—from the Western point of

28. *Izvestiia*, June 1, 1985.

29. Seweryn Bialer, "Politics and Priorities," in *Soviet Economy*, ed. Bergson and Levine, p. 403.

30. As quoted in Campbell, "Economy," p. 74.

view is the example of Solidarity. A period of rapid economic growth in the 1970s was followed by near-collapse; the Polish state's efforts to remedy the situation with belt-tightening met with popular resistance, strikes ensued, and Solidarity was born. The process is obviously not that simple, but the lesson to be drawn—that an economic downturn following a period of prosperity will produce rebellious attitudes and, perhaps, rebellion—is.

Students of logic will notice that the first view is based on a faulty understanding of if–then statements. If it is true that material well-being fosters popular acceptance of the state—an assumption made in Chapter 4—it is not necessarily true that a lack of prosperity will produce rejection. Another example will help illustrate the point. If youth means vigor, old age need not mean ossification. In other words, the statement "If A, then B" does not necessarily translate into "If not A, then not B."

Social scientists will notice that the second view is nothing other than a restatement of the relative deprivation theory of Ted Robert Gurr and especially of the J-curve theory of James C. Davies.[31] When expectations and capabilities are farthest apart, claims Gurr, men will rebel. Divergence may occur with any combination of rising, declining, or static expectations and rising, declining, or static capabilities. Davies's theory holds, in Harry Eckstein's words, that "revolution is likely when periods of prolonged improvement, the historical pattern most likely to raise expectations, are interrupted by abrupt reversals; then frustrations due to unrequited expectations become intolerable." Both arguments make a great deal of intuitive sense, and there is also some empirical evidence to back them up. However, "the chief problem with J-curve theory is the abundance of countercases. Consider, for example, the many countries in which the Great Depression of the 1930s did not increase political violence. Surely, the effects of sudden depression, following the orgiastic recovery of the 1920s, were crucial—and no more in Germany than in all the countercases."[32] As for a perception of relative deprivation, it, like all antistate attitudes taken on their own, is well-nigh meaningless. As I argued in Chapter 1, only the deprivatization of such attitudes and their adoption by

31. Ted Robert Gurr, Why Men Rebel (Princeton: Princeton University Press, 1971); James C. Davies, "The J-Curve and Power Struggle Theories of Collective Violence," American Sociological Review, no. 4 (August 1974), pp. 607–13.

32. Harry Eckstein, "Theoretical Approaches to Explaining Collective Political Violence," in Ted Robert Gurr, ed., Handbook of Political Conflict (New York: Free Press, 1980), pp. 157–58.

groups and leaders can transform them into significant and potentially destabilizing factors. Whether the Soviet citizenry's expectations are low or high, therefore, there is no a priori reason to believe
that continued economic stagnation or a decline in living standards
will necessarily result in antistate collective activity.

For the sake of argument, however, let us assume the worst of Gurr's
and Davies's worlds: a severe economic downturn coupled with protracted economic decline. Let us also assume that rebellious attitudes
are in the air and that a budgetary squeeze forces the state to curtail
certain stability-related activities or, minimally, to give preference to
some over others. Given this not too outlandish worst-case scenario,
how might potentially rebellious societal sectors and the state be expected to react?

Let us begin with the substate elites because they are easiest to
dispose of. Unless these people abruptly change their behavioral patterns, economic stringencies will probably only increase competition
among them for a greater share of the budget pie. An increase in
competition among the regional elites may have deleterious effects on
the functioning of the Soviet socioeconomic and political systems, but
it is unlikely to foster feelings of antistate solidarity among the competitors. More fundamentally, it is exceedingly hard to imagine that
republican elites will plunge to such depths of personal poverty and
disaffection as to opt for genuine antistate collective activity. Their
material privileges may suffer in a time of decline, but, as functionaries of the Soviet Russian state, they are not likely to bite the hand
that still feeds them better than the local population. Dimitri Simes is
right to say that "Ukrainian functionaries, as well as officials of other
national republics, depend heavily on the central government's support. Who could expect these people to be real separatists when an
actual separation from Russia would mean the end of their own political careers?"[33]

As for the peasantry, we do not have to share Karl Marx's jaundiced
view of it to see that its capacity for rebellion, under Soviet conditions, is very limited.[34] To an increasingly large degree, the present
Soviet countryside is the repository of an aged, female, and comparatively undereducated population. Most deficient are 15-to-19-

33. Carl A. Linden and Dimitri K. Simes, eds., *Nationalities and Nationalism in the
USSR: A Soviet Dilemma* (Washington, D.C.: Center for Strategic and International
Studies, 1977), p. 50.
34. Karl Marx, "The 18th Brumaire of Louis Napoleon."

year-olds in general and boys in particular, the very population group that seems to be most prone to violence throughout the world (the disturbances in South Africa in the mid-1980s are an excellent example).[35] Although several revolutions (Mexico, Vietnam, Algeria, Cuba, Nicaragua, China, Russia) have proven that peasants possess vast revolutionary potential,[36] the strength of that potential appears to be more or less determined by the degree to which the village is penetrated by both the state and some revolutionary organization. Where the state's coercive apparatus remains strong, revolutionaries will not be able to take root; where political autonomy exists and revolutionaries can engage in mobilization, peasants can become revolutionaries.[37] The Soviet countryside, organized as it is into collective and state farms possessing a small degree of autonomy, remains the preserve of the state. Lacking its own revolutionary cadres and isolated from potential rebels in the cities, the Soviet peasantry in general and any single non-Russian peasantry in particular would thus be fundamentally incapable of engaging in large-scale antistate actions even if serious economic decline were to set in.

In contrast to the peasantry, the young generation occupies a fairly high position on the state's list of trouble spots. The October 1984 plenum of the CPSU Central Committee devoted special attention to Komsomol and youth, scoring the less than satisfactory behavior of both. "Individual young people" in all the republics are supposed to be dissolute, parasitic, passive, rude, consumer-oriented, and enamored of Western pop culture; they engage in "annoying" conduct— "immorality, drunkenness, hooliganism, and other negative phenomena."[38] Especially disturbing is the widespread tendency to pursue a "high life" and little else. Rejection of the demands of socialist morality is not the only problem posed by Soviet youth. Perhaps even more serious is young people's insufficiently developed class consciousness, Soviet patriotism, and proletarian internationalism.[39]

35. Basile Kerblay, *Modern Soviet Society* (New York: Pantheon, 1983), pp. 75–76.

36. On peasant revolutions, see Eric R. Wolf, *Peasant Wars of the Twentieth Century* (New York: Harper Colophon, 1969).

37. Theda Skocpol, "What Makes Peasants Revolutionary?" *Comparative Politics*, no. 3 (April 1982), pp. 351–75; Joel S. Migdal, *Peasants, Politics, and Revolution* (Princeton: Princeton University Press, 1974); Roy Hofheinz, "The Ecology of Chinese Communist Success," in *Chinese Communist Politics in Action*, ed. A. Doak Barnett (Seattle: University of Washington Press, 1969), pp. 3–77.

38. *Soviet Nationality Survey*, no. 3 (March 1984), p. 5.

39. The dark hand of Western "propaganda and espionage centers" is supposed to be responsible for this deplorable state of affairs. As a Moldavian Party functionary put it:

That the youth problem contributes to a less than optimal functioning of Soviet society is undeniable. Politically, however, most deviant
youth behavior in the USSR and elsewhere is of little or no consequence. Withdrawal into the self—narcissism—is no threat to the
established order because it is predicated on political and social passivity. Careerists, high-lifeists, punks, and the Soviet equivalent of
yuppies will certainly affect the socioeconomic environment of the
Soviet system and perhaps redirect some of its priorities. But their
direct impact on the Soviet state and its survival is at most minuscule,
because the privatization of their passions leaves the public sphere
unaffected. Ironically, despite the Soviet state's obvious unhappi-
ness with its "me generation" citizens, politically they are a boon of
sorts.[40]

Politically interested youths may be a different matter. As in the
West and other parts of the world, young Soviet activists appear to be
drawn largely from the student population. May 1968 in Paris and
opposition to the Vietnam War testify to students' ability to cause
trouble for states; Polish and Czech students demonstrated a similar
aptitude in 1956 and 1968. Nevertheless, as a variety of university
revolutionaries belatedly learned, for all their verve, students are notoriously incapable of conducting successful rebellions in developed
capitalist and socialist countries, for several reasons: partly because
students represent a small and socioeconomically unimportant con-
stituency in such countries; partly because of their inability to develop ties with other, nonintellectual social strata; partly because they
almost never act with a monolithic unanimity of purpose and tend to
lack long-term organizational strength; and partly because student-
hood is a transitory phenomenon. In a word, students can become a
political nuisance but rarely a political threat in a developed country.

"A special task . . . is to perfect ideo-educational and propaganda work among the
young. We take account of the fact that our ideological adversaries bet on weakening the
class consciousness of youth by speculating on the particularities of their psychology
and age, their belated civic development, and on the political naiveté of a certain
segment of youth. All channels are utilized, including those that seem to be divorced
from politics, such as music and fashion. Take fashion, for example. Propaganda draw-
ings and texts are printed on many articles of foreign mass consumption. Sports shirts
with images of bourgeois state symbols and rock-music idols and portraits of popular
foreign singers and actors on bags and packages, which a certain part of our youth likes
to parade about, have a fully defined ideological function and are far from being so
inoffensive" (*Kommunist Moldavii,* no. 6 [June 1984]).

40. See Donna Bahry, "Politics, Generations, and Change in the USSR," Soviet Interview Project, Working Paper no. 20 (Urbana: University of Illinois, April 1986).

After all, despite Daniel Cohn-Bendit's expectations, youth movements in the United States and Western Europe, which were massive, well organized, well led, and openly hostile to their respective political systems, did not succeed in overthrowing them.[41] Surely, what is true of the countries of the West is all the more true of the USSR, where the state controls the educational system and uses it for its own political ends. This last point has special importance for the many non-Russians who flooded the educational system in the 1960s and 1970s. Are the educated offspring of uneducated workers and peasants likely to turn into revolutionaries? I doubt it. If such doubts are justified, non-Russian students' incapacity for rebellion may be matched by an unwillingness to risk their hard-won gains.

Professional intellectuals, on the other hand, have been and continue to be a political problem for the Soviet state. They formed the ranks of the national Communists in the 1920s and 1930s and of the dissidents in the 1960s and 1970s. Like students, intellectuals can articulate grievances; unlike students, they possess the maturity and experience to communicate with other classes and nations and the popular respect to be able to serve as an elite. And as an articulate group with access to resources, intellectuals are ideally situated to mobilize constituencies around inherent conflict tendencies and penetrate the public sphere. In this sense, intellectuals are indispensable to rebellions. On their own, however, intellectuals are powerless. They possess the strength of neither numbers nor economic importance. In a word, they need allies. As leaders, they need those who can be led.

Most successful revolutions have been the result of alliances between intellectuals and peasants, a necessary ingredient of what Samuel P. Huntington has called the "Green Uprising."[42] It may in fact be the case, as Huntington argues, that only such alliances are capable of producing revolutionary victories. If that is true, then revolution may be impossible in the USSR. There is, however, no reason why an alliance between intellectuals and *workers* should not produce at least a rebellion: Solidarity testifies to that. Like their Polish comrades, Soviet workers are objectively capable of shaking, if not overthrowing, the Soviet system. Their number, their concentration, their intimate relationship with the means of production, and their strate-

41. Daniel and Gabriel Cohn-Bendit, *Obsolete Communism: The Left-Wing Alternative* (New York: McGraw-Hill, 1968).
42. Samuel P. Huntington, *Political Order in Changing Societies* (New Haven: Yale University Press, 1968), pp. 74–78.

gic role in the society and economy permit them enormous potential power. Although non-Russian workers in general and Ukrainian and Belorussian workers in particular are the targets of an intensive Russification policy, they can ascend their ethnic ladders if elites who enjoy some autonomy appeal to and mobilize them. Indeed, if elites succeed in building bridges to workers (or vice versa), a potentially destabilizing situation could ensue.

How, then, might the Soviet state react at a time of uniformly rising mass discontent? It would pay extra-special attention to intellectuals and workers. Assuming that its normative, instrumental, and coercive capabilities remained unaffected (an assumption we shall dispense with below), the state could focus its ideological-behavioral message on these two groups, skew its distribution of material goods to their benefit, and intensify secret police surveillance. Under such circumstances, their disaffection would probably dissipate, the threat they posed would be neutralized, and overall resources would still be sufficient to enable the state to control other social groups.

Let us now shift the focus. How might a severe economic downturn affect the state and its capacity for self-maintenance? Naturally, its overall ability to distribute instrumental largess would suffer, and with fewer resources to spend on propaganda and socialization, its ideological message would become less pervasive. Consequently, antistate attitudes would intensify across the board. This much is obvious, but the political import of such a development is not. After all, would such attitudes, however intense, inevitably translate into massive antistate actions? That depends on the degree to which economic decline would undermine the state's occupation of the public sphere and reduce its coercive capacity vis-à-vis public individual time-space. Is this possibility plausible? Unless military defeat occurs—and we know what a nuclear conflict would mean for the non-Russians—alas, no.

Purges of the secret police have been common, both during Stalin's time and after, and a withdrawal from private to public time-space did occur after Stalin's death. At no time in Soviet history, however, not even in the immediate post-Stalin period, has the secret police's mandate to prevent and contain subversive activity been rescinded. Quite the contrary, police forces tend to flourish during declared and undeclared states of emergency—consider Poland after martial law or the Federal Republic of Germany during the Baader-Meinhof crisis—and there is no reason to think that the KGB would be an exception to this rule.

While the KGB would continue to guard the points of entrance into the public sphere, the state might undertake a temporary retreat from those sectors that involve the objectively more benign peasantry, substate, and youth. It could then center its organizational efforts on those boxes within which the working class and intelligentsia congregate. With respect to the former, this means intensified control of the workplace. The Law on Labor Collectives and official insistence that the "perfection of socialism" must begin at the production level may be signs that the Soviet state has already begun to move in this direction. With respect to intellectuals, their ability to express themselves autonomously in public, whether in the official press or by samizdat, would be still more strictly supervised. Glavlit's formidable powers might be enhanced at minimal financial cost, while the KGB would be unleashed on disseminators of clandestine literature. Once muzzled, the intelligentsia would lose its capacity to communicate and thus to form alliances and to lead. Even when the state is confronted with a crisis-like situation and limited resources, therefore, it is not at all evident why it should not be able to prevent and contain assaults against itself. Naturally, if we up the ante indefinitely, we can easily come up with the "right" destabilizing scenario. Needless to say, such an exercise of the imagination would be analytically worthless.

Will, then, the non-Russians rebel? Structural grounds for opposition are there: latent conflict tendencies are inherent in the ethnic pattern of domination of the Soviet Russian state. In time, if economic decline and ideological erosion set in and outside interference continues, behavioral reasons for rebellion may accumulate. At some point, non-Russians may massively want to rebel. But will they? As long as the public sphere is occupied and, more important, as long as the KGB remains intact, the deprivatization of antistate attitudes will be problematic, antistate collectivities and elites will be unlikely to mobilize, alliances between workers and intellectuals will not materialize, and rebellion, revolt, and insurrection will be well-nigh impossible. Because they *cannot* rebel, non-Russians *will not* rebel.

Selected Bibliography

A complete bibliography for an interpretive study such as this would approach the size of a small monograph and overwhelm the reader with references to obscure articles in obscure journals that probably deserve to go unread. A short bibliography runs the risk of providing references only to "great works" that everyone knows anyway. The selected bibliography that follows is an attempt to avoid the Scylla of the ponderous and the Charybdis of the obvious by focusing on the suggestive.

Adelman, Jonathan R., ed. *Terror and Communist Politics: The Role of the Secret Police in Communist States.* Boulder, Colo.: Westview, 1984.

Ake, Claude. "A Definition of Political Stability." *Comparative Politics*, no. 2 (January 1975), pp. 271–83.

Alexeyeva, Ludmilla. *Soviet Dissent: Contemporary Movements for National, Religious, and Human Rights.* Middletown, Conn.: Wesleyan University Press, 1985.

Allworth, Edward, ed. *Ethnic Russia in the USSR.* New York: Pergamon, 1980.

——, ed. *Nationality Group Survival in Multi-Ethnic States: Shifting Support Patterns in the Soviet Baltic Region.* New York: Praeger, 1977.

——, ed. *Soviet Nationality Problems.* New York: Columbia University Press, 1971.

Anderson, Barbara A., and Brian D. Silver. "Equality, Efficiency, and Politics in Soviet Bilingual Education Policy, 1934–1980." *American Political Science Review*, no. 4 (December 1984), pp. 1019–39.

Armstrong, John A. *Ukrainian Nationalism*. Littleton, Colo.: Ukrainian Academic Press, 1980.

Aspaturian, Vernon V. "Marxism and the Meanings of Modernization." In *The Politics of Modernization in Eastern Europe*, ed. Charles Gati. New York: Praeger, 1974.

Avtorkhanov, Abdurakhman. *The Communist Party Apparatus*. Chicago: Henry Regnery, 1966.

Azrael, Jeremy. "The 'Nationality Problem' in the USSR: Domestic Pressures and Foreign Policy Constraints." In *The Domestic Context of Soviet Foreign Policy*, ed. Seweryn Bialer. Boulder, Colo.: Westview, 1981.

——, ed. *Soviet Nationality Policies and Practices*. New York: Praeger, 1978.

Bahry, Donna, and Carol Nechemias. "Half Full or Half Empty? The Debate over Soviet Regional Equality." *Slavic Review*, no. 3 (Fall 1981), pp. 366–83.

Bandera, V. N., and Z. L. Melnyk, eds. *The Soviet Economy in Regional Perspective*. New York: Praeger, 1973.

Barghoorn, Frederick C. *Soviet Russian Nationalism*. New York: Oxford University Press, 1956.

Belotserkovskii, Vadim. "Robitnychi vystupy v SRSR." *Suchasnist'*, no. 10 (October 1978), pp. 32–43.

Bennigsen, Alexandre. "Mullahs, Mujahidin, and Soviet Muslims." *Problems of Communism*, no. 6 (November–December 1984), pp. 28–44.

—— and Marie Broxup. *The Islamic Threat to the Soviet State*. London: Croom Helm, 1983.

Bergson, Abram, and Herbert S. Levine, eds. *The Soviet Economy: Toward the Year 2000*. London: Allen & Unwin, 1983.

Bialer, Seweryn. "How Russians Rule Russia." *Problems of Communism*, no. 5 (September–October 1964), pp. 45–52.

——. *Stalin's Successors: Leadership, Stability, and Change in the Soviet Union*. Cambridge: Cambridge University Press, 1980.

Bilinsky, Yaroslav. "The Concept of the Soviet People and Its Implications for Soviet Nationality Policy." *Annals of the Ukrainian Academy of Arts and Sciences in the United States*, nos. 37–38 (1978–80), pp. 87–133.

——. "Expanding the Use of Russian or Russification?" *Russian Review*, no. 3 (1981), pp. 317–32.

——. *The Second Soviet Republic: The Ukraine after World War II*. New Brunswick: Rutgers University Press, 1964.

——. "Shcherbytskyi, Ukraine, and Kremlin Politics." *Problems of Communism*, no. 4 (July–August 1983), pp. 1–20.

Bilyns'kyi, Andrii. *Hromads'ki orhanizatsii v SRSR*. Chicago: Ukrainian Research and Information Institute, 1969.

Bornstein, Morris, ed. *The Soviet Economy*. Boulder, Colo.: Westview, 1982.

Borys, Jurij. *The Sovietization of Ukraine, 1917–1923*. Edmonton: Canadian Institute of Ukrainian Studies, 1980.

Brass, Paul. "Ethnicity and Nationality Formation." *Ethnicity*, no. 3 (September 1976), pp. 225–41.

Braverman, Harry. *Labor and Monopoly Capital*. New York: Monthly Review Press, 1974.

Breuilly, John. *Nationalism and the State*. Manchester: Manchester University Press, 1982.

Brinkley, George A. "Khrushchev Remembered: On the Theory of Soviet Statehood." *Soviet Studies*, no. 3 (January 1973), pp. 387–401.

Bromlei, Iu. V. "Etnichni aspekty dukhovnoi kul'tury v istorychnii perspektyvi." *Narodna tvorchist' ta etnohrafiia*, no. 2 (1984), pp. 3–10.

——. *Sovremennye etnicheskie protsessy v SSSR*. Moscow: Nauka, 1975.

Browne, Donald R. *International Radio Broadcasting*. New York: Praeger, 1982.

Browne, Michael, ed. *Ferment in the Ukraine*. London: Macmillan, 1971.

Brunner, Georg, and Boris Meissner, eds. *Nationalitäten-Probleme in der Sowjetunion und Osteuropa*. Cologne: Markus, 1982.

Bunce, Valerie, and John M. Echols. "Soviet Politics in the Brezhnev Era: 'Pluralism' or 'Corporatism'?" In *Soviet Politics in the Brezhnev Era*, ed. Donald R. Kelley. New York: Praeger, 1980.

Burlatsky, Fyodor. *The Modern State and Politics*. Moscow: Progress, 1978.

Carrère d'Encausse, Hélène. *Decline of an Empire: The Soviet Socialist Republics in Revolt*. New York: Newsweek Books, 1979.

Castles, Francis G. "Political Stability and the Dominant Image of Society." *Political Studies*, no. 3 (September 1974), pp. 289–98.

Chekharin, E. M. *The Soviet Political System under Developed Socialism*. Moscow: Progress, 1972.

Chernogolovkin, N. V. "Sotsialisticheskoe obshchenarodnoe gosudarstvo— vyrazitel' voli i interesov rabochikh, krest'ian i intelligentsii, trudiashchikhsia vsekh natsii i narodnostei strany." *Sovetskoe gosudarstvo i pravo*, no. 11 (November 1982), pp. 114–20.

Chkhikvadze, V. *The State, Democracy, and Legality in the USSR*. Moscow: Progress, 1972.

Chornovil, Vyacheslav. *The Chornovil Papers*. New York: McGraw-Hill, 1968.

Clem, Ralph S., ed. *The Soviet West*. New York: Praeger, 1975.

Connor, Walker. "Nationalism and Political Illegitimacy." *Canadian Review of Studies in Nationalism*, no. 2 (Fall 1981), pp. 201–28.

——. "Nation-Building or Nation-Destroying?" *World Politics*, no. 3 (April 1972), pp. 319–55.

Dahrendorf, Ralf. *Class and Class Conflict in Industrial Society*. Stanford: Stanford University Press, 1959.

Davies, James C. "The J-Curve and Power Struggle Theories of Collective Violence." *American Sociological Review*, no. 4 (August 1974), pp. 607–13.

Dellenbrant, Jan Ake. *Soviet Regional Policy*. Stockholm: Almqvist & Wiksell, 1980.

Desheriev, Iu. D. "Iazykovye problemy mnogonatsional'nogo sovetskogo obshchestva." *Voprosy iazykoznaniia*, no. 6 (1982), pp. 14–27.

——. "Vazhneishii faktor v sblizhenii vsekh natsii i narodnostei strany." *Partiinaia zhizn'*, no. 1 (January 1983), pp. 20–26.

Deutsch, Karl. *Nationalism and Social Communication*. Cambridge: M.I.T. Press, 1953.

Dmytryshyn, Basil. *Moscow and the Ukraine, 1918–1953*. New York: Bookman, 1956.

Dowding, Keith M., and Richard Kimber. "The Meaning and Use of 'Political Stability.'" *European Journal of Political Research*, no. 3 (1983), pp. 229–43.

Dunlop, John B. *The Faces of Contemporary Russian Nationalism*. Princeton: Princeton University Press, 1983.

Duvall, Raymond D. "Dependence and Dependencia Theory: Notes toward Precision of Concept and Argument." *International Organization*, no. 1 (Winter 1978), pp. 51–78.

Dzyuba, Ivan. *Internationalism or Russification?* New York: Monad, 1974.

Eberwein, Wolf-Dieter, ed. "Politische Stabilität und Konflikt: Neue Ergebnisse der makroquantitativen Politikforschung." *Politische Vierteljahresschrift*, no. 14 (1983).

Eckstein, Harry. "On the Etiology of Internal Wars." In *Why Revolution?* ed. Clifford T. Paynton and Robert Blackey. Cambridge, Mass.: Schenkman, 1971.

——. "Theoretical Approaches to Explaining Collective Political Violence." In *Handbook of Political Conflict*, ed. Ted Robert Gurr. New York: Free Press, 1980.

—— and Ted Robert Gurr. *Patterns of Authority: A Structural Basis for Political Inquiry*. New York: Wiley, 1975.

Enloe, Cynthia H. *Ethnic Conflict and Political Development*. Boston: Little, Brown, 1973.

Etzioni, Amitai. *A Comparative Analysis of Complex Organizations*. New York: Free Press, 1975.

Evans, Alfred, Jr. "The Decline of Developed Socialism? Some Trends in Recent Soviet Ideology." *Soviet Studies*, no. 1 (January 1986), pp. 1–23.

——. "Developed Socialism in Soviet Ideology." *Soviet Studies*, no. 3 (July 1977), pp. 409–28.

Farmer, Kenneth C. *Ukrainian Nationalism in the Post-Stalin Era*. The Hague: Martinus Nijhoff, 1980.

Fishman, Joshua. "Language Maintenance and Ethnicity." *Canadian Review of Studies in Nationalism*, no. 2 (Fall 1981), pp. 229–47.

Friedgut, Theodore H. *Political Participation in the USSR*. Princeton: Princeton University Press, 1979.

Galtung, Johan. "A Structural Theory of Imperialism." *Journal of Peace Research*, no. 2 (1971), pp. 81–117.

Gidwitz, Betsy. "Labor Unrest in the Soviet Union." *Problems of Communism*, no. 6 (November–December 1982), pp. 25–42.

Gitelman, Zvi. "Are Nations Merging in the USSR?" *Problems of Communism*, no. 5 (September–October 1983), pp. 35–47.

Glazer, Nathan, and Daniel P. Moynihan, eds. *Ethnicity.* Cambridge: Harvard University Press, 1975.

Goldhagen, Erich, ed. *Ethnic Minorities in the Soviet Union.* New York: Praeger, 1968.

Gouldner, Alvin. "Stalinism: A Study of Internal Colonialism." *Telos*, no. 34 (Winter 1977), pp. 5–48.

Grigorenko, Petro. *Memoirs.* New York: Norton, 1982.

Guboglo, M. N. "Leninskaia natsional'no-iazykovaia politika KPSS—internatsionalizm v deistvii." *Sovetskaia etnografiia*, no. 1 (January–February 1984), pp. 3–15.

Gurr, Ted Robert. "Persistence and Change in Political Systems, 1800–1971." *American Political Science Review*, no. 4 (December 1974), pp. 1482–1504.

——. *Why Men Rebel.* Princeton: Princeton University Press, 1970.

Harding, Neil, ed. *The State in Socialist Society.* Albany: SUNY Press, 1984.

Hechter, Michael. *Internal Colonialism: The Celtic Fringe in British National Development, 1536–1966.* Berkeley: University of California Press, 1975.

Hirszowicz, Maria. *The Bureaucratic Leviathan.* New York: New York University Press, 1980.

Hodnett, Grey, and Peter J. Potichnyj. *The Ukraine and the Czechoslovak Crisis.* Canberra: Australian National University, 1970.

Hoetink, H. *Two Variants in Caribbean Race Relations.* London: Oxford University Press, 1967.

Holub, Vsevolod. *Ukraina v Obiednanykh natsiiakh.* Munich: Suchasna Ukraina, 1953.

Holubnychyi, Vsevolod. "Tezy pro rusyfikatsiiu." *Journal of Ukrainian Graduate Studies*, no. 2 (Fall 1977), pp. 72–80.

Horowitz, Donald L. *Ethnic Groups in Conflict.* Berkeley: University of California Press, 1985.

Hough, Jerry F., and Merle Fainsod. *How the Soviet Union Is Governed.* Cambridge: Harvard University Press, 1979.

Huntington, Samuel P. *Political Order in Changing Societies.* New Haven: Yale University Press, 1969.

Hurwitz, Leon. "Contemporary Approaches to Political Stability." *Comparative Politics*, no. 3 (April 1973), pp. 449–63.

Isajiw, Wsevolod. "Urban Migration and Social Change in Contemporary Soviet Ukraine." *Canadian Slavonic Papers*, no. 1 (March 1980), pp. 56–66.

Istoriia derzhavy i prava Ukrains'koi RSR. Kiev: Naukova Dumka, 1967.

Jones, Ellen, and Fred W. Grupp. "Modernisation and Ethnic Equalisation in the USSR." *Soviet Studies*, no. 2 (April 1984), pp. 159–84.

K., B. "Nevdovolennia i sprotyv robitnychoi kliasy v Radians'komu Soiuzi s'ohodni." *Suchasnist'*, no. 2 (February 1980), pp. 127–41.

Kanet, Roger E. "The Rise and Fall of the 'All-People's State': Recent Changes in the Soviet Theory of the State." *Soviet Studies*, no. 1 (July 1968), pp. 81–93.

Katz, Zev, ed. *Handbook of Major Soviet Nationalities.* New York: Free Press, 1975.

Khalilov, A. M. "Puti sovershenstvovaniia sovetskoi natsional'noi gosudar-stvennosti." *Sovetskoe gosudarstvo i pravo,* no. 12 (December 1982), pp. 23–31.

Kirchheimer, Otto. "Confining Conditions and Revolutionary Breakthroughs." *American Political Science Review,* no. 4 (December 1965), pp. 964–74.

Kirsanova, O. A. *Rozvytok suspil'no-politychnoi aktyvnosti trudiashchykh zakhidnykh oblastei URSR u protsesi budivnytstva osnov sotsializmu.* Kiev: Naukova Dumka, 1981.

Knight, Amy W. "The Powers of the Soviet KGB." *Survey,* no. 3 (Summer 1980), pp. 138–55.

Kolasky, John. *Two Years in Soviet Ukraine.* Toronto: Peter Martin, 1970.

Kolesnik, V. P. *Internatsional'nye sviazi trudiashchikhsia prigranichnykh oblastei SSSR i evropeiskikh sotsialisticheskikh stran.* Lvov: Vyshcha Shkola, 1984.

Kondrats'kyi, A. A. *Suspil'no-politychna aktyvnist' robitnychoho klasu Ukrains'koi RSR v umovakh rozvynutoho sotsializmu.* Kiev: Naukova Dumka, 1978.

Kopeichikov, V. V. "Sotsialisticheskoe obshchenarodnoe gosudarstvo—glav-noe orudie postroeniia kommunizma." *Sovetskoe gosudarstvo i pravo,* no. 10 (October 1982), pp. 112–20.

Koropeckyj, I. S., ed. *The Ukraine within the USSR.* New York: Praeger, 1977.

—— and Gertrude Schroeder, eds. *Economics of Soviet Regions.* New York: Praeger, 1981.

Kovalenko, A. I. *Sovetskaia natsional'naia gosudarstvennost'.* Minsk: Vyshei-shaia Shkola, 1983.

Kowalewski, David, and Cheryl Johnson. "The Ukrainian Dissident: A Statis-tical Profile." *Ukrainian Quarterly,* no. 1 (Spring 1984), pp. 50–65.

Krawchenko, Bohdan. "The Impact of Industrialisation on the Social Struc-ture of Ukraine." *Canadian Slavonic Papers,* no. 3 (September 1980), pp. 338–57.

——. *Social Change and National Consciousness in Twentieth-Century Ukraine.* New York: St. Martin's Press, 1985.

——, ed. *Ukraine after Shelest.* Edmonton: Canadian Institute of Ukrainian Studies, 1983.

Kulichenko, M. I. *Natsional'nye otnosheniia v SSSR i tendentsii ikh razvitiia.* Moscow: Mysl', 1972.

——. *How the USSR Solved the Nationalities Question.* Moscow: Novosti, 1974.

Kupchyns'kyi, Roman, ed. *Natsional'nyi vopros v SSSR.* Munich: Suchas-nist', 1975.

——, ed. *Pohrom v Ukraini, 1972–1979.* Munich: Suchasnist', 1980.

Kuper, Leo. *Race, Class, and Power.* Chicago: Aldine, 1975.

Kushnirsky, Fyodor. *Soviet Economic Planning, 1965–1980.* Boulder, Colo.: Westview, 1982.

Kux, Ernst. "Contradictions in Soviet Socialism." *Problems of Communism,* no. 6 (November–December 1984), pp. 1–27.

Lapidus, Gail Warshofsky. "Ethnonationalism and Political Stability: The Soviet Case." *World Politics*, no. 4 (July 1984), pp. 355–80.

Lashin, A. *Socialism and the State*. Moscow: Progress, 1977.

Lazarev, B. M. "Demokraticheskii tsentralizm—vazhneishii printsip upravleniia sotsialisticheskim obshchestvom i gosudarstvom." *Sovetskoe gosudarstvo i pravo*, no. 12 (December 1982), pp. 115–24.

Lepeshkin, A. I. *Sovetskii federalizm*. Moscow: Iuridicheskaia Literatura, 1977.

Lewis, E. Glyn. *Multilingualism in the Soviet Union*. The Hague: Mouton, 1972.

Lewytzkyj, Borys. *Politics and Society in Soviet Ukraine, 1953–1980*. Edmonton: Canadian Institute of Ukrainian Studies, 1984.

——. "Radians'kyi biurokratychnyi model' panuvannia." *Suchasnist'*, nos. 10, 11 (October, November 1979), pp. 58–71, 104–17.

——. "Sovetskij narod"—"Das Sowjetvolk": Nationalitätenpolitik als Instrument des Sowjetimperialismus. Hamburg: Hoffmann & Campe, 1983.

——. *Die sowjetische Nationalitätenpolitik nach Stalins Tod (1953–1970)*. Munich: Ukrainische Freie Universität, 1970.

——. *Die Sowjetukraine, 1944–1963*. Cologne: Kiepenheuer & Witsch, 1964.

Likholat, A. V., and V. F. Panibud'laska. *V edinoi sem'e narodov*. Moscow: Mysl', 1979.

Linz, Juan J. *The Breakdown of Democratic Regimes: Crisis, Breakdown, and Reequilibration*. Baltimore: Johns Hopkins University Press, 1978.

Lubin, Nancy. *Labour and Nationality in Soviet Central Asia*. Princeton: Princeton University Press, 1984.

Lustick, Ian. "Stability in Deeply Divided Societies: Consociationalism versus Control." *World Politics*, no. 3 (April 1979), pp. 324–44.

McAuley, Mary. *Politics and the Soviet Union*. Harmondsworth: Penguin, 1977.

Mace, James E. *Communism and the Dilemmas of National Liberation: National Communism in Soviet Ukraine, 1918–1933*. Cambridge, Mass.: Ukrainian Research Institute, 1983.

Macridis, Roy C. "Comparative Politics and the Study of Government: The Search for Focus." *Comparative Politics*, no. 1 (October 1968), pp. 79–90.

Maistrenko, Ivan. *Natsional'naia politika KPSS*. Munich: Suchasnist', 1978.

Memmi, Albert. *The Colonizer and the Colonized*. Boston: Beacon, 1967.

Migdal, Joel S. *Peasants, Politics, and Revolutions*. Princeton: Princeton University Press, 1974.

Milgram, Stanley. *Obedience to Authority*. New York: Harper & Row, 1975.

Miliband, Ralph. *Marxism and Politics*. Oxford: Oxford University Press, 1977.

Misiunas, Romuald J., and Rein Taagepera. *The Baltic States: Years of Dependence, 1940–1980*. Berkeley: University of California Press, 1983.

Mlynar, Zdenek. *Krisen und Krisenbewältigung im Sowjetblock*. Cologne: Bund-Verlag, 1983.

Mnogonatsional'noe sovetskoe gosudarstvo. Moscow: Politizdat, 1972.

Mommsen, Wolfgang J. *Theories of Imperialism*. New York: Random House, 1980.

Moore, Barrington. *Injustice: The Social Bases of Obedience and Revolt*. White Plains, N.Y.: M. E. Sharpe, 1978.

Moroz, Valentyn. *Report from the Beria Reserve*. Chicago: Cataract, 1974.

Motyl, Alexander J. "The Foreign Relations of the Ukrainian SSR." *Harvard Ukrainian Studies*, no. 1 (March 1982), pp. 62–78.

——. *The Turn to the Right: The Ideological Origins and Development of Ukrainian Nationalism, 1919–1929*. Boulder, Colo.: East European Monographs, 1980.

Mova i protsesy suspil'noho rozvytku. Kiev: Naukova Dumka, 1980.

Nahorna, L. P. "Partiine kerivnytstvo internatsional'nymy i natsional'nymy protsesamy v suspil'stvi rozvynutoho sotsializmu." *Ukrains'kyi istorychnyi zhurnal*, no. 12 (December 1982), pp. 17–29.

Natsional'nye otnosheniia i gosudarstvo v sovremennyi period. Moscow: Nauka, 1972.

Naulko, V. I. *Razvitie mezhetnicheskikh sviazei na Ukraine*. Kiev: Naukova Dumka, 1975.

Neubauer, Deane E., and Lawrence D. Kastner. "The Study of Compliance Maintenance as a Strategy for Comparative Research." *World Politics*, no. 4 (July 1969), pp. 629–40.

Nordlinger, Eric. *On the Autonomy of the Democratic State*. Cambridge: Harvard University Press, 1981.

Pipes, Richard. *The Formation of the Soviet Union*. New York: Atheneum, 1974.

Plyushch, Leonid. *History's Carnival*. New York: Harcourt Brace Jovanovich, 1977.

Potichnyj, Peter J., ed. *Poland and Ukraine: Past and Present*. Edmonton: Canadian Institute of Ukrainian Studies, 1980.

——, ed. *Ukraine in the Seventies*. Oakville, Ont.: Mosaic, 1975.

Poulantzas, Nicos. *State, Power, Socialism*. London: Verso, 1980.

Pravda, Alex. "Is There a Soviet Working Class?" *Problems of Communism*, no. 6 (November–December 1982), pp. 1–24.

Present-Day Ethnic Processes in the USSR. Moscow: Progress, 1982.

Prokop, Myroslav. "Pro t. zv. radians'kyi narod." *Suchasnist'*, nos. 2, 3 (February, March 1976), pp. 70–79, 60–69.

——. *Ukraina i ukrains'ka polityka Moskvy*. Munich: Suchasnist', 1981.

Rabushka, Alvin, and Kenneth A. Shepsle. *Politics in Plural Societies*. Columbus, O.: Merrill, 1972.

Redzhepov, P. P., and N. P. Chirkov. *V edinom stroiu narodov-brat'ev*. Moscow: Mysl', 1980.

Rockett, Rocky L. *Ethnic Nationalism in the USSR*. New York: Praeger, 1981.

Rosenthal, Uriel. *Political Order: Rewards, Punishments, and Political Stability*. Alphen aan den Rijn: Sijthoff & Noordhoff, 1978.

Rothschild, Joseph. *Ethnopolitics: A Conceptual Framework*. New York: Columbia University Press, 1981.

Rymarenko, Iu. I. *Burzhuaznyi natsionalizm i ioho 'teoriia' natsii*. Kiev: Naukova Dumka, 1974.

Rywkin, Michael. *Moscow's Muslim Challenge*. Armonk, N.Y.: M. E. Sharpe, 1982.

Sadykov, M. B. *Edinstvo internatsional'nykh i natsional'nykh interesov v sovetskom mnogonatsional'nom gosudarstve*. Kazan: Izdatel'stvo Kazanskogo Universiteta, 1975.

Sanders, David. *Patterns of Political Instability*. London: Macmillan, 1981.

Sartori, Giovanni. "Concept Misformation in Comparative Politics." *American Political Science Review*, no. 4 (December 1970), pp. 1033–53.

Schmitter, Philippe C. "Still the Century of Corporatism?" In *The New Corporatism: Social-Political Structures in the Iberian World*, ed. Fredrick B. Pike and Thomas Stritch. Notre Dame: University of Notre Dame Press, 1974.

Schroeder, Friedrich-Christian, and Boris Meissner, eds. *Bundesstaat und Nationalitätenrecht in der Sowjetunion*. Berlin: Duncker & Humblot, 1974.

Semenov, V. S. "Dialektika sovershenstvovaniia sotsializma i prodvizheniia k kommunizmu." *Voprosy filosofii*, no. 1 (January 1986), pp. 21–36.

———. "Kurs na uskorenie sotsial'noekonomicheskogo razvitia, na sovershenstvovanie obshchestva razvitogo sotsializma." *Voprosy filosofii*, no. 5 (May 1985), pp. 15–34.

Sherstobitov, V. P. "Razvitie sovetskogo naroda—novoi istoricheskoi obshchnosti na sovremennom etape." *Istoriia SSSR*, no. 6 (1982), pp. 17–31.

Shevtsov, V. S. *National Sovereignty and the Soviet State*. Moscow: Progress, 1974.

Silver, Brian D. "Social Mobilization and the Russification of Soviet Nationalities." *American Political Science Review*, no. 1 (March 1974), pp. 45–66.

Skocpol, Theda. *States and Social Revolutions*. Cambridge: Cambridge University Press, 1979.

———. "What Makes Peasants Revolutionary?" *Comparative Politics*, no. 3 (April 1983), pp. 351–75.

Solchanyk, Roman. "Molding 'The Soviet People': The Role of Ukraine and Belorussia." *Journal of Ukrainian Studies*, no. 1 (Summer 1983), pp. 3–18.

Solomon, Susan Gross, ed. *Pluralism in the Soviet Union*. New York: St. Martin's Press, 1982.

Sovetskii narod—novaia istoricheskaia obshchnost' liudei. Moscow: Nauka, 1975.

Stepan, Alfred. *The State and Society: Peru in Comparative Perspective*. Princeton: Princeton University Press, 1978.

Sullivant, Robert S. *Soviet Politics and the Ukraine, 1917–1957*. New York: Columbia University Press, 1962.

Suspil'no-politychne zhyttia trudiashchykh Ukrains'koi RSR. Kiev: Naukova Dumka, 1974.

Szporluk, Roman. "Nationalities and the Russian Problem in the U.S.S.R.: An

Historical Outline." *Journal of International Affairs*, no. 1 (1973), pp. 22–40.

——. "West Ukraine and West Belorussia." *Soviet Studies*, no. 1 (January 1979), pp. 76–98.

——, ed. *The Influence of East Europe and the Soviet West on the USSR*. New York: Praeger, 1975.

Tadevosian, E. V. "Dvadtsat' shestoi s'ezd KPSS ob internatsionalistskoi sushchnosti sovetskoi gosudarstvennosti i ee natsional'nykh form." *Istoriia SSSR*, no. 4 (July–August 1982), pp. 3–19.

——. "Soiuz SSR—voploshchenie leninskikh printsipov proletarskogo, sotsialisticheskogo internatsionalizma." *Voprosy istorii KPSS*, no. 11 (November 1982), pp. 52–65.

——. *Sovetskaia natsional'naia gosudarstvennost'*. Moscow: Izdatel'stvo Moskovskogo Universiteta, 1972.

——. "Sovetskii narod—sotsial'naia osnova Sovetskogo mnogonatsional'nogo obshchenarodnogo gosudarstva." *Sovetskoe gosudarstvo i pravo*, no. 12 (December 1982), pp. 13–22.

Therborn, Göran. *What Does the Ruling Class Do When It Rules?* London: Verso, 1980.

Tilly, Charles. "Does Modernization Breed Revolution?" *Comparative Politics*, no. 3 (April 1973), pp. 425–47.

——. *From Mobilization to Revolution*. Reading, Mass.: Addison-Wesley, 1978.

Tsamerian, I. P. *Natsii i natsional'nye otnosheniia v razvitom sotsialisticheskom obshchestve*. Moscow: Nauka, 1979.

——. "Radians'ka bahatonatsional'na derzhava na etapi zriloho sotsializmu." *Filosofs'ka dumka*, no. 4 (July–August 1983), pp. 32–43.

Tykhyi, Oleksa, and Vasyl' Romaniuk. "Istorychna dolia ukraintsiv: Lyst ukrains'kykh politv'iazniv." *Ukrains'kyi pravozakhysnyi rukh*. Toronto: Smoloskyp, 1978.

V. I. Lenin, KPSS o sovetskom mnogonatsional'nom gosudarstve. Moscow: Politizdat, 1981.

Vardys, V. Stanley. "Polish Echoes in the Baltic." *Problems of Communism*, no. 4 (July–August 1983), pp. 21–34.

Velikii sovetskii narod. Kiev: Naukova Dumka, 1976.

Voslensky, Michael. *Nomenklatura: The Soviet Ruling Class*. Trans. Eric Mosbacher. New York: Doubleday, 1984.

White, Stephen. "The Effectiveness of Political Propaganda in the USSR." *Soviet Studies*, no. 3 (July 1980), pp. 323–48.

Wiarda, Howard, ed. *New Directions in Comparative Politics*. Boulder, Colo.: Westview, 1985.

Wimbush, S. Enders, ed. *Soviet Nationalities in Strategic Perspective*. London: Croom Helm, 1985.

Wixman, Ronald. *The Peoples of the USSR: An Ethnographic Handbook*. Armonk, N.Y.: M. E. Sharpe, 1984.

Yanov, Alexander. *The Russian New Right.* Berkeley: University of California Press, 1978.

Young, Crawford. *The Politics of Cultural Pluralism.* Madison: University of Wisconsin Press, 1976.

Za shcho usunuly Shelesta? Munich: Suchasnist', 1973.

Zaslavsky, Victor. "The Ethnic Question in the USSR." *Telos,* no. 45 (Fall 1980), pp. 45–76.

——. *The Neo-Stalinist State.* Armonk, N.Y.: M. E. Sharpe, 1982.

Zimmermann, Ekkart. *Political Violence, Crises, and Revolutions: Theories and Research.* Boston: G. K. Hall, 1983.

Zinkevych, Osyp, ed. *Ukrains'ka Hel'sinks'ka Hrupa, 1978–1982: Dokumenty i materiialy.* Baltimore: Smoloskyp, 1983.

Zinoviev, Aleksandr. "Stabil'no li sovetskoe obshchestvo?" *Kontinent,* no. 37 (1983), pp. 131–49.

Index

Library of Congress Cataloging-in-Publication Data

Motyl, Alexander J.
  Will the non-Russians rebel?
  (Studies in Soviet history and society)
  Bibliography: p.
  Includes index
  1. Soviet Union—Ethnic relations. I. Title. II. Series: Studies in Soviet
history and society (Ithaca, N.Y.)
DK33.M64   1987   305.8′00947   86-24386
ISBN 0-8014-1947-6 (alk. paper)